JAPAN

OPPOSING VIEWPOINTS®

JAPAN

OPPOSING VIEWPOINTS®

David L. Bender & Bruno Leone, *Series Editors*

William Dudley, *Book Editor*

OPPOSING VIEWPOINTS SERIES ®

Greenhaven Press, Inc.   PO Box 289009   San Diego, CA 92128-9009

Library of Congress Cataloging-in-Publication Data

Japan, opposing viewpoints / William Dudley, book editor.
   p.   cm. — (Opposing viewpoints series)
   Includes bibliographical references.
   Summary: Presents opposing viewpoints regarding Japan's business practices, society, position as a world power, and relationship with the United States. Includes critical thinking skills activities.
   ISBN 0-89908-444-3 (lib. bdg.) — ISBN 0-89908-419-2 (pbk.)
   1. Japan—Foreign relations—1945- 2. Industry and state—Japan.
3. Japan—Social conditions—1945- [1. Japan. 2. Critical thinking.]
I. Dudley, William, 1964-   . II. Series.
DS890.3.J36   1989
952.04'8—dc20   89-36620
                                                CIP
                                                AC

"Congress shall make no law... abridging the freedom of speech, or of the press."

First Amendment to the US Constitution

The basic foundation of our democracy is the first amendment guarantee of freedom of expression. The *Opposing Viewpoints Series* is dedicated to the concept of this basic freedom and the idea that it is more important to practice it than to enshrine it.

Contents

Why Consider Opposing Viewpoints?

"It is better to debate a question without settling it than to settle a question without debating it."

Joseph Joubert (1754-1824)

The Importance of Examining Opposing Viewpoints

The purpose of the Opposing Viewpoints Series, and this book in particular, is to present balanced, and often difficult to find, opposing points of view on complex and sensitive issues.

Probably the best way to become informed is to analyze the positions of those who are regarded as experts and well studied on issues. It is important to consider every variety of opinion in an attempt to determine the truth. Opinions from the mainstream of society should be examined. But also important are opinions that are considered radical, reactionary, or minority as well as those stigmatized by some other uncomplimentary label. An important lesson of history is the eventual acceptance of many unpopular and even despised opinions. The ideas of Socrates, Jesus, and Galileo are good examples of this.

Readers will approach this book with their own opinions on the issues debated within it. However, to have a good grasp of one's own viewpoint, it is necessary to understand the arguments of those with whom one disagrees. It can be said that those who do not completely understand their adversary's point of view do not fully understand their own.

A persuasive case for considering opposing viewpoints has been presented by John Stuart Mill in his work *On Liberty*. When examining controversial issues it may be helpful to reflect on this suggestion:

> The only way in which a human being can make some approach to knowing the whole of a subject, is by hearing what can be said about it by persons of every variety of opinion, and studying all modes in which it can be looked at by every character of mind. No wise man ever acquired his wisdom in any mode but this.

Analyzing Sources of Information

The Opposing Viewpoints Series includes diverse materials taken from magazines, journals, books, and newspapers, as well as statements and position papers from a wide range of individuals, organizations and governments. This broad spectrum of sources helps to develop patterns of thinking which are open to the consideration of a variety of opinions.

Pitfalls To Avoid

A pitfall to avoid in considering opposing points of view is that of regarding one's own opinion as being common sense and the most rational stance and the point of view of others as being only opinion and naturally wrong. It may be that another's opinion is correct and one's own is in error.

Another pitfall to avoid is that of closing one's mind to the opinions of those with whom one disagrees. The best way to approach a dialogue is to make one's primary purpose that of understanding the mind and arguments of the other person and not that of enlightening him or her with one's own solutions. More can be learned by listening than speaking.

It is my hope that after reading this book the reader will have a deeper understanding of the issues debated and will appreciate the complexity of even seemingly simple issues on which good and honest people disagree. This awareness is particularly important in a democratic society such as ours where people enter into public debate to determine the common good. Those with whom one disagrees should not necessarily be regarded as enemies, but perhaps simply as people who suggest different paths to a common goal.

Developing Basic Reading and Thinking Skills

In this book, carefully edited opposing viewpoints are purposely placed back to back to create a running debate; each viewpoint is preceded by a short quotation that best expresses the author's main argument. This format instantly plunges the reader into the midst of a controversial issue and greatly aids that reader in mastering the basic skill of recognizing an author's point of view.

A number of basic skills for critical thinking are practiced in the activities that appear throughout the books in the series. Some of the skills are:

Evaluating Sources of Information   The ability to choose from among alternative sources the most reliable and accurate source in relation to a given subject.

Separating Fact from Opinion   The ability to make the basic distinction between factual statements (those that can be demonstrated or verified empirically) and statements of opinion (those that are beliefs or attitudes that cannot be proved).

Identifying Stereotypes   The ability to identify oversimplified, exaggerated descriptions (favorable or unfavorable) about people and insulting statements about racial, religious or national groups, based upon misinformation or lack of information.

Recognizing Ethnocentrism   The ability to recognize attitudes or opinions that express the view that one's own race, culture, or group is inherently superior, or those attitudes that judge another culture or group in terms of one's own.

It is important to consider opposing viewpoints and equally important to be able to critically analyze those viewpoints. The activities in this book are designed to help the reader master these thinking skills. Statements are taken from the book's viewpoints and the reader is asked to analyze them. This technique aids the reader in developing skills that not only can be applied to the viewpoints in this book, but also to situations where opinionated spokespersons comment on controversial issues. Although the activities are helpful to the solitary reader, they are most useful when the reader can benefit from the interaction of group discussion.

Using this book and others in the series should help readers develop basic reading and thinking skills. These skills should improve the reader's ability to understand what they read. Readers should be better able to separate fact from opinion, substance from rhetoric and become better consumers of information in our media-centered culture.

This volume of the Opposing Viewpoints Series does not advocate a particular point of view. Quite the contrary! The very nature of the book leaves it to the reader to formulate the opinions he or she finds most suitable. My purpose as publisher is to see that this is made possible by offering a wide range of viewpoints which are fairly presented.

David L. Bender
Publisher

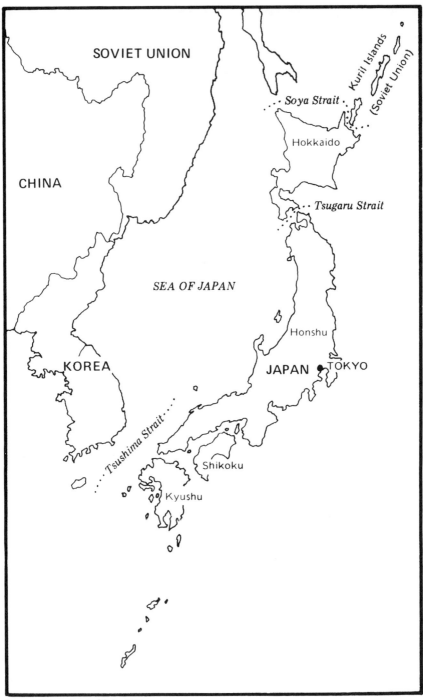

Source: US Department of State, 1986.

Introduction

"Japan remains a reluctant power, unsure of its place, fearful of speaking out too loudly. . . . But habits of timidity and parochialism are giving way."

Susan Chira, *The New York Times*, March 7, 1989.

US naval officer Matthew Perry steamed into Tokyo Bay in 1853 with a mission to establish relations with Japan for the United States. What he found was a centuries-old society that had been isolated from the rest of the world since the early 1600s. On his mission, Perry demonstrated a steam locomotive, the telegraph, and other new Western technologies. The exposure to these technologies ended Japan's complete isolation and precipitated many changes in its society, government, economy, and culture. Japan now strove to imitate the West. Today, it is one of the world's most powerful and wealthy nations. Yet Japan has also remained almost completely homogeneous with long-held traditions and beliefs. As syndicated columnist William Pfaff argues, "Japan remains a culturally and morally isolated nation." This tension between Japan's international status and its lingering isolationism remains a controversial problem facing Japan today.

From 1853 to 1945 Japan gained international status through warfare. Only a few decades after Perry's fateful arrival, Japan stunned the world by defeating China in 1894 and Russia in 1905 in two successive wars. Following World War I, Japan was recognized as a major power, but its attempt to create an Asian empire in the 1930s culminated in the disaster of World War II. Not only was it defeated by the United States in 1945, but Japan's reputation for military brutality in World War II "continues to stunt its political life, both domestically and internationally," according to historian Barry Buzan. In addition, the massive destruction of Hiroshima and Nagasaki left the Japanese disillusioned by war. Japan reverted to its previous isolationism as it largely abandoned a political and military role in Asia.

Since its defeat in 1945, Japan's world reputation is an economic, not a military one. Japan has built powerful industries in steel, automobiles, electronics, and other technological fields. Its success in exporting its products has resulted in Japan's possession of "the largest cache of wealth in the world," according to economist R. Taggart Murphy. In response to its relative affluence other nations now want Japan to participate in solving international problems such as sending aid to developing nations, solving the world debt crisis, and managing the world economy. But while Japan has increased its foreign aid and has begun to propose solutions to these problems, it is reluctant to become involved in global concerns. "Japan is like a dinosaur," says Japanese political science professor Masataka Kosaka. "It has a huge body and tiny brain." Kosaka and others believe Japan's economic wealth has grown faster than its ability to participate actively and constructively in global affairs.

Whether Japan will significantly change the way it confronts the outside world remains to be seen. But its status as an economic giant is placing enormous pressures on its homogeneous population and culture. The viewpoints in *Japan: Opposing Viewpoints* include the works of Japanese and Western economists, politicians, and scholars. They examine Japan and its changing role in the world from several perspectives. The questions discussed are Is Japan a World Power? Are Japan's Economic Policies Fair? Is Japan an Internally Troubled Society? Should Japan Increase Its International Role? Is Cooperation Between the US and Japan Beneficial? It is hoped that the diverse viewpoints in this book will increase understanding of this important country that in many ways remains as mysterious now as it was when Matthew Perry saw it over one hundred and thirty years ago.

Is Japan a
World Power?

Chapter Preface

After its surrender to the Allies in World War II, Japan became the only major industrialized country to officially renounce war. It has refused to develop or deploy nuclear weapons, and its military forces are designed for defense rather than conquest. Many people have concluded that its limited military capacity prevents Japan from being a true world power.

Others argue that military strength is less important than economic strength today. Japan's economy produces more goods and services than any other nation except the US, and Japan is a leader in world finance, new technologies, and exports. Daniel Burstein, an American journalist, is one of many people who argue that economic success proves Japan is definitely a world power and could perhaps become the world's number one power.

The viewpoints in the following chapter debate Japan's status in the world today.

"Japan may find it possible to lead the world without an American-style global military machine."

Japan Is a Superpower

Daniel Burstein

Japan's success in the world economy has led many to speculate whether it has become a global superpower. In the following viewpoint, Daniel Burstein argues that Japan's economic strength and its leadership role in Asia are indications that Japan is a superpower. Burstein is a New York-based journalist who writes extensively on Japan and other Asian countries.

As you read, consider the following questions:

1. Why does Burstein place so much emphasis on Japan's creditor status?
2. How does Burstein respond to arguments that the world will not be dominated by any single superpower?
3. According to the author, why might the "Pacific century" be more accurately called the "Japanese century"?

Daniel Burstein, *YEN! Japan's Financial Empire and Its Threat to America.* Copyright ©
1988 by Burstein & O'Connor, Inc. Reprinted by permission of Simon & Schuster, Inc.

Masaaki Kurokawa is not exactly a household name in the United States, but he is one of the most important financial executives in the world. He works for Nomura Securities—a company whose own name was barely known on Wall Street just a few years ago. Today Nomura is not only Japan's largest securities company, it is the largest in the world. It dwarfs all those companies whose names are so much more familiar in the West. "In a takeover financed with stock," *Fortune* remarked, "Nomura could swallow Merrill Lynch like a bit of predinner *sashimi*." . . .

[One evening], Kurokawa entertained American guests in a restaurant at the top of one of the several buildings owned by Nomura in Tokyo. This one was in the Shinjuku district, fifty stories above the city's swirling neon and never-ending sprawl. His voice was deep and resonant. The drama of what he had to say was reaching its crescendo.

A Proposal

"We Japanese will have to come up with much bolder ideas to play our role properly in the world," he asserted, pausing to watch as his guests attempted to eat the live lobster sashimi in front of them. Kurokawa said he had a plan for how Japan could help the United States solve its trade deficit: the already mighty yen, which was then trading around 140 to the dollar, should be strengthened further until it reaches 100 to the dollar. This, he said, would make Japan incapable of earning a profit on export products. The United States would no longer see its domestic industries threatened by Japanese imports.

Next, a single joint currency would be created, "dollar on one side, yen on the other." This way Japan could invest freely in the United States without worrying that American fiscal profligacy would weaken the dollar and thereby lower the value of investment portfolios. And what would Japan get in return? "California," he said. . . .

The World's Leading Creditor

That Nomura could make the transition from a firm virtually unknown on Wall Street in 1983 to one whose executives brainstorm about ideas as far-reaching as a joint U.S.-Japan currency or a Californian common market is a product of Japan's new role as the world's leading creditor nation.

A creditor nation is one whose investments abroad exceed the size of foreign investments in its own economy. A debtor nation is one that owes foreigners more than the sum of its own assets abroad. Creditor nations obviously have a lot of leverage over those to whom they lend their money; debtor nations often become subservient to the interests of their creditors.

Japan replaced the United States as the world's leading creditor in 1986. The scope of Japanese capital outflows has been likened to the period in the 1950s and 1960s when the United States bought up much of Western European industry, but Japanese acquisitions over the last few years have actually far outstripped the American expansion of those days. In fact, Japan's net external assets already surpass by 20 percent the American record established over a thirty-seven-year period.

Every single working day, Japanese individuals and corporations generate over a billion dollars' worth of savings. This excess cash

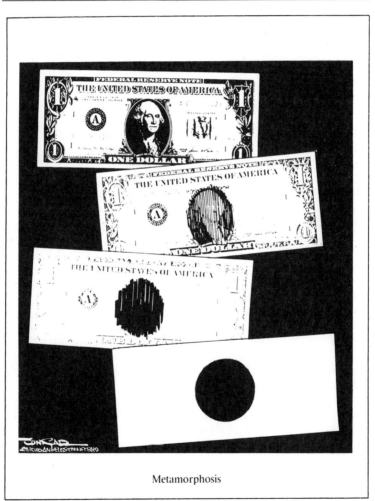

Metamorphosis

Paul Conrad. Copyright 1989 The Times. Reprinted by Permission of Los Angeles Times Syndicate.

rushes into domestic bank accounts, stocks, insurance premiums, and real estate speculation, but even these institutions can't hold it all. Like water seeking its own level, a large amount of it *must* flow abroad. In 1981 Japanese traded foreign securities worth a total of $15 billion for the year. In 1986 the figure was $2.6 trillion—growth by a factor of 175 in five years' time. A newly popular Japanese saying summarizes the situation: "It took Britain one hundred years and the United States fifty years to become the richest country in the world, but it only took Japan five."

Japan's ascendancy to world leadership on the positive side of the ledger has been mirrored by America's fall into debt. A creditor nation since 1914, the United States became a net debtor for the first time in the 1980s. Its red ink ran quickly past Brazil, Mexico, and Argentina all the way to the position of world's leading debtor. By the year 2000, Japanese net external assets may reach +$1,000,000,000,000 (positive one trillion dollars). The figure for the United States could be −$1,000,000,000,000 (negative one trillion dollars).

A Role Reversal

To begin to grasp what this historic role reversal means, a short review of some of the ways Japan's financial influence is currently manifesting itself is in order:

• The United States has come to depend on Japanese investors to directly finance as much as 30 percent of the American government's budget deficit. Throughout 1985-87, the leading Japanese securities firms were almost always among the largest buyers of long-term U.S. Treasury bonds at auction. Several Japanese-owned firms are primary dealers in securities issued by the U.S. government. Without Japanese participation, it is safe to say the Treasury would have an extremely difficult time financing American debt.

• All ten of the world's ten largest banks (ranked by deposits) are today Japanese. Only one American bank—Citicorp—even makes the somewhat more broadly defined list of the world's top ten bank holding companies. Thirty years ago not a single Japanese bank was counted in the world's top fifty; as recently as 1980 only one Japanese bank ranked in the American-led top ten. . . .

• If U.S. subsidiaries of Japanese-owned companies (Nissan, Honda, Sony, and the like) were ranked in the *Fortune* 500, they would already account for thirty of the biggest U.S. industrial corporations. The Japanese-owned sector is growing 400 percent faster than the rest of the U.S. economy on the strength of direct investments approaching $10 billion for 1987.

• A quarter-million Americans already work for Japanese employers in the United States. Economists expect that number to rise to a million in the 1990s.

• The total value of all stocks listed on the Tokyo Stock Exchange surpassed the total value of all stocks listed on the New York Stock Exchange early in 1987. Tokyo's lead has continued to widen since. A single Japanese company—Nippon Telegraph & Telephone (NTT)—is worth more than IBM, AT&T, General Motors, General Electric, and Exxon *combined*. . . .

The World's Dominant Economic Power

Future historians may well mark the mid-1980s as the time when Japan surpassed the United States to become the world's dominant economic power. Japan achieved superior industrial competitiveness several years earlier, but by the mid-1980s its high-technology exports to the United States far exceeded imports, and annual trade surpluses approached $50 billion a year. Meanwhile, America's trade deficits mushroomed to $150 billion a year. By late 1985, Japan's international lending already exceeded $640 billion, about ten percent more than America's, and it is growing rapidly. By 1986 the United States became the world's largest debtor nation and Japan surpassed the United States and Saudi Arabia to become the world's largest creditor. . . .

America's GNP may remain larger than Japan's well into the 1990s (depending on exchange rate measurements), but there are many reasons to believe that Japan will extend its lead as the world's dominant economic power in the years ahead.

Ezra F. Vogel, *Foreign Affairs*, Spring 1986.

• Japanese investors bought about $18 billion worth of prime U.S. real estate between 1985 and 1988. Among the notables in New York: the Tiffany, Mobil, Exxon, and ABC buildings, 666 Fifth Avenue, and a chunk of the Citicorp tower; in southern California, Arco Plaza, La Costa Spa Resort, and one-third of all downtown L.A. office buildings; in Washington, D.C., the U.S. News & World Report Building; in Las Vegas, the Dunes Hotel. Continuing to buy such high-visibility flagships, Japanese investors are now moving into office and commercial real estate in cities such as Atlanta, Boston, Indianapolis, Cleveland, and Charlotte.

• In Hawaii, Japanese investors own more than 75 percent of the equity in the twenty hotels along the Waikiki beachfront—just a small part of their $6.5 billion Hawaiian realty portfolio. "Although the U.S. flag still flies there, Hawaii looks to be well on the way to becoming an economic colony of Japan," observed *Forbes*. . . .

Money and Power

It is no mere accident of history that the world's leading creditor nation generally proves to be the world's most influential nation as well. The ability to export capital provides an extraordinarily efficient lever controlling events around the globe. This trend can be seen in its primitive form going back at least as far as the Spanish and Dutch empires. It is more relevant after the birth of modern finance, when Britain's role as leading creditor (and the pound sterling's role as key currency) lay at the very foundation of the empire and of the period of nineteenth-century history known as "Pax Britannica."

In the twentieth century, a nearly one-to-one correspondence exists between America's role as creditor and its level of influence on the global scene. As soon as the United States became a creditor nation in 1914, it immediately found good reason to raise an army and involve itself in a European war. After World War II, when the United States took over Britain's former role as leading creditor, the dollar became the key currency, and a "Pax Americana" ensued. Since the mid-1980s, as the United States has become a debtor nation, the dollar's influence has waned, and America can no longer lead the world as forcefully as it once did.

Obviously this history cannot be reliably reduced into a mechanical formula, "Leading Creditor = Leading Global Power." Too many other forces are at work, and it is often hard to tell the causes from the effects. But history does emphasize a close correlation between the country that dominates world finance and the country that most influences the world in other ways—industrially, technologically, and politically. The experience of England is particularly instructive because it shows that a country need not have a large land area or extensive natural resources to build a global economic empire.

A Pax Nipponica?

But can Japan recapitulate the pattern of Pax Britannica and Pax Americana with a "Pax Nipponica"?

As students of history know, the "Pax"—both Britannica and Americana—was a peace born of war. Both prior eras of global hegemony relied not only on financial leadership, but on many other kinds of power, the most visible being military. Japan today is not widely considered to be a military power, since its American-imposed postwar constitution specifically prohibits it from such a role, and the one percent of GNP [gross national product] that constitutes its defense budget is the lowest such allocation of any major economy. The gross disparity between Japan's strength as an economic power and its weakness as a military power would at first blush seem to render the idea of Pax Nipponica impossible.

Yet a compelling case for Pax Nipponica can be made, depending on exactly how the concept is defined and bearing in mind that since no two periods of world history are alike, no two styles of world leadership need be similar to achieve the same effects. Just as the United States managed to lead the world without Britain's

22

extensive system of physical colonies, Japan may find it possible to lead the world without an American-style global military machine.

If one assumes that (1) the risk of global war is low because of the nuclear balance of terror, (2) the likelihood of a Soviet or Chinese threat to Japan is minimal as a result of internal changes in those countries, and (3) in the era of high-tech warfare, Japan is perfectly capable of building adequate conventional defense systems at reasonable cost, then development of a grand military strategy becomes largely irrelevant to the exercise of Japanese influence on a world scale.

Under those assumptions Japan could avoid the pitfalls of heavy military spending and continue using its surplus capital to reinvest in its own global economic leadership. Meanwhile the superpowers would continue to bankrupt their own economies through the arms race and thus diminish their global influence.

An Empire Being Born

Blinded by wartime victory and our long-standing role as senior partner in the U.S.-Japan relationship, we ignore the obvious: Japan is becoming a global superpower in its own right. We casually acknowledge Japan as a great manufacturing and trading nation that has surpassed us in certain product areas. We even accept the idea that "Made in Japan" means higher quality than "Made in USA." But we still shrink from recognizing the essential reality. A Japanese empire is being born that will pose a fundamental challenge to American power in every sphere.

Daniel Burstein, *Yen: Japan's Financial Empire and Its Threat to America*, 1988.

Ezra Vogel, the Harvard scholar whose book *Japan as Number One* shocked many American businessmen just by its title when it appeared in 1979, envisions a certain kind of Pax Nipponica arising from such conditions. He predicts that the already vast competitive strengths of Japanese industry and trade could become so awesome that future world development would necessitate a system of self-imposed Japanese restraints. Japan's ability to dictate the terms of such solutions—rather than armies, navies, or missiles—could become the basis of a "limited" Pax Nipponica, Vogel argues. . . .

Military Power

Military power is supposed to be the one area of clear-cut American strength and explicit Japanese weakness. The unstated assumption behind the blithe attitude exhibited by much of America's power elite in the face of Japan's growing economic strength is that Japan cannot pose a real threat to American interests as long as its own security is dependent on a defense treaty with the United States.

Yet Japan's wealth will inevitably alter even this seemingly institutionalized relationship. It has already begun to do so. The commitment of one percent of Japan's GNP to national defense seemed like a token sum when the limit was first set. Yet today one percent of Japan's huge GNP places it in a dead heat with Britain as the world's third biggest military spender. What's more, as Washington tries to reduce the chasm between the far-reaching nature of current American military commitments and dwindling economic resources to finance them, Japan, like other American allies, is being encouraged to "burden-share." . . .

Japan and Other Nations

The military issue is not the only one determining whether or not there will be a Pax Nipponica. The consensus of contemporary economists and political scientists holds that the world is moving away from the long-standing bipolarity of American and Soviet spheres of interest. A multipolar arrangement is already beginning to take shape in which a greater variety of countries and regional blocs share power. According to this view, neither Japan nor any other country is likely to again achieve the degree of single-nation dominance experienced at the height of Pax Americana. . . .

Yet while the world of tomorrow is likely to have a multiplicity of power centers, one should not rush to conclude that such diffusion prevents a single nation from exerting a predominant influence—especially when that nation is Japan. Precisely because power will be more differentiated than it has been in the past, Japan need not monopolize it to exert extraordinary influence. . . . Being just one rank above the rest of the world's leading economies may be a suitably subtle Japanese way of asserting itself. It could also be a very cost-beneficial one, enabling Japan to enjoy most of the benefits of world economic leadership without being obliged to pay for the rest of the world's security or development.

In the end, the crystallization of Pax Nipponica may have much to do with Japan's relationships to other Asian countries. Lately it has become fashionable to speak of the twenty-first century as the "Pacific Century." And for good reason. Many east Asian countries—not only Japan—have been at the top of the world's economic growth charts for the last two decades. Nearly 2,500 years after the death of Confucius, his influence is still deeply felt in this part of the world, encouraging such virtues as hard work; productivity; education; consensus building; national unity; the willingness to sacrifice for family, company, and country; long-term planning; high-quality civil service; and a preference for saving rather than consuming and for prosperity rather than politics. Mastering the complexities inherent in character writing and the abacus, among other factors, seems to predispose the children of these cultures to an affinity for mathematics, engineering, and other valuable technical skills. . . .

The Japanese Century

But there is also a sense in which the "Pacific Century" is more properly viewed as a euphemism for the "Japanese Century." The popular image of the "little dragons" hot on Japan's heels is not quite accurate. Singapore and Hong Kong, while exceedingly successful, are both city-states where domestic output is less than in Japan's third largest city, Osaka. Taiwan and South Korea, while very important as trading states, are a long way from approximating the scope and diversity of Japanese industry. Both are highly militarized economies facing large unanswered political questions about their future. As for the biggest potential dragon of all, China, even her most optimistic planners believe two more decades of uninterrupted peace and continued reform are needed to obtain the level of economic development typical of Japan around 1980. . . .

The appropriate analogy here is the American relationship to Western Europe in the 1950s and 1960s. The domination of Atlantic markets by American multinational corporations and the immense political leverage obtained in Europe was integrally bound up with the rise of the United States to global supremacy. Even though individual European economies were themselves among the world's strongest, European leaders from Gaullists to socialists frequently decried their exploitation at American hands.

Today, from Thailand to China, complaints of Japanese exploitation of local economies are heard with increasing frequency. The prospect of the "Pacific Century" serving largely as veneer and context to what will actually be a "Japanese Century" (at least until China matures) is quite real.

"Japan obviously hasn't replaced the U.S. as the pre-eminent global power—and it probably never will."

Japan Is Not a Superpower

Karen Elliott House

Some people have speculated that Japan is replacing the United States as the most powerful and wealthiest country in the world. In the following viewpoint, Karen Elliott House offers several reasons why such speculation is unwarranted. Japan, she argues, lacks military strength, is resented by other Asian nations, and relies too much on other countries for trade and technological innovation. House is a staff reporter for *The Wall Street Journal*, an American business newspaper.

As you read, consider the following questions:

1. Why does House call Japan a one-dimensional power?
2. What significance does the author attach to Japanese investment in the US?
3. Why does House believe the formation of a Japan-led Asian block is unlikely?

They are the world's new plutocrats, buying up Rembrandts and real estate with their rock-hard yen—the new highfliers in an age of high technology, the new elite in an era in which money is a major measure of power.

They are an insecure people from an insular nation no bigger than California, hiding their national vulnerabilities behind a veil of yen, escaping their crowded cities to roam a world in which they increasingly are resented and even reviled—ambassadors of a nation notably devoid of the idealism or ideology that has motivated great powers in the past.

They are the richest of people and the poorest of people; the most envied of leaders and the most eager of followers; the strongest of global competitors and the most fragile of global powers. In the increasingly intense struggle for world leadership, Japan is winning many of the battles. But can it win the war?

The Japanese miracle is well-known. A country that only a generation ago was disparaged as a producer of tinny transistor radios has turned itself into one of the wealthiest and most technologically advanced on Earth, a transformation accomplished through sheer hard work and a social organization so cohesive and centrally managed that an Italian journalist here laughingly calls Japan "the only communist nation that works."

Unburdened by defense spending or, until recently, a consumer culture, Japanese saved and invested in industry. With methodical precision and market perceptivity, Japan began industry by industry to take leadership, moving rapidly from heavy industries on to high technology. Now, finally, the yen has replaced the dollar as the symbol of financial strength, enabling Japan to go on an unprecedented global buying binge.

This lock-step national march from war-torn poverty to economic prominence has set off an urgent debate in the West: Is this seemingly invincible economic engine destined in the next generation to simply roll over the world, establishing Japan's unchallenged dominance? Or do Japan's limits—the scarcity of its natural resources, the narrowness of its political vision and the animosity it stirs—foreclose true global leadership? Japan's future is a question that weighs not only on experts but on ordinary individuals: What American or European consumer hasn't felt, along with admiration for a Japanese car or VCR, a twinge of fear for his own country's future?

Words of Warning

"At the rate things are going, we are all going to wind up working for the Japanese," says Lester Thurow, an economist at Massachusetts Institute of Technology.

"Japan will be the No. 1 financial power in the next generation," declares Alfred Herrhausen, chairman of Deutsche Bank, in his office atop its shimmering new Frankfurt headquarters, from which he tracks the rise of Japanese banking. (Nine of the world's 10 largest banks, ranked by 1987 assets, are Japanese.)

Yet despite all this yen-inspired awe, Japan obviously hasn't replaced the U.S. as the pre-eminent global power—and it probably never will. This is the conclusion that emerges from talks with more than a hundred government officials, scholars and other experts in the U.S., Russia, Europe and Asia. There are dissenting voices, certainly, but the predominant view is that while Japan will wield greater influence, especially economic, a broader global leadership will elude it. Japan's deficiencies are simply too great.

For starters, Japan is a one-dimensional power. Its economic might isn't bolstered by either military, political or ideological clout, elements that have always been essential for a nation to shape international events. Nor is there much prospect of Japanese rearmament in the next generation, so opposed is the entire world even four decades after World War II. While the international community does insist Japan play a larger political role, Japanese so far lack the confidence or will to do so. Japan keeps its head down. It is content to have a Mitsui policy, not a Mideast policy; a foreign-exchange policy, but not a true foreign policy.

Japan Lacks Ideology

There is the question "Will the 21st century be led by Japan?" I unfortunately do not think so, if things remain as is.

Although there are various reasons, one major reason is that Japan does not have an ideology which will impress people. There never has been and probably never will be one. Having money and material goods will not do for Japan to assume any kind of leadership in the 21st century. I think that information and human resources will not do, either. This is to say that there must be something spiritual.

Fuji Kamiya, *Shokun*, February 1987.

In the few instances where Japan has tried to expand its political role, as it did in offering proposals for handling Third World debt, the international reaction has ranged from skepticism to hostility. That is largely because Japan is seen as standing for no ideal other than a quest for self-enrichment, hardly a globally appealing philosophy.

"The Japanese will find out money isn't everything just as we found out armaments aren't everything," says Soviet deputy foreign minister Anatoli Adamishin.

Even in the field where the Japanese are strongest, economics, it is far from clear they are winning. For Japan's wealth is dependent on access to others' markets, a dependency that makes it vulnerable. By contrast, America's enormous domestic market provides greater self-sufficiency, as well as leverage over Japan and others who rely on it.

"Japan is like a thin-bottomed pan on a hot fire—very vulnerable to external forces," says Chung Hoon Mok, president of Hyundai Construction Co., over dinner in Seoul.

Technology

Many in the U.S., of course, worry these days about Japan's feats on the frontiers of high technology, once virtually the exclusive preserve of America. Having some years ago all but abandoned consumer electronics to big Japanese companies like Sony, Toshiba and Hitachi, U.S. industry now is being challenged in futuristic technologies like fiber optics, genetic engineering and superconductivity. These are fields that require heavy investment in research and development, and they lend themselves to the kind of cooperation among industrial giants that is a hallmark of Japanese success.

Regardless, many businessmen who envy Japan's technological prowess and marketing might remain confident the high-tech battle is far from lost. One reason is America's pre-eminence in the realm of pure science where technologies are born. "We still have a commanding lead in pushing the frontiers of science," says Bobby Inman, chairman of Westmark, an electronics holding company in Texas. "Where we've fallen short frequently is in the speed with which we turn technology into product. But we're waking up."

Much of Japan's success has been based on rapid commercialization of technology developed in America. But these days American companies are working harder to protect their patents, to cooperate in the development of new technologies and to turn their discoveries into products more quickly. Government and industry have begun to work together on research too, though at a level far below that of Japan. The Bush administration has signaled that helping U.S. industry compete in technology is a top priority.

"Six years ago I was pretty pessimistic," says Mr. Inman, former deputy director of the Central Intelligence Agency. "Today I am cautiously optimistic because of the level of attention I see the problem beginning to get."

Japanese Investment

It's even more fashionable in America these days to lament Japan's frequent and flashy purchases of pieces of America and of American corporations. In fact, this buying spree is as much a manifestation of Japanese weaknesses as of strength. It's true

29

the low dollar makes U.S. assets cheap, but the Japanese also rush to America for what they can't find at home.

"The U.S. is a land of opportunity and Japan is a land of lack of opportunity," says Jiro Tokuyama, senior adviser to the Mitsui Research Center. "We close our market because opportunities are scarce and we don't want to share them with others. Already our college graduates don't have the same opportunities as those 20 years ago." But, he adds, "being closed is a weakness. This is our dilemma."

Japan Is Second

Although Japan is strong economically and financially, it is not yet prepared for the responsibility of global leadership.

[A] global power will have to possess many elements, including size and diversity of population, financial strength, military strength and scientific capability. Our differences from the US in some of these areas limit our potential as a world leader. For example, the same cultural homogeneity that has brought competitive strength to our industry detracts from the capacity to be a global leader. I'm afraid this is one of our shortcomings compared to the multi-cultural character of the United States. In military strength we of course play a small role internationally. So, in overall strength, Japan is likely to stay second in line behind the United States. And that is desirable.

Saburo Okita, *New Perspectives Quarterly*, Spring 1987.

Indeed, Japanese investment at levels America is likely to tolerate is a blessing, not a curse. Ironically, given America's low savings rate (less than one-fourth that of Japan), it is Japanese money that is financing the investment that is rebuilding America's competitiveness, including new thrusts in high-tech fields. Also, for all the concern about buying of U.S. assets, Japanese investment in America still ranks below that of Britain and Holland. (More broadly, total American ownership of assets abroad is about $1 trillion, while total foreign ownership of American assets stands at about $1.5 trillion.)

Most important, there is the obvious fact that the assets so avidly purchased by Japanese these days remain in America. "We sold the top of these two buildings to the Japanese," says Citicorp Chairman John Reed in his glass-walled New York office. "But these two buildings are in Manhattan, and the fact they they own them doesn't mean very much."

Just as some fret that there is too much Japanese investment in the U.S., others worry that it might suddenly end. "Even a rumor that investment might stop sends the market into a tizzy," says Fred Bergsten, director of the Institute for International Economics in Washington. "We are hostage to foreigners."

While possible, an investment halt is hardly likely. Japan is at least as reliant on the American consumer market for its exports as America is dependent on Japanese investment. An abrupt end to Japanese lending to America could precipitate a U.S. recession that most economists believe would rapidly send shock waves through Japan's economy.

"An American recession affects the whole world," says Toyoo Gyohten, Japan's vice minister of finance. "Nobody wants an American recession."

Moreover, many individual Japanese investors and companies have spent so heavily in America they can ill afford to stop supporting its currency and economy. "The more the Japanese invest, the more committed they are to the American economy," says John Welch Jr., chairman of General Electric Co. "If you buy a home in my neighborhood, you care how I keep my neighborhood. If the Japanese own our assets, they don't want values to drop or currencies to drop."

Mitoji Yabunaka, an America-watcher in Tokyo's foreign ministry, acknowledges the U.S. leverage: "It's a very tough decision for Japanese investors. They've already invested so heavily that if they stop and get a free fall of the dollar, they lose a lot."

The Asian Bloc

The Japan-will-win school relies on yet another facile assumption. In the next century, this theory goes, Japan will lead an Asian bloc—two billion hard-working, self-sacrificing people, a full two-thirds of the world's population, all harnessed to Japan's economic ambitions. In reality, this 1990s version of the 1930s Greater Co-Prosperity Sphere imposed by Japan's armies grows less likely every day. For as Japan gets stronger, so does Asian suspicion, resentment and fear.

"Japanese may feel patriotic sentiments when they see the rising sun on Japan's flag," says Wu Ningkun, a professor at Beijing's Institute of International Relations. "But to Chinese it is just blood and murder." (He then launches into a recitation of Japan's wartime brutalities, which he says killed 30 million Chinese.)

In no sense is Asia a monolith. Culturally and historically, its divisions are far deeper than those in Europe. And the distances among those diverse neighbors are great. Europeans, using the code term, "1992," talk ceaselessly these days of economic unity. Asians do not. At New York conferences of the Council on Foreign Relations, in university seminars and even in some corporate board rooms, experts discuss with great seriousness the emergence of a new Asian trading bloc. But here in Asia, a visitor finds that concept draws only blank stares. When it is explained, the reaction is a combination of horror and bemusement.

"Japan's view is always a flying-geese format with Japan as the head goose," says Ding Xinghao, director of American studies at Shanghai's Institute of International Studies. "Our memories are long, so we aren't about to fly in Japan's formation."

Korean economist Park Ungsuh offers a practical, if less colorful, analysis. "It's simply not possible for Asian nations to be a viable bloc," he says, "because there is too much disparity between economies. You have one giant, Japan, and many peanuts."

Statistics underscore the point that, unlike Europe, Asia isn't a region of nearby neighbors and near-equals. The two largest economies in Asia are Japan, with annual per capita income of more than $13,000, and China, with only $270. Other economies, while booming, are dwarfed by these two; the increase in China's economic output in 1984 exceeded the entire gross national product of South Korea.

The same point is made by many others who look beneath the statistics on Japan's trade surpluses with most of the rest of Asia. A 1989 world economic survey by Coopers & Lybrand, the big American accounting firm, stresses that "no unified 'Pacific Rim' exists." It argues that the region is "simply a collection of high-growth, competitive countries that have yet to achieve any sense of economic coherence.

Resentment

Beyond practical obstacles to an Asian bloc are even greater political ones. Generally, proximity to Japan raises, rather than reduces, anti-Japanese sentiment. If Europe reacts to Japan with cool envy and America with occasional angry outbursts, in Asia, from businessmen to bar girls, it's open season on Japan.

At the Cotton Club, a Bangkok bar that caters to Japanese businessmen, Thai hostesses dressed in pseudo-kimonos tell Western visitors how much they despise the Japanese men who pay them for drinks and dances.

In the glistening Seoul headquarters of Lucky Gold Star, a Korean electronics and chemical products company, corporate president Lee Hun Jo frets over predictions emanating from America that Japan will play a greater role in Asia: "If that's so, I'm afraid we won't have a very stable next decade."

Zhao Fusan, a vice president of the Chinese Academy of Social Sciences in Beijing, is more blunt. A picture of the Virgin Mary adorns his cluttered office but doesn't temper his harsh views of Japan. "The Japanese are an aggressive people," he says. "They exploited us in the '40s with force and now with finance. They sell us inferior goods and deny us technology to try to keep China backward. But Asians have memories that can't be rubbed out with money."

A group of young Chinese economists at Shanghai's Asia Institute gleefully predict those memories will more and more manifest themselves in anti-Japanese government policies. "As democracy spreads in Asia, the people's hatred of Japan will carry more and more weight," predicts Chen Lebo, an economist at the institute.

Almost certainly, the greatest problem confronting Japan in the next several decades is the Japanese. Felix Rohatyn, a New York investment banker who believes Japan's economic power already exceeds America's, says, "Japan may have trouble adjusting to victory. The Japanese are going to have to give a lot back to the world. There's no history of their doing so."

Former West German Chancellor Helmut Schmidt echoes the point. "If I were Japanese, my top priority would be establishing friendly relations with my neighbors by learning to say 'I'm sorry.' They never have."

Japanese acknowledge this constraint on their nation. "We can sell cars and VCRs but who loves Japan? Who loves Japanese?" says Mr. Tokuyama. "We are winning the battle but losing the war."

No Inevitable Dominance

In view of all this, there seems little justification for the American elite's attraction to the idea of Japanese invulnerability and inevitable dominance. That analysis largely rests on taking a snapshot of Japan's sudden, sharp accumulation of wealth since 1981 and projecting it forward into the future, forgetting that in 1980 Japan had a trade deficit of $10 billion, not todays $80 billion surplus.

"I'd guess that the next decade may not be as favorable for Japan as this one has been," says Citicorp's Mr. Reed. The costs of commodities Japan imports such as oil and coal have been low in much of the 1980s, he notes, while the prices of Japanese exports like cars and computers have been relatively high. Besides, he adds, three-quarters of the $90 billion swing in Japan's fortunes between 1980 and 1988 was due to currency realignments and only 25% to increased export volume. "If you think that what exists today is permanent and forever true, you inevitably get your head handed to you," says Mr. Reed.

The Japanese know better than anyone that the race for economic pre-eminence is only now beginning. For the past 40 years, Japan has mainly followed in America's footsteps, doing, in the words of management guru Peter Drucker, "better what the West was already doing well."

"Closing the gap with America was easy," says Wataru Hiraizumi, a member of the Japanese parliament. "Now the race begins."

That race almost certainly isn't as lopsided as some handicappers think. America's economy remains nearly twice the size of Japan's. Japan's annual economic growth, which averaged 11% in the '60s and just under 5% in the '70s, has slowed to a modest 3.8% in the '80s, almost exactly the same as America's.

Japan no longer boasts the low labor costs of a developing country and the high labor productivity of a developed one. Labor costs in America now are lower than in Japan, and productivity higher. Just as in America a decade ago, labor costs are prompting Japanese industries to move offshore, taking jobs with them, to Korea, Singapore, Taiwan—even the U.S. And Japan's hoard of dollar assets has lost 60% of its value in just three years through the U.S. currency's decline.

Beyond all that, Japan's vaunted corporate loyalty is fraying as its job opportunities decline and Japanese business leaders seek to reward initiative, not longevity. After all, to excel, Japan now has to innovate, not imitate. Yet nothing in its educational system or, until very recently, its corporate culture encourages independent thinking or creativity. So, significantly, Japan is once again imitating America, this time by trying to motivate individual excellence, not reward group unity.

America More Trusted

But it is America, not Japan, for which Asians cheer. That's not merely because they like America more, though many do, but because they need America more. America, not Japan, is Asia's major market. And it is America only that offers a counterweight to both Soviet and Japanese ambitions in Asia.

"America is far more trusted than Japan," says South Korean Foreign Minister Choi Kwang Soo. "Japan harbors ambitions to be a major power, and that worries not just us but the Soviets and China."

And, short of their unlikely full-scale rearmament, Japan, too, needs America. "The next decades will be marked by competition between the U.S. and Japan rather than confrontation between the U.S. and the Soviets," says Mr. Ding, the America expert at Shanghai's Institute of International Studies. "But the world hasn't yet reached a point where military power isn't required to maintain global equilibrium, and that's America's task."

"The belief in their uniqueness . . . can paralyze Japanese when they come to grips with the outside world."

Japan's Ethnocentrism Inhibits Its Global Status

Clyde Haberman

A striking feature of Japanese culture is the strong belief held by many Japanese that they are a unique and homogeneous people. In the following viewpoint, Clyde Haberman argues that despite the country's increasing influence and involvement in international politics, Japan's self-image as a nation set apart prevents Japan from behaving like a true world power. Haberman spent five years in Japan as a reporter for *The New York Times.*

As you read, consider the following questions:

1. How has Japan's self-image changed in the 1980s, according to Haberman?
2. According to the author, how has pressure from other governments affected Japan?
3. What examples of the Japanese presumption of uniqueness does Haberman examine?

Clyde Haberman, "The Presumed Uniqueness of Japan," *The New York Times*, August 28, 1988. Copyright © 1988 by The New York Times Company. Reprinted by permission.

Five years in Japan have left me thinking a good deal about Bernstein, the scratchy-voiced business manager in the movie *Citizen Kane*. When a visitor speaks admiringly of a wealthy man, Bernstein waves him off. "It's no trick to make a lot of money," he says, "if all you want is to make a lot of money."

Japan in the late 1980's understands Bernstein. It is fabulously rich, and sure to get richer. It is so rich that even its own people have come to believe it. That wasn't the case when I arrived in 1983. Then, many Japanese took refuge in the worn cliché that this was a resource-poor island country, prone to earthquakes and typhoons, a vulnerable outpost where good fortune could disappear in a flash.

Japanese still tend to remind foreigners that despite the national wealth, they themselves don't live well—look at their cramped houses, they say, or their sky-high prices. But with their vast trade surpluses, enormous capital reserves and bulging portfolios of overseas real estate, the Japanese are no longer fooling themselves, or anyone else, about how wealthy they have become. And, like Bernstein, they have concluded that making a lot of money isn't good enough.

New Wealth

It has taken them most of the 1980's to reach this stage. Wealth has produced self-confidence and a surge of nationalism. It is time, Japanese say, to assert themselves on the world stage in at least rough equivalence to their economic might—even though the way they should assert themselves, or Japan's precise world role, isn't clear to them.

There is no grand debate on this score, certainly no intellectual debate as there might be in the United States. Intellectuals are a conspicuously weak force in Japan. Scholars, writers, professors all have far less influence in shaping public policy than their counterparts in the West, or even elsewhere in Asia. In South Korea and Burma, militant students are a key element in setting the political agenda; these days, Japanese students are stone silent.

In the special brand of democracy that distinguishes postwar Japan, where the same party has governed for 33 years and may well govern for another 33, the range of opinions on any subject is extremely narrow. When it comes to national direction, an elusive yet indispensable consensus somehow develops among big business, government bureaucrats, ruling-party politicians and, to a lesser extent, the national newspapers. That led long ago to the concept of Japan Inc. Although it is a simplistic notion, it is not a completely inaccurate one. Business, government and press work together in Japan to a degree unmatched in other major industrialized countries. All these power blocs now agree that Japan must speak out more forcefully. And apparently it has. During the widespread anti-Government demonstrations in Burma, Japan—which is Burma's largest aid donor—exerted pressure on the Burmese Government to restore stability by instituting necessary economic reforms.

A Blind Giant

A Japan as powerful diplomatically as it is economically would be an awesome force. Few Japanese, however, seem ready for that. In traditionally insular Japan, an overwhelming majority of people do not even think about the rest of the world. Many businessmen—now being pushed reluctantly toward the center of the world stage—regret the passing of a simpler time when they were left to the single-minded pursuit of profits.

There are, of course, Japanese who worry that they are moving too slowly. The country is like "a blind giant," a university professor in Tokyo said to me. He argued that the longer Japan took to find its world role, the longer it would invite misunderstanding and suspicion overseas about its true intentions. It's time to speak up, he said, and he is not alone.

Japan's Shortsightedness

Japan's economic sphere is broadening to encompass the whole world. Shamefully, however, we feel no need to be grateful for what we get from outside Japan. . . .

Our biggest problem is that we cannot see beyond our borders. Our shortsightedness is preventing us from becoming full-fledged members of a much greater world community.

Kenichi Ohmae, *Beyond National Borders*, 1987.

A vivid expression of this point of view came from Naohiro Amaya, a former senior planner in the Ministry of International Trade and Industry. "Does Japan have the soul of a merchant or a samurai?" he wrote in a newspaper column. "It's time to decide if we are a nation of salesmen or statesmen. There's no glory in an abacus, so I vote for grandeur."

Japan has slowly come to accept its obligation to recycle some of its enormous trade and capital surpluses. Foreign economic aid, once meager, swelled to $10 billion in the 1988 budget, pushing Japan past the United States as the world's No. 1 donor. The annual increases in aid are actually much less dramatic than they appear because the yen has been much stronger than the dollar in recent years, so the aid translates into a lot more dollars. Still, it amounts to a good deal of money. . . .

In order to live up to its global responsibilities, Japan has also begun to transform the way it does business. Official policy is to restructure the economy by encouraging domestic demand, restraining exports and welcoming imports. Although the gates have hardly been flung wide open to foreign products and financial services, in Tokyo these days one does find American investment houses, South Korean television sets and West German cars that were not there in sizable numbers a few years ago.

Diplomatically, Japan is moving cautiously into a few uncharted areas. Heavily dependent on Arab oil, Japan had long maintained distant relations with Israel; in late June 1988, however, Sosuke Uno, the first Japanese Foreign Minister to visit Israel, announced a "new phase" in the two countries' relationship.

In a number of instances, Tokyo is stepping out a bit from Washington's shadow, especially when Asian interests are at stake. Foreign Ministry officials have begun to complain that Washington is leaning too hard on such newly industrialized countries as South Korea to reshape their economies and their exchange rates in favor of the United States. Washington may "scare off" these countries, the officials say.

Of course, none of this amounts to revolutionary innovation. Each step is so carefully measured that no one can state with confidence that fundamental change is underway. . . .

Outside Pressure

In assessing Japan's enthusiasm for global responsibility, it may be useful to bear in mind that many of what have been construed as important Japanese initiatives were not taken by the Japanese. For decades, the impetus for major shifts—toward increased domestic consumption, or expanded foreign aid, or strengthened armed forces—has originated elsewhere, usually in the United States.

Now and then, foreign demands coincided with Japan's perceived self-interest. When Yasuhiro Nakasone was Prime Minister, he was more than glad to use the United States as a scapegoat for a military buildup that he himself wanted. Outside pressure, however, has become such an integral part of the Japanese political process that it is doubtful whether anything of consequence can be accomplished without it.

The endless trade friction with the United States is the clearest example. The pattern is the same each time. Washington asks for something and Tokyo says no. Often, it invokes cultural or historical imperatives. Every step of the process produces angst and a flurry of hand-wringing newspaper editorials. Yet each time, Japan has yielded—sometimes a bit, sometimes more.

Its basic purpose is always to keep the world off its back for a while longer. Politicians then explain to their constituents that they have no choice but to give in. Japan, after all, must preserve "international harmony," to use a favorite locution. Washington thereby becomes a handy whipping boy for officials who are too timid to exercise leadership.

Besides, Japan has long been uncomfortable with unequivocal expressions of principle—a point even ardent nationalists (Nakasone being one of the most prominent figures in this group) agree with, and they are the most forceful advocates of a Japan that stands for something other than money-making.

The Japanese Spirit

Nakasone talked often about the need to promote the "Japanese spirit." The problem is that no one can explain to the rest of the world exactly what "Japanese spirit" means, or how it translates into specific policies. Each of the military superpowers—the United States and the Soviet Union—has a political system and a set of values with worldwide applicability. Japan, the economic superpower, believes, above all, in the specialness of being Japanese.

The Japanese Tribe

For all the current talk about the "internationalization" of Japan, it remains, in some respects, nothing but talk. The Japanese may embrace American technology, European fashion and Chinese philosophy, but when "internationalization" means close contact with non-Japanese, many Japanese still react with a mixture of fear and loathing.

Says Hideaki Kase, the English-speaking son of a former ambassador to the United Nations, "Japanese are very tribal."

Bernard Wysocki Jr., *The Wall Street Journal*, November 13, 1986.

The belief in their uniqueness is so powerful that it can paralyze Japanese when they come to grips with the outside world. Once, I asked a meteorologist why so many Japanese, even in big cities, seemed preoccupied with the weather. Probably, he replied, because Japan used to be an agrarian society. It apparently never occurred to him that every country was once an agrarian society. I've even heard Japanese say they could not live anywhere else because they would miss the four seasons.

This fetish for presumed uniqueness is limitless. A physician became a best-selling author with a book arguing that the Japanese brain processes certain sounds differently from all other brains. Bureaucrats at the trade ministry rejected European-made skis as unsuitable for the "unique" Japanese snow. A former Cabinet minister declared that Japanese cannot consume higher levels of American beef because their intestines are longer than anyone else's.

The lack of kinship the Japanese feel toward the rest of the world can mask an element of amorality. One example was the scandal involving the Toshiba Machine Company, which slunk around Japanese law to sell militarily sensitive technology to the Soviet Union. While the threat to overall Western security was debatable, the Toshiba case reinforced the doubts that many Americans already had about Japan's reliability as far as international covenants and loyalty to allies are concerned.

A similar myopia accounts for its racial attitudes and its burgeoning trade with South Africa. . . .

Michio Watanabe, a leader of the ruling Liberal Democratic Party, [stated] that American blacks are nonchalant about going bankrupt to avoid paying debts. The incident recalled an earlier gaffe by then-Prime Minister Nakasone; [in 1986] he said that blacks and Hispanics in the United States lowered the nation's "level" (of intelligence or literacy).

As for South Africa, the Japanese Government denounces apartheid and has no diplomatic relations with Pretoria, but that has not interfered with business. In 1987, Japan replaced the United States as South Africa's top trading partner. What really ruffles Japanese officials is not so much the trade itself as the awkwardness of being No. 1. Japanese, in general, don't care at all. To my knowledge, there has not been a single protest demonstration anywhere in Japan demanding business disinvestment from South Africa. . . .

A friend, a Japanese newspaper editor, said that he was discomfited by a new arrogance that he detects among his countrymen. His concern is well-placed.

A growing number of Japanese are convinced that they alone know how to do things right. Quite a few times, I have heard businessmen and bureaucrats say that Japan has nothing more to learn from the United States or any other country.

A Modern Industrial State

No country can turn on a dime like Japan.

It transformed itself in the late 19th century from a quasi-feudal kingdom into a modern industrial state, one that was capable as early as 1905 of defeating Russia at war. After World War II, it spun around again, acquiescing to its American conquerors, accepting imposed reforms and then turning them to incredible advantage.

No one can rule out still another sudden shift, perhaps even toward acceptance of a leadership role. Whatever happens, you can be sure Japan will see that it comes out ahead.

"The contradictory pulls between uniqueness and internationalism that so grip the Japanese today will be resolved in favor of internationalism."

Japan Can Overcome Its Ethnocentrism

Edwin O. Reischauer

Edwin O. Reischauer is a former US ambassador to Japan, and is professor emeritus and director of the Edwin O. Reischauer Institute of Japan Studies at Harvard University in Cambridge, Massachusetts. In the following viewpoint, he argues that Japan is caught between its traditional ethnocentric view of itself as a unique nation and its increasing international concerns and responsibilities as a world power. Reischauer cites two trends that he believes will make Japan less insular in the future. One is the successful modernization of Japan's economy, and the other is its younger generation's growing interest in foreign products and trends.

As you read, consider the following questions:

1. How is Japan viewed by other nations, according to Reischauer?
2. Why must Japan change its attitude towards other countries, according to the author?
3. What three reasons does Reischauer provide to support his belief that Japan can successfully change its ethnocentric attitudes?

Reprinted by permission of the publisher from *The Japanese Today*, by Edwin O. Reischauer. Cambridge, MA: The Belknap Press of Harvard University Press. Copyright © 1988 by the President and Fellows of Harvard College.

Japan stands out in some ways as the most international major country in the world. Economically it is prominent almost everywhere. It depends for its livelihood on its economic relations with distant parts of the world, and its products are valued everywhere. It has blended with unparalleled success its own native culture with elements from the West. Japan seems almost the model of what a modern international country should be.

And yet the greatest single problem the Japanese face today is their relationship with other peoples. During the past century and a half they have overcome truly mountainous problems, but they now find themselves struggling with the largely self-created psychological problem of their own self-image and the attitude of other nations toward them.

Admired but Not Liked

Japan naturally is much admired, but it is not widely liked or trusted. It is feared both for its past military record and for its current unprecedented economic success. Its low political posture in world politics is looked on with suspicion as an attempt to avoid responsibilities and concentrate on its own narrow advantages. To others Japan's low posture seems a form of trickery rather than a positive effort to promote peace, as it is seen in Japanese eyes. Most non-Western peoples perceive the Japanese to be more Western than Asian, while to Occidentals they appear to be the epitome of the mysterious and menacing "East." Less-developed countries feel Japan should be more sympathetic and generous, while the other advanced countries see it as uncooperative in facing world problems. On both sides it is recognized as an economically dominant power, but it is not well understood and is felt to be uncommunicative and to hold itself self-consciously apart.

Lingering feelings of separateness and uniqueness are still serious problems for the Japanese themselves. Once the problems Japan faced were quite different. They centered on technological backwardness, strategic defense, and massive reforms of society and government. Now they concern successful communication and cooperation with the other peoples of the world. If world peace crumbles, Japan will collapse with it. If the world trading system stagnates, Japan's future will be at risk. Even continued brilliant economic success, such as Japan has enjoyed during the past few decades, could bring on catastrophe if it is not balanced by worldwide growth and understanding. It could produce retaliatory trade restrictions and possibly a trade war, which could plunge the world into a descending spiral toward economic collapse. It certainly would concentrate the ill will of other nations on Japan. The country's narrow emphasis on its own economic growth, which has been its chief policy ever since World War II, has become positively dangerous. Japan as a world leader must adopt broader aims, which embrace the other nations of the world. International understanding is not just a pleasantly innocuous catchphrase for Japanese policy but has become a practical necessity.

Sense of Uniqueness

The Japanese are intellectually aware of this situation, but they find their own sense of uniqueness difficult to shake off. It is not easy for them to give up their past cozy life, safely insulated by their language barrier and thriving economy, for a more adventurous life dealing with the problems of world peace and the global economy. To put it in dramatic terms, they find it hard to join the human race. For one thing, they still have inadequate skills of communication. More seriously, they have a strong sense of separateness.

Changing Generations

Generations are changing, and attitudes will change with them. Young people in Japan today have had more exposure to foreigners than their parents had. Their attitude toward foreigners seems to be somewhat more tolerant and relaxed, even disinterested. They appear to be more open-minded on the subject of marriage to foreigners, for example. Surveys have found that over half of the respondents in their thirties accept the idea, while only about a third of those in their forties approve.

Young Japanese currently studying abroad are also likely to make a difference. Some 300,000 are studying in the United States; about 50,000 are in West Germany; and another 50,000 or so are in the United Kingdom. They represent a small minority, but they are likely to assume positions of leadership when they return to Japan.

Ellen L. Frost, *For Richer, For Poorer*, 1987.

A good illustration of the latter point was provided by Prime Minister Yasuhiro Nakasone in October 1986 when he made slighting references to certain American ethnic groups as lowering overall American intellectual standards. He unquestionably expressed attitudes taken for granted by most Japanese, but he also revealed an appalling lack of understanding that Japanese leaders, now that they are world leaders as well, will have to be more circumspect in their public utterances, since the whole world now pays attention to what they say. It is to be hoped that the resulting outcry to this incident in the United States taught the Japanese a needed lesson.

Much depends on Japan's choice between continued separateness and a genuine internationalization of its attitudes.

Its own stable democracy, smoothly operating social system, and commitment to peace, when combined with its tremendous economic power, can do much to help solve the problems the world faces. However, if it continues to be resented by the less-developed countries and to be seen as uncooperative by the advanced ones, economic frictions could escalate and bring on a general decline in international relations. In these days of growing complexity in world affairs such a decline could all too easily end in catastrophe.

Reasons for Optimism

Only time will reveal the outcome, but there are good reasons for optimism. The Japanese have already fitted themselves with remarkable success into the dominant "first world" of the industrialized democracies. Their history shows that for the past century and a half they have risen to meet whatever challenge Japan faced as soon as they could clearly see the problem. When superior Western military and economic technology threatened Japan's future in the nineteenth century, the Japanese proved themselves equal to the situation, fundamentally transforming their polticial, social, and economic systems in order to achieve technological equality. When the age of rampant imperialism threatened Japan's future, the country concentrated on building sufficient military power to become one of the five great powers of the world, though its failure to perceive in time the ending of this age led to Japan's one great disaster in modern times. When it found itself at the end of World War II a devastated land living under greatly changed global conditions, it concentrated with unprecedented success on economic growth, once again reforming its whole political, social, and economic systems.

Today the great problem for Japan is to become a fully cooperative member of world society, serving as a leader in helping to develop a peaceful world order. To do this will require the abandonment of its sense of uniqueness. It will also require greater efforts to help the less-developed countries, a bolder stance on world peace, and sacrifices of some economic advantages to create a more smoothly operating international economic system. But these are relatively small changes compared with the ones Japan made to achieve earlier goals. There is no reason to believe that a country that has been so successful in attaining its main objectives in the past cannot do so again.

A second reason for optimism is the fact that most Japanese are intellectually aware of the need to be more international, even though they may not be emotionally prepared for it. A host of small moves are being made toward the internationalization of Japan. There is inevitably a degree of self-congratulatory pride and arrogance toward other countries because of Japan's extraordinary economic success, but there are no movements leading toward the strengthening of Japanese separateness from the rest of the world. Such attempts would obviously be suicidal, and even the most flagrantly self-confident Japanese realize that increased international cooperation is the only hope for Japan's future success. It is also quite clear to everyone that a prosperous Japan can exist only in a prosperous world. There are many current efforts at internationalizing education in Japan, making Japanese more internationally minded, and getting the people out of their familiar national cocoon. These efforts are all admittedly small and feeble when compared to the needs, but all the motion is in the right direction. World conditions also draw the Japanese inevitably outward.

Japan's Internationalization

The internationalization of Japanese society is likely to progress in the exchange of both goods and people. It has been noted already that an increasing number of Japanese enterprises, including some major corporations, are beginning to seek and hire Japanese graduates from European and U.S. universities, who possess non-Japanese thinking patterns and behavioral style. This is a rather expected consequence of the internationalizaton of the behavior of Japanese enterprises. In the not too distant future these Japanese firms doing business within Japan will also start hiring foreigners as their regular staff employees. Such a policy shift in hiring and employment is expected to have an inevitable impact on the nation's educational system, exerting a strong force to make it become progressively open to the outside world.

Seizaburo Sato, *The United States and Japan*, 1987.

The chief factor, however, that makes one believe that Japan will become more international, and at an increasingly rapid rate, is the shift in generations. Most great changes in the world are basically generational. What older people who knew the old conditions accept reluctantly if at all, new generations, which did not personally experience the past, take up quite unconsciously and often with enthusiasm. Today there are vast psychological differences between the prewar generation and the several successive postwar generations. The younger generations are decidedly more internationally minded than their elders. They eagerly roam the world. They feel themselves part of worldwide youth movements. They accept the differences of the outside world with ease. In fact, they feel bottled up in Japan until they have had a chance to see and participate in what lies outside. They look on their own cities not as different from the rest of the world but as centers of world culture. Just as an American looks on New York and a Frenchman on Paris, they see Tokyo as an international city. The very thought that they feel themselves to be different from others is distasteful or even laughable.

Barring the occurrence of a worldwide catastrophe, it is certain that the Japanese will continue to be a major and increasingly unselfconscious part of the world. The contradictory pulls between uniqueness and internationalism that so grip the Japanese today will be resolved in favor of internationalism. And with the economic power and technical skills of the Japanese clearly lending themselves to that trend, Japan and the rest of the world will come appreciably closer to a viable world order.

"Japan . . . to an extent is a colony of the West; it is equal only as an economic power."

Japan Must Rearm To Be a Superpower

Richard Nixon

The Japanese Constitution, drafted by the United States after World War II, includes a provision to renounce war and the use of military force. Since World War II, Japan has depended on the United States for military protection. In the following viewpoint, Richard Nixon argues that this has left Japan vulnerable and dependent, and it cannot be considered a fully developed superpower. Richard Nixon was president of the United States from 1969 until his resignation in 1974.

As you read, consider the following questions:

1. Why are the Japanese reluctant to pursue a major military buildup, according to the author?
2. Why does Nixon believe Japan should increase its military power?
3. How serious a threat is the Soviet Union towards Japan, according to Nixon?

Richard Nixon, *1999: Victory Without War.* Copyright © 1988 by East-West Research. Reprinted by permission of Simon & Schuster, Inc.

Only one new economic superpower has emerged in the world since World War II. Only one Asian country in history has entered the first rank of modern industrial powers. That same country has the most stable democracy in Asia. It is Japan, an ancient storied land whose economic and political success stories in the last forty years can only be described as mind-boggling. . . .

The Western alliance is immeasurably stronger with Japan than it would be without it. Both the United States and Japan should be proud of the partnership that produced a democratic Japan out of the bitterness and destruction of war. But the war and the American military occupation that followed it—and the period of Japan's dependency on the United States that followed the occupation and that continues today—have had negative results as well as positive ones.

Lack of Military Power

Japan is now governed by a constitution written and translated into somewhat awkward Japanese by Americans. It contains an antiwar provision that at the time sparked little controversy in a country that was exhausted by war but that today, with a healthy sense of national pride on the rise, some Japanese find insulting. In the meantime Japan, like West Germany, remains dependent on the United States for critical elements of its national defense. . . .

Some of Japan's critics in the United States are too quick to jump on Japan for adhering to the forty-year-old American-imposed proscriptions on military activities. It is true that the balance of power in the world has changed profoundly since World War II. But we should not expect the Japanese to deal with the psychological scars left by the war as easily as the balance of power. Relations between nations can change with the grasp of a hand, the flourish of a pen, or the flash of a bomb. Relations between people take longer.

When I visited Tokyo as Vice President in 1953, Japanese newspapers gave eight-column headlines to my statement that the United States had "made a mistake" in imposing constitutional restrictions on defense spending on the Japanese after World War II. I believed then that Japan should do more to provide for its own defense. Because of Japan's enormously increased wealth and the fact that the Soviet Union is "reaching out its hand" in the Pacific, the case for what I urged thirty-five years ago is far stronger today. But there are understandable reasons why the Japanese have been slow to take such advice.

In the 1950s, with full American acquiescence, Japan adopted a policy that permitted it to devote virtually all of its resources to its domestic economy. Military expenditures were kept at a minimum, both because of Japan's made-in-America constitution, which strictly limits its military activities, and because of our protective nuclear umbrella. But as the growth of our economy slowed in the 1970s and the growth of our defense budget shrank after the Vietnam War, Japan's low defense spending became an issue in the United States. The key slogan of the argument was, "No more free ride."

Psychological Scars

What many fail to realize is that the Japanese are still not psychologically equipped for a major military buildup, for reasons Americans ought to be able to grasp. Recently, and especially during the tenure of Prime Minister Yasuhiro Nakasone, the Japanese have begun to emerge from the shadow of their shattering defeat in 1945. But to understand why for over three decades the Japanese were reluctant to extend themselves militarily and why to this day they remain profoundly ambivalent about defense spending, all we have to do is examine what happened in the United States in the wake of Vietnam.

Failed Effort

There is little question that Tokyo could relieve the United States of most of its heavy security burden in the Far East. Japan is already an economic superpower, and with even a modest effort it could certainly become a daunting regional political and military power if not actually join the exclusive superpower club. Yet, because of domestic political factors and perverse incentives created by U.S. foreign policy, Japan has consistently failed to make the requisite effort.

Ted Galen Carpenter, *An American Vision*, 1989.

For five years after our failure in Indochina the United States became increasingly isolationist as military budgets were slashed and every use of American forces abroad was examined with such a hypercritical eye that the U.S. was effectively rendered impotent as a world power. Thirteen years after the end of the war, even the smallest commitment of American military power to protect our interests in Central America or the Persian Gulf is bitterly criticized by the media and by isolationists in Congress. Such is the impact that defeat in war can have. Before we preach to the Japanese—who lost 1.2 million people in battle in World War II—about devoting more to defense, we should remember the paralyzing bout of indecision and isolationism that the United States suffered after losing 55,000 men, and for a time our national pride, in Vietnam.

To the extent that Japan's reluctance to rearm is a product of the traumas of defeat in war, we should sympathize with them.

To the extent that it is a rationalization that enables them to enjoy the status of an economic superpower without the responsibilities of a military one, it is unacceptable. While the Japanese reluctance to rearm is to an extent understandable, it is also true that by depending on the United States for its security Japan has had the luxury of diverting more of its resources to building an economy that now competes with, and in some areas outcompetes, our own.

Three Reasons

There are three purely practical reasons why the Japanese must eventually abandon the essentially passive role they have played on the world scene ever since it was imposed on them by defeat in war and by policies established by the victors. Each reason has to do not only with our national interest but with theirs.

First, the United States that took the responsibility for defending Japan controlled almost 50 percent of the world's economy. The United States that sustains that commitment today controls only 27 percent. As a result, Japan's free ride on defense is becoming far too tempting a target for American Japan-bashers. Eventually, if such resentment spreads, our critically important and mutually beneficial relationship with Japan could be harmed.

Second, Japan must realize that, for a great power, playing a role on the world stage is not a privilege; it is a responsibility. There is nothing pleasant about having to divert resources to defense spending and foreign aid that could be applied to problems at home. We do it because we have to, not because we want to. This is the burden that weighs on any prosperous and free society that wants to protect its interests in a world that is by and large inhospitable to freedom. The United States was an isolationist power before World War II; the war made it a world power in spite of its natural inclinations. Japan must also rise to do its duty as a world power.

The third and by far most important reason is that unless Japan does do its duty as a major power, it can never hope to have real national security.

The Soviet Threat

Geographically Japan is an island. But if it continues to attempt to function as an island geopolitically, it cannot survive. A commentator has said that Japan strives to be ''no man's enemy, and a salesman to all.'' This is a worthy but hopelessly impractical goal. The reason is brutally simple: the position Japan occupies on the globe makes it a de-facto target of the Soviet Union. Japan plays an integral part both in Soviet planning for a possible war in the Pacific and in the Western alliance's scheme for deterring and if necessary fighting such a war.

The Soviet conventional buildup in the Far East over the last decade has been ominous. Between a quarter and a third of Soviet

Money for the Military

3.5 trillion yen							
3.0							
2.5							
2.0	**While Japan is Spending More . . .** Military budget for each fiscal year, in trillions of yen.						
1.5							
1.0							
0.5	At current exchange rates, 1989 budget is $31.4 billion. Yen's value against dollar has more than doubled since 1982.						
0.0	'82	'83	'84	'85	'86	'87	'88 '89

. . . It is Still Far Behind Other Countries

Military spending as a percentage of gross domestic product. Figures for 1986.

Japan	1.5%*
West Germany	3.1%
France	3.9%
United Kingdom	4.9%
United States	6.7%

*Includes military spending costs, which Japan separates from other military spending

Sources: Japanese Management and Coordination Agency, International Institute for Strategic Studies

military power is now aimed at the Pacific theater. In 1976 its Asia force was 31 tank divisions, 2,000 combat aircraft, and a 755-ship Navy. Today it has 41 divisions, 85 new Backfire bombers armed with nuclear missiles, 2,400 combat aircraft, and 840 ships. Even after its medium-range nuclear missiles are removed from Asia according to the terms of the INF [intermediate-range nuclear forces] treaty, every key target in Japan will be covered by the Soviet Union's strategic nuclear weapons.

Even more troubling is that, Gorbachev's Asian "peace offensive" notwithstanding, the Russians have been flexing their substantial muscle. In 1986 Soviet aircraft intruded into Japanese airspace 350 times; estimates were even higher for 1987. In 1986 the Soviets also staged exercises in the Kurile Islands, which they seized from Japan in 1948, that simulated an invasion of Japan's northenmost island of Hokkaido. . . .

Japan Should Rearm

In the short term a major military buildup by Japan would cause more problems than it would solve: it would relieve a relatively insignificant portion of the American burden for defending Japan while at the same time fostering regional unrest, especially among nations such as China and Korea that fear a militarily resurgent Japan. But in the long term it is both inevitable and proper that Japan take on a military role in Asia commensurate with its economic power. In view of Japan's actions during and before World War II, China's and Korea's misgivings are understandable, but each should ponder what it fears more: Japan's 180,000-man Self-Defense Force or the Soviets' 785,000-man Asian army, Japan's 270-plane air force or the 2,700 aircraft in the Soviets' Far Eastern department.

The new postwar world demands a reassessment of the balance of power in Asia. For the foreseeable future, the stronger Japan is, the safer Asia will be. Japan is the indispensable linchpin for any strategy for peace in Asia.

Today Japan's Self-Defense Forces could hold out as few as two days against a surprise Soviet conventional invasion. Some commentators who counsel against a major Japanese buildup say that the United States's security guarantee is sufficient to stop such a Soviet move. Regrettably, it would not be. Since the United States does not have enough ground forces in place to match the Soviets, stopping such an invasion would be difficult at best. The United States would quickly be faced with the necessity of considering the use of nuclear weapons based at sea or on the American mainland.

While these weapons are loaded and ready, the danger is that the Soviets would see the threat of their use as an empty cannon. The concern that the United States would not risk a nuclear World War III by using U.S.-based strategic nuclear weapons against a Soviet army marching on Western Europe was the principal reason the United States deployed intermediate-range nuclear weapons in Europe in 1979. The same holds true in the Far East, only more so. An American President who used nuclear weapons to halt a Soviet conventional attack on Japan would be risking a massive nuclear attack on the United States—a risk a President would be unlikely to take. The Soviets know this. As a result, Japan today is dangerously vulnerable to such an attack. Eventually Japan must develop the capacity to defend itself *by* itself against Soviet conventional forces. It does not have to match the Soviets man to man. It only has to do enough to make a Soviet invasion too costly to contemplate.

Japan cannot undertake a full-scale military buildup now. The memory of World War II is still too strong among its neighbors. But that will change—especially if Japan begins to play a greater role as a supplier of development aid and investment to Third World nations in Asia and elsewhere. When Japan shows the world that it is willing to invest in a peaceful, prosperous, and free Asia, its neighbors' misgivings about its military posture will slowly but surely fade. If it follows this course in the twenty-first century Japan will be a true superpower—willing and able to defend its own interests and those of its friends and allies. . . .

A Partial Superpower

One observer in Japan said, "For Japan to be equal requires Japan to be separate. If Japan were not separate, it could only be inferior, and would soon be a colony of the West." The irony of this statement is that because Japan depends upon another nation for its security it to an extent is a colony of the West; it is equal only as an economic power. Thus the Japanese have the opposite dilemma to that of the Soviet Union, whose status as a superpower comes only from its military strength. Just as the Japanese are self-conscious about depending on the United States for their security, the Soviets are self-conscious about their economic backwardness. The problem with the Soviet economy is communism. The problem with Japanese national security is Japan's inability to protect itself as a result of both political and psychological constraints.

What will help banish Japan's fear of losing its individuality is a more activist role on the world stage—diplomatically, developmentally, and eventually militarily. The Japanese people have good reason to be repelled by the thought of war, and many do not want their nation to rearm. Americans are also repelled by war. The difference is that Americans support a level of national-security spending that is adequate to protect their country against any aggressor. The Japanese attitude will inevitably change, especially if Japan's neighbors become less concerned about its reemergence. With the change will come a new self-confidence among Japanese, born of the certain knowledge that Japan is once again a truly independent nation.

> *"Japan is betting that it can continue to increase its global influence . . .by relying primarily on economic rather than military power."*

Japan Need Not Rearm To Be a Superpower

Paul Kreisberg

Paul Kreisberg is a senior associate at the Carnegie Endowment for International Peace. In the following viewpoint, he argues that Japan's world power status stems from financial and economic clout rather than military force. Kreisberg states that Japan has succeeded in increasing its global influence and protecting its national interests without a fully developed military.

As you read, consider the following questions:

1. How does Japan's global influence differ from the influence of the United States and Soviet Union, according to the author?
2. According to Kreisberg, why does Japan believe increasing its military power might actually decrease its national security?
3. Why does Kreisberg believe Japan's status is advantageous for the United States?

Paul Kriesberg, "Japan: A Superpower Minus Military Power," *Los Angeles Times*, December 11, 1988. Reprinted with permission.

For 40 years the United States and the Soviet Union have set new standards for power: military capability to wage war across the globe, to wholly destroy their enemies, to provide virtually unlimited arms to their allies, to "bear any burden" in a prolonged contest for influence and strength. The United States for much of this same period possessed enormous economic resources to influence and affect the economic and political policies of other countries, to dominate world markets and to compete for influence in ways no other country, even the Soviet Union, could match.

A New Sort of Superpower

But now there is Japan, a new sort of superpower, relying on technological and financial clout to protect increasingly global interests while remaining heavily dependent on the United States for military protection. Can Japan be an active and effective political player in the international community without an independent and powerful military capability?

Japan is the second-largest economy in the world but spends less of its gross national product on defense than Austria, Malta or Jamaica. The Japanese people consistently tell pollsters they want this to continue. Even the current level of expenditure enables Japan to field highly sophisticated conventional forces in its own defense. But its treaty agreement with the United States and its own constitution leave open whether Japan would ever come to the aid of America even if the United States was under attack in the Pacific, so long as Japan itself was not under assault. Nor has Japan taken any part in international peacekeeping activities; this was the first year it contributed funds for such actions.

At the same time Japan underwrites the U.S. budget deficit, buying between 20%-40% of U.S. Treasury securities each month. It is now the largest aid donor to the developing world, also the largest contributor of new capital to the World Bank and the International Monetary Fund. The dollar remains the key international reserve currency but the yen is in increasing demand except for those countries committed to propping up the dollar.

Japanese banks and insurance companies are the world's largest. Japanese investors are the most active in Asia and most other parts of the world. Even the Japanese domestic market, once virtually impenetrable to products from abroad, is rapidly becoming more important not only to other Asian countries (where imports are often manufactured by Japanese companies) but to the West.

Since the early 1970s Japan has gradually accepted its responsibility in discussions on global economic policy, in supporting developing countries and even on some international political issues. It remains uneasy over how to use the political influence and power inevitably attached to economic power but is beginning to adjust to this.

When virtually any international event has an economic cost, the first question now asked is, "Will Japan pay?" This is the ultimate "power" question that was once asked only of the United States. It is forcing Japanese to think about what *they* want to achieve in more and more situations.

Japan thus far has used its influence primarily to further its own economic interests and objectives, but in recent years it has also taken account—usually under U.S. pressure—of how it can contribute to American or Western interests in Egypt, Jordan, Turkey, Pakistan or the Persian Gulf—or the interests of friendly Asian groups in Cambodia, the Korean peninsula and Burma.

Different Assumptions

We in the United States make three assumptions about a strong military force that the Japanese do not make.

The first is we assume that a strong military force benefits foreign policy. However, that may not be so for Japan, at least as regards East Asia. All of the Asian countries have told the Japanese that a Japanese military build-up is not necessarily in their best interests.

The second assumption is that a strong military force enhances domestic security and tranquility. That may be true in the United States but it certainly is not true in Japan. The Japanese fear a resurgence of militarism. . . .

The third assumption is that Japan should take as serious a view of the Soviet threat as the United States does. The Japanese do not take this threat so seriously. . . .

On this score, the Japanese ask three questions. The first is why would the Soviet Union ever attack on its weakest and most distant front? Of all the places in the world, it would be most difficult for the Soviets to do anything in Japan, so why would they start there? The second question is what do the Soviets want from Japan? Could it be their technology? Is a war the way to acquire it? The third question is does the Soviet Union really have the capability to mount a sustained conventional attack on Japan?

Nathaniel B. Thayer, *Toward a Better Understanding: US—Japan Relations*, 1986.

Japanese privately insist that they are particularly sensitive to U.S. views on virtually all political issues; and this generally seems to be true. But there are signs of change and more Japanese legislators privately insist that their government look at Japanese, not U.S. interests. Japan has consistently distanced itself from a number of U.S. positions on the Middle East, including Iran and the Palestine Liberation Organization, because of Tokyo's dependence on the region for oil and markets. Until recently Japan has declined to alter trading relationships with South Africa despite U.S. pressures and, according to published figures, is still South Africa's largest trading partner. Japan has its own positions on a wide range of environmental and ecological issues and has almost always resisted joining in international economic sanctions.

Japan's Influence

But Japan is capable of pursuing a far broader foreign-policy agenda of its own, using the levers of Japanese investment, economic assistance, technology transfers and contributions to international organizations. And Japan is gradually—almost everything in Japan is gradual—about to undertake more independent initiatives. Foreign Minister Sosuke Uno, for example, in July 1988 offered to pay for actual peacekeeping forces in Cambodia, a step some Japanese officials are still not sure was thought through, since it runs counter to a 1978 resolution prohibiting support for military forces in other countries.

Japan's help is sought on all sides—by the communist world and by developing countries of all political complexions in Asia, Africa, Latin America, the Middle East, and the West. The respect given its officials and diplomats, the attention given its views and the care and consideration extended to its private citizens are at superpower levels.

Japanese comments on economic policy issues are treated on a par with those of America—and sometimes with even greater respect. Japan's voting power in both the International Monetary Fund and the World Bank will surely increase in the next few years, commensurate with Japanese contributions; Japanese policy influence in both organizations will grow. Even quiet hints, or silence, on policy issues are increasingly taken note of. *This* is political influence.

Japanese officials have been the most skeptical in the world about Soviet intentions and objectives, and of Mikhail S. Gorbachev himself. But the United States cannot assume that Japan will not shift its policy toward Moscow. Gorbachev's . . . conciliatory tone will play well to Japanese audiences. . . .

Military Power

The foundation of Japanese security policy continues to be, as it has been for the last 40 years, military dependence on the United States. For Japan, the question has been whether increased defense spending and a change in defense policy will strengthen its economic and political security or weaken it. Its answer thus far is that if it is seen by the rest of the world—particularly by the Chinese and Soviets—as becoming a more potent military power, both America and Japan would be less, not more, secure. This answer is almost certainly right.

Ironically peace, stability and an easing of tensions in Asia—just as in Europe—could also erode vital elements in the U.S.-Japan relationship, diminishing the importance of security ties and causing more Japanese to reconsider the strategic bargain they have maintained, especially if the arrangement itself caused Washington-Tokyo economic strains.

Global war seems increasingly distant. All major powers are likely to avoid involvement in regional conflicts and are likely to try helping settle those that do occur. Economic development and reform are given priority in the policies of virtually every country. It seems inevitable that the political influence of strong economic powers should increase relative to those dependent on military power.

Japan a Forerunner

Military power may very well become a less important component of international influence in the 21st century, and the current revulsion toward and rejection of nuclear weapons may grow. Japan's postwar decision to be an exclusively defensive power and to base its security on non-nuclear principles may well be a forerunner of global trends.

Saburo Okita, *Foreign Policy*, Summer 1989.

This argues strongly for a restoration of a vital and innovative U.S. economy as quickly as possible. But it also argues for continuing to take advantage of the current situation: The political influence generated by Japan generally enhances the geopolitical and international economic interests of the United States. This is likely to continue, assuming the two countries adjust psychologically to the special symbiotic power relationship that has developed between them. As one close adviser to President George Bush observed in private, the mutual economic damage that might be done if this breaks down might resemble in its own way the consequences of a confrontation between the two great military superpowers.

When other states understand that U.S. views on how or whether Japan should use its financial or economic weight are essential elements in Japanese decision making, and when they see the bilateral cooperation on global issues, the political and economic objectives of both countries are served.

All this is easier to write than to do and the day-by-day political challenges for both countries are enormous. But Japan is betting that it can continue to increase its global influence and strengthen its economic and political interests by relying primarily on economic rather than military power, even while preserving strong U.S. relations.

Recognizing Statements That Are Provable

From various sources of information we are constantly confronted with statements and generalizations about social and moral problems. In order to think clearly about these problems, it is useful if one can make a basic distinction between statements for which evidence can be found and other statements which cannot be verified or proved because evidence is not available, or the issue is so controversial that it cannot be definitely proved.

Readers should constantly be aware that magazines, newspapers, and other sources often contain statements of a controversial nature. The following activity is designed to allow experimentation with statements that are provable and those that are not.

The following statements are taken from the viewpoints in this chapter. Consider each statement carefully. *Mark P for any statement you believe is provable. Mark U for any statement you feel is unprovable because of the lack of evidence. Mark C for any statements you think are too controversial to be proved to everyone's satisfaction.*

If you are doing this activity as a member of a class or group, compare your answers with those of other class or group members. Be able to defend your answers. You may discover that others will come to different conclusions than you. Listening to the reasons others present for their answers may give you valuable insights in recognizing statements that are provable.

> P = *provable*
> U = *unprovable*
> C = *too controversial*

1. Japan will be the number one financial power of the next generation.

2. Nine out of ten of the world's largest banks are Japanese.

3. Japan may find it possible to lead the world without a global military machine.

4. By the year 2000, Japan's net external assets may reach one trillion dollars.

5. The two largest economies in Asia are Japan's and China's.

6. Many Asians view the US more positively than Japan.

7. In 1986 Soviet aircraft intruded into Japanese airspace over 350 times.

8. Japan's reluctance to increase its military spending stems from memories of World War II.

9. Japan spends a smaller percentage of its gross national product on defense than Jamaica.

10. Global war seems increasingly distant.

11. An overwhelming majority of Japanese do not even think about the rest of the world.

12. The Japanese belief in their society's uniqueness paralyzes their relationship with the outside world.

13. Economic power is becoming more important than military power.

14. The younger generations in Japan are more internationally minded than their elders.

15. If world trade declines, Japan will suffer greatly.

16. Japan finances about 30 percent of the US government's budget deficit.

17. The basic purpose of Japan's trade concessions is to keep the world off its back for a while longer.

18. When superior Western military technology threatened Japan in the 1800s, the Japanese successfully reformed their society to achieve technological equality.

Periodical Bibliography

The following articles have been selected to supplement the diverse views presented in this chapter.

Ian Buruma — "Not To Be Confused with Confucius," *The Spectator*, November 5, 1988.

Barry Buzan — "Japan's Future: Old History Versus New Roles," *International Affairs*, Autumn 1988.

John Greenwald — "From Superrich to Superpower," *Time*, July 4, 1988.

Peter Hartcher — "Guess Who's Carrying a Bigger Stick," *World Press Review*, July 1988.

Takashi Inoguchi — "Four Japanese Scenarios for the Future," *International Affairs*, Winter 1989.

Donald Kirk — "Japan Feels Its 'Uniqueness' in the Land of the Rising Yen," *The New Leader*, September 5, 1988. Available from the American Labor Conference on International Affairs, 275 Seventh Ave., New York, NY 10001.

Larry Martz — "Hour of Power?" *Newsweek*, February 27, 1989.

William J. Mazzocco — "Japan, the USSR, and Eurasia," *Global Affairs*, Winter 1989.

George R. Packard — "The Status & Power of Japan," *The National Interest*, Winter 1986/1987.

Klaus H. Pringsheim — "Japan and the Superpowers," *Global Affairs*, Winter 1987.

Carla Rapoport — "Will the Yen Push Aside the Dollar?" *Fortune*, December 5, 1988.

Murray Sayle — "The Powers That Might Be," *Far Eastern Economic Review*, August 4, 1988.

Tsugio Tajiri — "Japan Is 'Accepted but Not Respected,'" *World Press Review*, February 1988.

Mike Tharp and Jim Impoco — "Japan's Diplomatic Pouch of Gold," *U.S. News & World Report*, September 26, 1988.

Jiro Tokuyama — "Creating 'Ameripan,'" *New Perspectives Quarterly*, Summer 1988.

Dori Jones Yang and Neil Gross — "Japan Builds a New Power Base," *Business Week*, April 10, 1989.

Are Japan's Economic Policies Fair?

Chapter Preface

Japan runs large trade surpluses with many countries, including the US. In 1986, for instance, Japan sold $211 billion worth of goods and services to other countries, and bought only $127 billion. Many people believe these trade imbalances threaten the stability of the world economy, and want them reduced. They accuse the Japanese of protecting their industries from foreign competition. They also believe the Japanese take unfair advantage of the relatively open world markets.

Those who agree often argue that Japan's trade surpluses result from unfair collusion between Japanese government and business. Management expert Peter Drucker states that the Japanese government targets certain industries for development, provides assistance to these companies, and shelters them from foreign competition in order to dominate the world market in these industries. Drucker and other critics of Japan describe a complex system of corporations and government bureaucracies sometimes labeled "Japan, Inc."

Other people argue that "Japan, Inc." is a myth, and assert that the government's role in Japan's economy has been exaggerated. Japan's trade successes, these people argue, result instead from Japanese superiority in work habits, business management, thriftiness, and education.

Is Japan an unfair competitor? The viewpoints in the following chapter debate this issue.

"Japan has the lowest number of restricted import items and the lowest tariff rates among the industrialized nations."

Japan Supports Free Trade

Shoichi Saba

Shoichi Saba is a former president of the Toshiba Corporation. In the following viewpoint, Saba argues that Japan does not prevent foreign goods from entering its domestic markets. He writes that American and European products do not succeed in the Japanese market because they do not satisfy the needs of Japanese consumers.

As you read, consider the following questions:

1. According to the author, how does the Japanese electronics industry contribute to free-market economies?
2. How does the Toshiba Corporation promote fair competition with foreign electronics companies, according to the author?

Reprinted with permission from Shoichi Saba, "The U.S. and Japanese Electronics Industries: Competition and Cooperation," *Issues in Science and Technology*, Volume II, Number 3, Spring 1986. Copyright 1986 by the National Academy of Sciences, Washington, DC.

There is a heated international debate concerning the relationship between the electronics industries in the United States and Japan. Unfortunately, the thrust of the discussion focuses almost exclusively on the competitive, as opposed to the cooperative, aspects of this relationship. Many of the loudest advocates appear to be basing their arguments on only partial information. The realities are naturally much more complex. To understand the true nature of the problems and to achieve workable solutions, both sides need a better grasp of the driving forces at work. The operating environment, the nature of technological change, the role of the electronics industry, and fair trade are each aspects of the debate and are explored in this article. Toshiba's policies for its electronics businesses are also considered here in an effort to shed light on how we at Toshiba are trying to work as responsible participants in the world electronics industry. . . .

Although Japan and the West have numerous cultural differences, their political and economic philosophies are remarkably similar. A fundamental assumption of both cultures is that there are efficiencies in a free market. The workings of the free market are based on fair competition among private companies, which should lead to higher productivity, technological innovation, and added value to the goods produced. The ultimate beneficiary of this system is the consumer.

Global Trading System

The intensification of the debate over trade, however, clearly indicates that the system is not working properly. Companies that participate in this global trading system need to reassess whether they are living up to their responsibilities as international corporate citizens. A number of developments indicate that such reassessments are being made.

One important step consists of the decisions reached at the September 1985 meeting of the Group of Five that involved leading economic officials from the United States, Britain, France, West Germany, and Japan. These decisions outlined a series of basic measures aimed at supporting free and fair trade. Each participating country must now in good faith guarantee to implement the terms of the agreement. For Japan's part the appreciation of the yen and higher domestic interest rates should make a positive contribution to rectifying some of today's imbalances.

When assessing Japan's role in the world electronics industry, it is important to understand the driving forces of the Japanese economy. Because Japan is a resource-poor nation, it must export to pay for its not inconsiderable imports. Often overlooked is the fact that Japan is a major importer of fossil fuels, other raw materials, and foodstuffs, in addition to finished manufactured products. It should also not be forgotten that while exporting,

65

Japan adds significant value to the goods it produces, thereby benefiting consumers in the process. . . .

One of the essential strengths of Japan's economy is that industry and government can agree on certain basic solutions, but that it is up to the private sector to carry out the needed responses. In other words, the Japanese government may help coordinate consensus, but clearly it does not intervene, for example, to nationalize industries, as sometimes occurs in other countries. Additionally, most studies of Japanese government subsidies provided to industry show that these subsidies are small by comparison with those of other countries.

The electronics industry is an important pillar of both Japan's and the world's future economic growth. In Japan the electronics industry is probably the main force accelerating the change in the composition of an economy from one that is industry based to one that is information based. As Japan's electronics industry has matured, it has responded to the challenge of more open competition.

In line with successive agreements reached under the auspices of the General Agreement on Tariffs and Trade, Japan has sought to open its markets further. To respond effectively Japan has established a broad-based action program. It is true (and the record

© J.D. Phillips/Rothco Cartoons

will show) that Japan has the lowest number of restricted import items and the lowest tariff rates among the industrialized nations. Japan also is making an effort to expand its domestic economy, as indicated by increases in public spending, to realign the more export-oriented economy of the past. . . .

Technological Changes

New technologies form the basis for a new information-oriented industrial structure. Through trade, advances in high technology and information systems in one country can quickly affect the industrial status quo in other countries. Technological innovation knows few national boundaries. As the information society develops, the world's economy will become increasingly interdependent. In the near future, trade frictions may cease to be limited to goods and may also extend to services and other information-intensive fields. If anything, left unresolved, the atmosphere of the trade conflict is quite likely to deteriorate further. The time to squarely address trade-related problems and their solutions is now. . . .

Internationalization, deregulation, and free trade are indispensable to the healthy development of the world's electronics industry. Toshiba's view is that the electronics industry will serve to continue to improve the quality of life of the individual. In short, the electronics industry occupies a central place, with concomitant responsibilities, in regard to the vitality of the economies of the free world.

These economies are based on free trade. A reading of history will show that the protectionism of the 1930s fueled rather than alleviated the protracted worldwide depression of that era, and it would be a mistake of major proportions to return to protectionism. Including consumer electronics products and control systems for power plants, more than 50 percent of Toshiba's business is accounted for by electronics. We are concerned, therefore, about the trade-friction debate and are attempting to contribute to resolving the problems. . . .

Promotes Fair Competition

As one of Japan's leading electronics manufacturers, Toshiba believes that international cooperation is an important part of the world electronics industry's future. In line with this belief, our companywide policy is to promote fair competition and to contribute to the development of the industry through technological exchange and the encouragement of bilateral and multilateral market access. This policy is more than just words: Our company is now implementing several programs to achieve these broader goals. Our three objectives may be summed up as follows:

Toshiba's first objective is to encourage greater technological exchange and cooperation with foreign companies. We are doing this in a number of ways. In semiconductors, for example, we are engaged in technological and other exchanges with non-Japanese corporations. We are proud of our cooperative efforts with such innovative and leading corporations as Intel Corp., LSI Logic Corporation, Motorola, and Zilog, in the United States; SGS Microelettronica, in Italy; and Siemens, in West Germany. We also plan to expand the scale and scope of these activities. . . .

Toshiba's second objective is to expand local production activities in hardware and software engineering, design, and R&D [Research and Development]. The company now has local production operations, either independently or jointly with local companies, in 12 countries and plans to increase this number. In the United States, for example, we produce semiconductors, color television sets, and microwave ovens, and we are planning to begin production soon of color picture tubes, key telephones, and medical equipment. To internationalize our business activities in electronics, we have established semiconductor design centers in the United States, and we will broaden the scope of the activities of these centers in the future.

Success of Giants

The Japanese consumer likes foreign goods. The attraction of a foreign trademark is very real. It is increasing, not diminishing, as witness not merely the success of giants like Dow Chemical, Texas Instruments, Mitsubishi-Caterpillar, and IBM, but also fast-food chains like McDonald's and Kentucky Fried Chicken. But the consumer has a mind and culture of his own. The cultural gravitational pull in Japan is probably the strongest in the world, and concessions must be made to it. Dealing with the Japanese market takes patience and induces a certain amount of humility. The left-hand drive syndrome—the naive assumption that what sells in New York or Los Angeles will sell in Tokyo, without any alterations—is doomed to fail.

Frank Gibney, *Miracle by Design*, 1982.

Toshiba's third objective is to promote imports of foreign products into Japan. This objective differs somewhat from the previous two, but our management feels it is of equal if not greater importance. In May 1985, to help resolve the problem of trade conflicts in electronics, we set up an in-house group called the Corporate Import Promotion Committee. Separately, our company sponsored an import fair in Japan and sent import missions to the United States, Europe, and Southeast Asia. In fact, Toshiba has also implemented a policy of emphasizing import-based purchases whenever sale conditions and product qualities are equal.

At the same time, however, the above-mentioned import fair did provide a good case study of some of the shortcomings of foreign companies when they participate in the Japanese market. Held in October 1985, this fair exhibited the goods of 180 overseas companies and was visited by about 2,000 Toshiba purchasing staff and design engineers. Frankly speaking, this particular fair illustrated rather strikingly a certain lack of forethought on the part of the foreign sales personnel involved. Many of our staff reported that many sellers lacked either an understanding of, and preparation for, what Japanese customers really need or an understanding of how the purchase decision in Japan actually takes place. It seemed clear to many Toshiba people at the fair that with more careful preparation, the foreign participants could have been much more successful in generating business in Japan. . . .

The future of the world electronics industry must be based on fair competition and cooperation among the participants. Both the Japanese and U.S. sides still have a distance to go in resolving their differences. Some of the main points for consideration by both sides are discussed below.

There are several areas in which Japan should seek to do more to solve the remaining trade problems in electronics:

• The Japanese government and Japanese companies should provide timely responses to requests from responsible parties overseas for information and clarification.

• Japanese companies should behave as responsible corporate citizens in the world community by investing overseas. Overseas investment provides a number of benefits to the host country in terms of funding new investment opportunities and creating new jobs.

• Japanese companies should seek to make trade in electronics a two-way street. One method of doing this is through increased international cooperation. The company-to-company technological ties established by Toshiba and other Japanese companies are a further step in this direction.

Long-Term Thinking

There are certain actions that the U.S. side could consider to improve the situation surrounding international trade in electronics:

• U.S. companies should reconsider their preoccupation with short-term profits. It is often said, and perhaps correctly so, that Japanese companies take the long-term view. Conversely, the Japanese view is that when inevitable economic downturns occur, U.S. companies seem somewhat too ready to trade long-term market position for short-term profit performance. There are numerous instances of U.S companies closing down plants or business operations altogether, whereas these are relatively rare occurrences in Japan.

• U.S. companies should understand the implications of moving manufacturing offshore. Many U.S. companies are apparently moving the production of certain electronics products out of the United States to countries in the Far East. If these decisions are based solely on short-term profit motivations, we at Toshiba would submit that it is shortsighted to move the production of important electronics offshore and to stress software and service businesses in the United States instead. In our opinion, hands-on manufacturing experience is one of the keys to designing advanced electronics and to competing in today's markets.

American Inroads

The depth of penetration of U.S. exports into the Japanese market is greater than generally perceived. American penetration into Japanese manufacturing sectors has been less obvious than Japan's penetration into America's, but it has encompassed a wider range of industries. Although many U.S. exports to Japan are in the primary sector (agricultural and mining goods), American inroads into Japan have not been limited to this sector. Japan is America's number one foreign purchaser of commercial aircraft, organic and inorganic chemicals, pharmaceuticals, and photographic supplies. It is the second largest foreign purchaser of medical and scientific supplies, measuring and testing devices, pulp and wood products, and semiconductors.

Kenichi Ohmae, *Triad Power*, 1985.

• U.S. companies should make greater efforts to translate their advanced R&D capabilities into commercial products. Despite the leading position of U.S. companies in many new technology areas, these companies sometimes show an insufficient amount of follow-through when it comes to commercialization. . . .

In conclusion, it is clear that the pace of technological innovation is contributing to the growth of the world economy and to the internationalization of important industries, such as electronics. Fair competition, international cooperation among companies, and the establishment of an equitable trade system are all part of the process. However, the debate over the world electronics industry strongly suggests that difficult problems exist and that the solutions will not be easy. The results of trade friction between the United States and Japan are not confined to our two countries but affect all the free world. The undeniable trends are that the economies and the industries of the United States and Japan are becoming increasingly interdependent. Neither side will benefit from a continuation of the problems now facing both sides.

"Japan has absolutely no incentive to import the most competitive products manufactured by American companies."

Japan Inhibits Free Trade

Robert T. Green and Trina L. Larsen

Robert T. Green is the H. Timothy Harkings Professor of Business at Harvard University in Cambridge, Massachusetts. Trina L. Larsen is a lecturer in international business and marketing at the University of Texas at Austin. In the following viewpoint, they argue that Japan has not kept its promises to open its domestic markets to foreign products. Green and Larsen believe that Japanese restrictions prevent inexpensive, high-quality US goods from entering Japanese markets.

As you read, consider the following questions:

1. How has Japan failed to follow the principles of free trade, according to the authors?
2. How does Japan protect its domestic markets from foreign products, according to Green and Larsen?

For more than a decade, Japan has been promising to open its markets to U.S. products. And for more than a decade, the U.S. trade deficit with Japan has grown. The reason for this discrepancy between promise and performance is clear: the United States' most competitive exports—especially high-tech products—are the same ones Japan has targeted for its own export market. To keep its domestic industries producing for a worldwide market. Japan shields them at home from U.S. imports. It's time U.S. producers wake up to the fact that there is no Japanese market in their future. Japan will not voluntarily sacrifice its strategic domestic targeting for the sake of the U.S. trade deficit.

Our country's burgeoning trade deficit has meant the loss of more and more U.S. businesses, jobs, and technology. To halt this dangerous erosion of our economy, the United States must adopt a finely tuned retaliatory—not protectionist—trade policy and do some carefully planned industrial targeting. This two-pronged approach will finally equip American managers and companies with the tools they need to compete fairly and effectively with their Japanese counterparts.

Japan's Open Market?

A brief recitation of Japan's trade promises and performance over the past ten years shows the way it plays the global economic game:

• In January 1977, the Japanese government announces a package of economic stimulants to offset the country's huge trade surplus.

In 1977, the U.S. trade deficit with Japan soars to a record $7.6 billion.

• In 1981, the Japanese government solemnly commits itself to increase imports; it adopts a trade package, including tariff cuts, to open the Japanese market.

The 1981 U.S. trade deficit with Japan reaches a $13.6 billion high.

• In 1982, the Japanese redouble their efforts to reduce the embarrassingly large U.S. trade deficit. The Japanese trade minister pledges to take drastic action to cut nontariff barriers to imports. The Japanese government again adopts a trade package, including new tariff cuts, to open Japan's market to foreign goods. Prime Minister Yasahiro Nakasone publicly instructs his cabinet to increase imports.

The 1982 U.S. trade deficit with Japan eases slightly to $12.4 billion.

• In 1983, Japan adopts trade programs designed to stimulate domestic consumption and to reduce tariffs and nontariff barriers.

The 1983 U.S. trade deficit with Japan again swells, to $18.5 billion.

• From 1984 to 1986, the U.S. dollar drops 40% to 50% in value against the yen as the two countries manipulate their currencies in an effort to cut the trade imbalance.

In 1984, the U.S. trade deficit with Japan grows to $33.5 billion; in 1985, to $40.6 billion; in 1986, to $60 billion.

The story that these recurring headlines tell is clear. Beneath Japan's surface pronouncements of concern for the U.S. trade problem are deep economic interests that Japan simply cannot afford to jeopardize. Consequently, it should come as no surprise that U.S. goods still cannot penetrate the Japanese market, even when those goods begin to cost much less: Japan has absolutely no incentive to import the most competitive products manufactured by American companies.

Don Wright, *Palm Beach Post*. Reprinted with permission.

A comparison of U.S. and West German exports with Japanese imports for 1985 illustrates Japan's national economic strategy in practice. The largest category of exports for all three nations is machines and transportation equipment—automobiles, machine tools, and high-tech products like semiconductors, telecommunications equipment, and computers—as might be expected of industrially advanced nations. Despite a greatly overvalued dollar, U.S. exporters have still been internationally competitive for the last decade in many types of machines and transportation equipment; these two categories accounted for almost 50% of 1985 U.S. exports.

Yet as is typical of most developed nations, the United States and West Germany were also substantial importers of machines and transportation equipment. Japan, however, made itself a major exception to this rule: less than 10% of Japanese imports were in the machines and transportation equipment categories.

Some have argued that Japan imports so little high technology simply because Japanese companies make these products better and more cheaply than anyone else. But that doesn't seem to be the case when we look at the numbers in certain product categories. In 1984, the United States' semiconductor industry enjoyed a 55% share of the European market, while Japan's own semiconductors could win no more than a 12% market share in Europe. Yet in spite of the reputation of American-made semiconductors as being superior to Japan's, the United States could gain only 11% of Japan's market.

Proof that U.S. producers can compete on a worldwide basis can also be found in the data from 1985, when the United States' deficit with the world set a record. Even in this bleak period, some U.S. exports continued to grow fast. Four high-tech products alone—office machines, transistors and valves, the most technologically advanced category of telecommunications equipment, and statistical machines—accounted for 11.5% of U.S. exports in 1985, up from 6.5% in 1984. Obviously, U.S. producers were highly competitive in these goods. Yet in 1985, the number of these products coming into Japan amounted to just 2.3% of total imports, primarily because Japan was protecting its own industries.

Japan Avoids Imports

As everyone knows, Japan's Ministry of International Trade and Industry (MITI) identifies growth industries and nurtures them with low-interest loans, subsidies, amortization benefits, and, most significant for U.S. trade, protection from imports. One weapon in Japan's arsenal of formal and informal trade barriers is "administrative guidance," which uses persuasion and veiled threats to get local businesses to avoid imports. Other weapons include debilitating customs procedures that can draw out action for several months; restrictive standards and certification requirements that can be set unrealistically high or changed without notice so that foreign producers have no time to react; and discriminatory public procurement policies, which are an especially effective impediment to imports since the public sector constitutes the lion's share of Japan's market for several product categories.

The procurement record of Nippon Telegraph and Telephone (NTT) illustrates how Japan protects its industries against threatening imports. In 1984, NTT controlled 60% of the $5 billion Japanese telecommunications market. Yet only a paltry 8% of the company's procurements came from outside Japan, and most of that went for such low-tech items as telephone poles. When it came to satellite equipment, the government strongly urged NTT to purchase only local equipment in compliance with the 1983 National Development Policy, which was designed to protect domestic industries. This guidance came in spite of the fact that U.S. satellites were commonly acknowledged to be better and cheaper than Japan's.

The tremendous success of Japan's economic strategy and its effect on U.S. trade is particularly evident in the categories of office machines, telecommunications equipment, and electro-medical equipment. Although Japanese imports in these categories rose only slightly from 1977 to 1985, exports soared. In two of the three industries, the United States retained competitiveness with the rest of the world despite the huge handicap of an overvalued dollar. In trade with Japan, however, the United States was the victim of Japanese targeting while Japanese imports swamped the U.S. market.

Of course, Japan is not the only nation that nurtures growth industries. In 1985, Brazil, Taiwan, South Korea, and Hong Kong, using Japanese methods of industrial targeting, had a collective trade surplus with the United States of about $30 billion. But these nations do not pose as serious a threat to U.S. competitiveness. Their market amounts to only a fraction of the size of the potential Japanese market. Nevertheless, the collective impact of these nations' trade policies has further exacerbated U.S. deficit and competitiveness problems.

Endangering Western Unity

Japan's rapid recovery from the destruction of World War II occurred at the height of the Cold War. The U.S. needed an economically strong ally in East Asia and turned a blind eye to Japan's protectionist, export-oriented economic policies. Today such "me-first" practices endanger Western unity.

Akira Sono, *World Press Review*, December 1988.

While Japan and other nations aggressively pursue export markets and limit imports, the United States remains reasonably faithful to the tenets of free trade. Indeed, the size of the U.S. trade deficit proves the relative openness of the U.S. market to imports, an openness that has greatly aided our competitors. Japan's automotive, home electronics, and semiconductor industries could not have developed as they have without access to the U.S. market. Now that access is hastening the demise of many U.S. industries.

Most of the solutions suggested for the U.S. trade deficit have focused on the long term: restructuring the economy, improving the educational system, retraining workers, orienting businesses to global marketing. Our attempts to moderate the immediate consequences of the trade deficit have failed miserably. The largely ad hoc, bilateral, product- and situation-specific measures taken to avoid protectionist legislation have done nothing to reduce the deficit's threat to U.S. competitiveness. For example, we let our dollar drop more than 40% in value against the yen from 1984 to 1986 in order to make U.S. goods more price competitive overseas. Yet exports expanded hardly at all—a clear indication of the exclusion of our products from several markets.

To compound the problem, many of our new competitors—South Korea and Taiwan, for instance—have not adjusted the values of their currencies against the dollar. By maintaining their undervalued currencies, they shut U.S. products out while enjoying an unwarranted competitive edge in the U.S. market.

Reduce the Trade Deficit

The United States must, therefore, act immediately to reduce the trade deficit and prevent further deterioration of our competitiveness through a dual program of retaliatory trade policies and industry targeting. The seriousness of the crisis demands immediate relief while we continue to explore long-term solutions.

But our actions must fit today's complex international economic and political circumstances. Japan, after all, supplies much of the capital to finance the U.S. budget deficit while keeping U.S. interest and inflation rates low. Our close relationship with Japan requires sensitive management in dealing with the trade problem without creating new global political problems. We must, as well, resist domestic pressures for blatant protectionism that invites foreign retaliation and raises the danger of another Hawley-Smoot tariff debacle.

We should also be mindful of the benefits of free trade while finding ways to limit it. When everybody is playing by the same rules, free trade offers more and better goods at lower prices. U.S. consumers are, no doubt, beneficiaries of our continued adherence to a free-trade policy. They enjoy a choice of goods and products from around the world at competitive prices. But this well-being has been achieved at an enormous cost to U.S. industry. In too many cases, U.S. businesses that should be competitive by world standards have been hurt. We have lost thousands of jobs and suffered a diminished standard of living. Therefore, the logical solution is to strike back only where we have been severely injured, thereby recognizing our legitimate interests and preserving as much as possible the system of free trade.

A fundamental issue in the debate over trade legislation is whether the United States should pursue a policy that is basically protectionist or retaliatory. As defined here, protectionist policy is product-specific and applies to all U.S. trading partners. For example, a tariff or quota might be placed on automobiles or clothing regardless of country of origin. Retaliatory policies, on the other hand, are country-specific. They focus only on nations whose practices hurt U.S. trade.

Although trade policy is rarely all protectionist or all retaliatory, we must avoid legislation that is basically protectionist. Protectionism retards U.S. competitiveness by allowing inefficient industries to continue and even expand, thus consuming resources that could be used more efficiently elsewhere. Once an industry receives protection, vested interests make it difficult to take the protection away. Further, protectionist legislation cuts so wide a path that it can injure nations whose trade practices are hardly affecting U.S. trade, thus hurting economic allies and inviting retaliation.

Measured retaliatory measures are more appropriate under the current circumstances. The trade deficit is the problem at hand, and one nation—Japan—accounts for more than a quarter of this deficit. Another handful of nations—Brazil, South Korea, Taiwan, West Germany, and Hong Kong—account for an additional 25%. To hit the deficit where it hurts us most, we need a target rifle, not a shotgun. . . .

To be sure, there are enormous complexities in developing trade legislation that reduces the deficit but remains essentially fair to both domestic and foreign producers. Nevertheless, retaliatory policies are consistent with the joint goals of providing immediate relief for the trade deficit and not interfering with—and perhaps even enhancing—efforts to make the country's economy more globally competitive.

The Need To Target

The second strategy element is targeting selected U.S. industries. Although targeting is associated with national industrial planning, which many find political distasteful, some form of targeting is now necessary, particularly in high technology. Targeting particular industries has enabled Japan to go from being a producer of cheap toys in the 1950s to rivaling, and even exceeding, the United States in technological capabilities in many industries. Now other nations are employing a targeting strategy to achieve economic growth.

How would the United States support industries targeted as crucial to its economic future? Here again, we should learn from Japan and use subsidies and domestic market protection to nurture key industries. Subsidies, for example, can be direct infusions of cash, such as the Europeans use to support their targeted Airbus company, or indirect forms like low-cost loans, tax relief, and R&D [research and development] grants.

Target industries might also benefit from the U.S. government's systematic exclusion of competing imports, thereby assuring U.S. producers of a profitable domestic market and a secure base from which to capture world markets. The methods available to protect domestic industries are infinite. Even though such formal restrictions as tariffs and quotas are proscribed by the General Agreement on Trade and Tariffs (GATT), we can look to Japan for other ways to protect targeted industries, such as the administrative guidance, customs procedures, certification requirements, and public procurement policies described earlier.

Of course, Japan has no monopoly on these protective devices. The United States has used all of them at various times, but less systematically than Japan. However, if we do not start using retaliation and targeting as part of a carefully devised policy, we will lose economic ground to those countries that do. . . .

Retaliate Now

The United States needs to identify industries that are critical to our economy and provide them with the protection, controls, and incentives necessary to maintain competitiveness. We don't want to shelter noncompetitive industries, but we do want to maintain a competitive advantage in already successful businesses.

U.S. producers will not find new Japanese markets for their products because Japan has no incentive to import our products. The Japanese have targeted most of the industries in which U.S. companies are the most globally competitive. If the Japanese do not intend to open their doors to us, we can no longer afford to keep ours wide open to them. If our government doesn't take action soon, the trade deficit will grow while U.S. global competitiveness deteriorates. We must retaliate now against those nations that have hurt our economy the most. And we must make some tough decisions about which industries are most essential to our future.

"All of Japan's domestic policies serve the goal of building its industrial strength."

Japan's Government Subsidies Unfairly Aid Business

Clyde Prestowitz

Clyde Prestowitz is a senior associate at the Carnegie Endowment for International Peace in Washington, DC. During the Reagan administration, Prestowitz was the principal adviser on Japanese affairs to the US secretary of commerce. In the following viewpoint, he outlines how Japan's government has intervened to ensure the success of its key industries. Prestowitz argues that these policies have led to Japan's sustained economic success while they have unfairly excluded foreign products from the Japanese market.

As you read, consider the following questions:

1. Why does Prestowitz disagree with the argument that the Japanese simply are better businesspeople than Westerners?
2. What is the motivation behind the Japanese government's economic policies, according to the author?
3. What measures has Japan taken to restrain competition within Japan, according to Prestowitz?

Adapted from *Trading Places: How We Allowed Japan To Take the Lead*, by Clyde Prestowitz, Jr. Copyright © 1988 by Clyde Prestowitz. Used by permission of Basic Books, Inc., Publishers.

Under great pressure from the United States as a result of rising trade frictions, in 1981 Nippon Telegraph and Telephone (NTT), the Japanese telecommunications company, agreed to open its annual procurement of $6 billion to foreign bidders. However, NTT's chairman at the time maintained that the only thing his company could buy from foreign firms would be buckets, mops, and telephone poles. Indeed, in the next two years, the firm purchased only about $30 million of U.S. goods, mostly in the bucket-and-mop category. In 1983, again under pressure from the United States, NTT finally decided to buy something significant from a U.S. manufacturer. Thus, on July 23, 1983, a delegation from the company arrived at Hughes Aerospace Corp. in El Segundo, Calif. Its stated mission was to buy software.

The Japanese and U.S. accounts of this meeting differ as night and day. As counselor to Secretary of Commerce Malcolm Baldrige, I received an irate telephone call from a Hughes executive that evening. Did I know, he asked, that the Japanese group, which the U.S. government had encouraged him to receive, was trying to obtain the technology for constructing its own telecommunications satellite? No, I responded, I understood they were looking for software. "Well," said the executive, "they described the software and it essentially involves teaching them how to build a satellite." Furthermore, he said, "We know they're in the market for a satellite, and when we asked if we could bid, they told us that they couldn't buy an American satellite because it is Japanese government policy to develop one of their own."

NTT later expressed surprise at Hughes's reaction, maintaining that it was interested only in software that would make satellites work better.

Whatever the truth of the situation, the subsequent facts are not in doubt. News of the meeting sent a shock wave through Washington. The U.S. government immediately asked the Japanese government to explain its policy. If, in fact, NTT could not buy a satellite, all the praise the government had earlier heaped on Japan for opening its telecommunications market would be shown to have been misplaced. More important, the incident would support the belief of many Americans that Japan's important markets remain closed because its leaders target certain industries for development.

The National Interest

After several months of crashing silence, the Japanese finally admitted that they did have an "infant industry" policy aimed at promoting indigenous satellite production. Long, hard negotiations ensued, at the end of which Japan agreed to buy two U.S. satellites. But the most interesting aspect of the talks was that despite the obvious contradiction with free-trade doctrine, Japan did not abandon its infant-industry policy. All government users of satellites had to continue to buy Japanese, and other users were directed to "consider the national interest" in their purchases. These events exemplify some of the strategies that the Japanese have used to gain a foothold in many key industries. The basis of these strategies was spelled out in 1983, when MITI [Ministry of International Trade and Industry] officials told U.S. negotiators that in key technologies the government must intervene to make its firms competitive, thereby assuring the security of the country's economy. Nor are the Japanese policies limited to encouraging new industries. Companies beset by the problems common to mature industries are often directed to set certain production levels and to engage in joint buying, marketing, and stockpiling.

Public-Private Balance

The government played a major role in guiding Japan's postwar economic recovery. As we have seen, it first encouraged a few selected basic areas of industrial activity and then, as the economy prospered, moved on to other more advanced fields. It has had a steadily shifting strategy as economic conditions have changed. . . .

The government in its economic guidance, however, was wise enough to leave actual business initiatives up to private industry. Thus, unlike the countries with fully planned economies, it permitted free enterprise to escape from governmental miscalculations and to exploit fields that the government had overlooked. The balance between private initiative and government aid and guidance seems to have been a happy one—perhaps the best such balance struck anywhere in the world.

Edwin O. Reischauer, *The Japanese Today*, 1988.

Many U.S. commentators deny the efficacy of these policies and argue that the Japanese simply do the things that create business success better than Americans or other Westerners. They point to Japan's high savings rates, well-educated labor force, and large population, and say that Japan would have achieved success with or without its industrial strategies. The fallacy of this view is evidenced by the fact that no Japanese hold it. As the economist Hiroya Ueno has noted, the Japanese government has always intervened to obtain a specific economic order viewed as favorable to the national interest. Few Americans understand these wide-ranging efforts or how directly they contradict Western economic doctrine and expose its weaknesses.

Western economic doctrine holds that consumption is the main purpose of economic activity. The demands of consumers are reflected in the unseen hand of the free market, which allocates resources most efficiently. Many firms, having no market power, compete on prices until they drop to a level that covers only costs. Internationally, the theory goes, nations should specialize in the goods they are best endowed to produce and trade for the rest. According to this doctrine of "comparative advantage," if a nation has a large unskilled labor force, for example, it should concentrate on making textiles or other labor-intensive goods. It should buy technologically advanced items such as airplanes from the United States, say, which has a resource base better-suited to making them.

The whole point of free trade is to enable an entrepreneur or a firm to exploit its particular capability worldwide. Free-trade doctrine says this is a benefit, not a threat, because it allows consumers everywhere to enjoy the fruits of efficiency and discovery. It is on this hallowed thinking that the international trade system rests.

The Japanese have difficulties with this theory. Since it assumes that a nation's products are determined by its resource endowment, the theory implies that national economic activity will remain relatively static. And because profits are driven down by extreme price competition, there is no return to invest in R&D [research and development]. This means that advanced countries will always retain their position and formalizes a kind of colonial relationship with less developed nations. Indeed, based on the writings of the British economists Adam Smith and David Ricardo, the theory justified England's dominance of world trade during the Industrial Revolution.

An Alternative Theory

Joseph Schumpeter, an Austrian economist and Harvard professor who wrote in the 1940s, formulated an alternative view of capitalist dynamics often ignored in the West. In his theory, what matters is not price competition or resource endowment but the competition arising from new technology, sources of supply, and industrial organization. An example of what Schumpeter meant is the Toyota just-in-time manufacturing system, which has led to a doubling and even tripling of productivity. The severe price competition of perfectly free markets may actually retard the R&D necessary for this kind of advance because a company will not have the profits to invest.

Schumpeter's concept of dynamic competition suggests that less industrialized nations can catch up, and that governments can legitimately intervene to make this happen. This is music to Japanese ears. As Naohiro Amaya, a former vice-minister of the Ministry of International Trade and Industry (MITI), indicated to me, "Businessmen are risk averse. Therefore, if the invisible hand cannot drive the enterprise to R&D, the visible hand must."

U.S. observers usually describe such an industrial policy as one of picking winners and losers, and most firmly believe that bureaucrats never do anything except pick losers. But the Japanese, aiming to attain as much autonomy as possible, attempt to foster development of as many industries as possible. According to Myohei Shinohara, a longtime member of Japan's Industrial Structure Council, it is especially desirable to encourage industries with high technology content, in which costs decline rapidly with increases in production. It is also important to promote industries that have ripple effects on other sectors. Semiconductors, for example, both have high technology content and are used in key products such as computers. These criteria seem simple and straightforward to the Japanese, whose bureaucrats do not feel that they rely on a mystical laying on of hands and do not claim any special clairvoyance.

Bruce Beattie. Reprinted by permission of Copley News Service.

All of Japan's domestic policies serve the goal of building its industrial strength. The education system provides an example. The Confucian tradition that Japan inherited from China emphasizes education, but technology never loomed large in this system. The thousands of engineers pouring out of Japanese universities today result from policies that deliberately encourage students to pursue engineering. This is borne out by the fact that Japan graduates relatively few chemists and physicists.

Japan's economic policies also serve its industrial policy. Japan maintains low interest rates for industry, but consumer loans, if available at all, usually carry high interest charges. Japan sets energy prices relatively high for consumers but keeps them low for industry. Everything is structured with one objective: to achieve industrial strength. This is the opposite of the U.S. approach where the consumer is king; in Japan, the consumer comes last.

Such an outlook accords well with the Samurai ethic of the Japanese, who cannot accept that their country will remain behind in any area of endeavor. It also reflects their view of economic health as national security. Since the time of Commodore Matthew Perry, the Japanese have seen foreign economic intrusion as a form of colonialism. Their dependence on the United States for defense makes them especially anxious to avoid economic domination. In lieu of a significant military establishment, an industrial policy aimed at achieving economic "security," by which they mean autonomy, has become Japan's strategy and its only assurance of some degree of independence on the international stage. Japan formulates its economic policies with an eye not only to their economic effect but also toward its overall power.

Tools of the Government

Japan puts these tenets into practice through an extraordinary domestic network that extends well beyond the efforts of the well-known MITI. Some of the main tools are the Industrial Structure Council, the Telecommunications Advisory Council, and other similar councils, which constantly study key industries and their relationships with others. These councils—which usually consist of members chosen from among leaders in business, consumer groups, labor unions, academia, government, and the press—issue a steady stream of white papers, often termed "visions," which form the basis for legislation for promoting or restructuring industries and encouraging R&D. MITI and other ministries also develop "elevation plans," which specify production levels for export, as well as R&D spending for specific projects from the visions. The elevation plans look much like the two- or three-year plans of major corporations and are in fact drawn up with industry representatives.

Many U.S. observers dismiss the plans as mere exhortation. But in Japan's group-oriented hierarchy, these procedures create a powerful consensus for achieving the objectives. The violent reaction to U.S. proposals in 1984 for placing Japanese nationals working for the Japanese subsidiaries of U.S. companies on the councils is strong evidence of their importance. Many Americans viewed as hyperbole the Japanese comparison of the Industrial Structure Council, which advises MITI, to the National Security Council. In fact, it was apt.

Japanese ministries have many tools at their disposal to achieve the goals established in the visions. They can set up companies such as the Japan Electronic Computer Corp., the government-backed leasing company established by MITI in the early 1960s to promote the Japanese computer industry in its battles with IBM. The Japan Electronic Computer Corp. provided immediate cash payments for computers manufactured by the financially strapped Japanese producers, and the company then leased the computers to customers.

Government's Active Role

An important consideration concerning Japanese economics is that, in contrast to the philosophy of laissez-faire that historically has prevailed in countries like Britain and the United States, in Japan, since the 1868 Meiji Restoration, government has taken an active and aggressive role in shaping the economy. And while certain business corporations have occasionally chafed at what they viewed as needless interference in their business matters by government bureaucrats, business has generally welcomed the government's activist economic role.

T.J. Pempel, *Japan: The Dilemmas of Success*, 1986.

MITI also often sets standards for industrial products that differ from those of other nations, automatically protecting the Japanese market from invasion by outsiders. And the Japan Development Bank makes low-interest loans to specific projects. Western economists often dismiss these loans as unimportant because they are usually just below the market rate, and because they fund only a small part of any R&D project. What outsiders do not realize is that by long tradition the loans are a signal to the financial community that it should give preference to targeted industries. The banks are willing to do so because the government backing reduces their risk. Companies can also draw up legal agreements to cooperate in cartels on deciding what goods to produce. Japanese machine-tool manufacturers have used such an agreement for the past 30 years to determine what sorts of machine tools each would make, as well as what direction the industry should take.

Socializing the Risk

All these devices are important because they encourage investment and reduce risk. Even though Japan is a conformist, risk-averse society, it nevertheless produces business leaders lauded the world over for their long-term strategic thinking. The solution to the paradox is that the government socializes the risk, removing it from individual firms. In such circumstances, it is easy to be a long-term thinker. . . .

Japan has developed an elaborate set of tools to restrain competition, including allowing companies to form cartels to jointly restrict production and capacity. An important characteristic of the cartels is that they reduce production in relation to each company's market share. This virtually guarantees market dominance in perpetuity to those who dominate at maturity. Companies thus tend to overinvest in an attempt to gain dominance. The risk is low even for the eventual losers because they know every effort will be made to keep them alive.

Reduce Production

Moves to jointly reduce production require even greater cooperation between government and business than efforts to promote specific industries. The steel industry provides perhaps the best example of this policy. In 1977 MITI directed 52 electric-furnace steel producers to cut production by 35 percent or face a fine. They complied. Then in mid-1982, MITI issued a "guideline" to reduce steel production while raising prices, in an effort to restore profitability. Japan's Fair Trade Commission investigated from time to time but took no action.

The mechanics of the guidelines to the steel industry reveal the close coordination between industry and government. Every Monday at noon, black limousines swarm around the Iron and Steel Building in Tokyo. From them emerge men from Japan's eight major steel companies. They go to room 704, where a sign reads "Regular Monday Club Meeting." The men take their places at a large, rectangular table, at whose head is the chief of MITI's Iron and Steel section. This group has met every Monday since 1958 to iron out a consensus on the MITI guideline for appropriate levels of investment and production. During this time, and even today, Japan's steel industry has been the world's most powerful. . . .

The result of Japan's policies has been one of the strongest sustained economic performances of all time—along with a rising tide of resentment from its trading partners. The Japanese have not been able to understand this and believe it is due to misperception. A major task of Japan's leaders is therefore to explain their industrial policies in a way that reconciles them with the free-trade system. Such explanations are difficult: having rejected the economic theories of the West, Japan nevertheless tries to show that its policies do not conflict with them.

86

"The Japanese success story is based on high savings, hard work, and excellent business leadership."

Japan's Government Subsidies Have Not Aided Business

C. Brandon Crocker

C. Brandon Crocker is a financial planner in San Diego, California. In the following viewpoint, he argues that the most successful businesses in Japan have not been the beneficiaries of government subsidies. He instead attributes Japan's economic success to its work ethic, frugal consumption, and superior management techniques.

As you read, consider the following questions:

1. What are the three questions that should be asked about government assistance to business, according to Crocker?
2. According to the author, what role does the Japanese government play in assisting industries?
3. What does Crocker believe the United States could learn from Japan's economic successes?

C. Brandon Crocker, "The Myth of Japanese Industrial Policy," *The Freeman*, April 1988.

It is incumbent upon industrial policy proponents to answer three questions: First, under ideal circumstances, can industrial policy work? Second, in the real political world, will industrial policy degenerate into yet another means for politicians to pass pork-barrel legislation? And third, is the sacrifice of individual liberty involved in implementing a serious industrial policy worth the supposed gains? This article is concerned with the first two questions, for if the advocates of industrial policy fail on these two points, the last question is moot.

The Japanese Example

Proponents of national industrial policy often point to Japan as a showcase of what such policies can do. The Japanese government, through such agencies as the Ministry of International Trade and Industry (MITI) and the Ministry of Finance, has played a powerful role in the economy, the argument goes, turning a war-battered Japan into an economic juggernaut in 25 years. The reality of the Japanese experience, however, does not provide support for a U.S. industrial policy.

During the 1950s and 1960s, the Japanese banking system wasn't well developed, nor did Japanese companies have access to an efficient capital market. This enabled the government, mainly through the Ministry of Finance and the Bank of Japan, to influence the availability of funds to specific industries. The government controlled a vast pool of private savings deposited with the post office, which had a virtual monopoly on private savings deposits.

With this power, the Japanese government effectively rationed credit, giving greater amounts to targeted industries such as steel, utilities, and communications. As domestic credit markets matured, however, and Japanese firms expanded and were able to tap foreign capital markets, the Japanese government lost the ability to control the flow of capital. Nevertheless, the government still controls a substantial amount of private savings which it uses for subsidized loans and loan guarantees.

MITI has long tried to influence company policies, while attempting to coordinate some industry activities, such as research and development. This role has grown in importance as credit rationing is no longer practicable. MITI has also loosened antitrust laws to allow firms to engage in joint research activities and to permit firms in troubled industries to cooperate.

Policy Has Not Altered the Market

However, the fact that a government has attempted to play an active role in an economy does not necessarily mean that it has significantly altered the final workings of the market. This seems to be the case in Japan.

During the 1950s and 1960s, when the Japanese government

used credit rationing to allocate capital to target industries, Japan was rebuilding its industrial infrastructure which had been battered during the war. This made it relatively easy to see which industries needed to be developed in order to catch up with other industrialized countries. A private commercial banking system, however, probably would have targeted these same industries since they offered profitable returns at low risk. But even if the government's efforts at targeting industries after World War II hastened Japan's economic rebirth, such a policy would not be relevant to an already developed economy such as the United States in 1988.

THE NEW JAPANESE/DETROIT CAR....

THESE PARTS WERE ASSEMBLED BY THE JAPANESE...

THESE PARTS WERE ASSEMBLED BY DETROIT...

© Raeside/Rothco Cartoons

MITI's influence over Japanese businesses is often overstated. Japanese firms generally follow only the MITI proposals with which they concur. MITI, for instance, did not want Mitsubishi and Honda to build cars, and did not want Sony to purchase U.S. transistor technology. The companies, however, went ahead, and entire industries were transformed.

MITI has not had any real power over Japanese industry since the Japanese government lost its near monopoly on the supply of credit in the early 1970s. Since then, MITI has made only suggestions, or has ruled on proposals from business leaders concerning industry cooperation and government loans. As Sadanori Yamanaka, Minister of International Trade and Industry, stated in 1983, "MITI works in an indirect fashion. When it guides industry, it is with soft hands. It has no real coercive power anymore. The main player is private industry."

The savings still controlled by the Japanese government are spread so thin among special interests that they are not an effective tool for industrial policy. Charles Schultze, chairman of the Council of Economic Advisors under President Carter, has concluded, "In Japan as in any other democratic country, the public investment budget has been divvied up in response to diverse political pressures. It has not been a major instrument for concentrating investment resources in carefully selected growth industries."

A case in point is semiconductors. This industry has been lauded as an example of the successful use of government financing for research and development. Yet the government's main investment arm, the Japanese Development Bank, has spent only one per cent of its budget for semiconductor research and development, which represents only a few percentage points of total research and development in the industry.

In addition to being spread thin, Japan's public investment budget is relatively small. During the 1970s, net lending by the Japan Development Bank amounted to only one per cent of private non-housing capital formation. The Japanese government is responsible for about 28 per cent of its nation's non-defense research and development—four per cent *less* than what the U.S. government supplies. Far from being an aggressive partner in funding industrial research and development, the Japanese government is actually *less* active than is the U.S. government.

One true success story of Japan's industrial policy has been the government's ability to assist distressed industries. The Japanese government has achieved this by relaxing antitrust laws so that firms can work together in industries burdened by over-capacity and reduce research and development expenditures by entering into joint research projects. But this is not an argument for an increased government presence in the market; it is quite the opposite. The success of this policy comes from *reducing* government intervention.

No Causal Relationship

Though the extent of Japanese industrial policy has been exaggerated, it cannot be denied that it has had some effect on the Japanese economy during the past 35 years. There is no convincing evidence, however, of a causal relationship between industrial policy and Japan's economic success. In fact, the argument could be made that the Japanese economy has flourished *despite* the activities of agencies such as MITI.

Aside from targeting basic industries after World War II, the performance of Japan's economic planners has left much to be desired, by the planner's own standards. In contrast to the examples of Mitsubishi, Honda, and Sony, which had the determination and foresight to disobey MITI, some of Japan's big industrial disappointments such as shipbuilding and aerospace received much government favor and funding. The Japanese cement, paper, glass, bicycle, and motorcycle industries—all of which are success stories—never received much assistance, and occasionally encountered some resistance from MITI. The two industries most associated by Americans with Japanese success—automobiles and consumer electronics—were never selected by the Japanese government as priority industries.

Japanese Industrial Policy Overrated

In my judgment, industrial policy has been somewhat beneficial for the Japanese economy but its extent and efficacy have been overrated by many. Japan has pursued a relatively coherent industrial policy, but its effect has not always been as intended, in degree or in direction. MITI has supported a number of specific industries and has had some notable successes. It has had some important failures—even aside from the promotion of petrochemical, aluminum, and other energy-intensive industries in the 1960s which were made uncompetitive by the sharp rises in energy prices in the 1970s. And there are a number of important industries, such as automobiles and consumer electronics—indeed virtually all consumer goods—in which the government did not take any differentially supportive role but which have succeeded on their own.

Hugh Patrick, *Japan's High Technology Industries*, 1986.

The Japanese economy has benefited from a number of factors since the early 1950s, none of which have had anything to do with industrial policy.

High Savings

First, encouraged by low tax rates (especially on interest income, which for most individuals is tax-free) and the absence of a social security system, the Japanese have saved at a high rate. Over the past 25 years, the Japanese individual savings rate has ranged between 17 per cent to more than 20 per cent of after-tax income; over the same period Americans saved only four to seven per cent.

Second, the Japanese have had access to relatively cheap labor until recently, as economic growth has bid up wages. This labor force has a strong work ethic, with most Japanese working six-day weeks and rarely taking holidays.

Third, Japanese management has done an excellent job in controlling production costs, recognizing and meeting consumers' desires, and in formulating human resource policies which have kept worker morale and productivity relatively high, and the power of labor unions low. With so many favorable variables at work, there is little cause for hailing industrial policy as the reason for Japan's economic robustness. . . .

The Japanese government no longer "targets" industries as some industrial policy proponents would like to see the U.S. government do. The reason for this has been the realization by the Japanese government that it cannot predict what the best industries will be for Japan.

Aneel Karnani, Professor of Corporate Strategy at the University of Michigan, states the issue clearly: "What will be the better growth industry in the next decade, computers or biotechnology? Do you want some bureaucrat somewhere making that decision?"

The Market Works

Austrian economist Friedrich Hayek has provided the answer: "It is through the mutually adjusted efforts of many people that more knowledge is utilized than any one individual possesses or than it is possible to synthesize intellectually; and it is through such utilization of dispersed knowledge that achievements are made possible greater than any single mind can foresee."

The market brings together the information possessed by all individuals in the market and, therefore, is able to make better decisions on questions of optimal resource allocation than can any group of bureaucrats. To try to identify "winners" and "losers" beforehand is folly.

Japan's economic success is not due to industrial policy. The Japanese success story is based on high savings, hard work, and excellent business leadership. These are the areas in which the United States must improve to remain competitive in the world market. The U.S. government can make positive contributions by reducing the budget deficit, repealing burdensome regulations, and implementing tax policies which encourage work and productive investment. But attempts at "planned" meddling will not help.

"Japan would 'grow' its own technology . . .through concerted and government facilitated R&D programs."

Government Support Has Aided Japanese Technology

Peter Cannon

Japan has become recognized as a world leader in technology in such fields as robotics, computers, and electronics. In the following viewpoint, Peter Cannon argues that one of the main forces behind Japan's technological development is the assistance the government gives to high technology businesses. He describes several methods used by the government, including the shielding of Japanese companies from foreign competition and monetary support of technology research and development. Cannon is vice president and chief scientist of Rockwell International Corporation, a US company.

As you read, consider the following questions:

1. What stark choice does Cannon believe Japan has faced in modern times?
2. How have Japanese government policies differed from those of other countries, according to the author?
3. What are the seven steps of Japan's industrial development strategy, according to Cannon?

Peter Cannon, a speech delivered to the Seventeenth Annual Matthews Business Management Forum at California Lutheran University on March 5, 1987.

Let's take a close look at America's most visible foreign competitor: Japan—the exemplar of our nation's external challenge.

The first thing we should note in looking at Japan is unsurprising though pregnant with oft-overlooked meaning. Japan is a small island about the size of California but with five times the population and without the state's rich endowment of natural resources.

In modern times, Japan has been faced with a stark choice: export or die. Japan had necessity placed upon it by geography and demography. It has lived with the sort of predicament that America has up until recently had the luxury of avoiding.

Well, how has Japan done it? How has this small island nation become so successful at exporting? How has it acquired the second largest economy in the world?

A Planned Strategy

Very deliberately. Without going into a lengthy historical review, suffice it to say that Japanese government bureaucrats and business executives, surveying the ruins of World War II and assessing their future prospects, embarked upon a very deliberate strategy whose aim was the construction of a technology-intensive, export-oriented, industrial infrastructure. Nothing less than rapid industrialization was the aim.

Logic bid them to design a strategy to generate savings for use in capital investment. Japan avoided the more popular and detrimental paths that most nations have chosen.

Unlike nations such as Brazil and Mexico, Japan refused the option of heavy foreign borrowing. Unlike many third world nations, Japan also refused the policy option of allowing extensive direct foreign investment by multinational corporations. Finally, Japan spurned the industrialization path—a la Sweden and France—that emphasized state capitalism.

Instead, in pursuit of their goal of rapid industrialization, Japan adopted what Thomas McCraw of the Harvard Business School economically terms a "pay-as-you-go" strategy.

This "pay-as-you-go" strategy was not so much a series of codified policies as it was an agglomeration of devices designed to promote habits of saving. McCraw points to five such devices.

First, by taxing interest payments and exempting from taxation most of the income from savings accounts, the Japanese government penalized consumer borrowing and installment plan purchases while rewarding consumer saving.

Second, by requiring large cash down payments for housing purchases, the government forced prospective homeowners to save for long periods, thereby effectively delaying widespread home ownership and allowing for the growth of a pool of funds that could later be used for more significant industrial investment.

Third, through a compensation system that paid Japanese

workers via proportionally large bonuses—in essence lump sum salaries—Japanese companies encouraged employers to save.

Further, many will be surprised to learn that, until the 1970s, Japan maintained a public welfare system that by western standards appeared underdeveloped—a fourth critical savings-oriented device.

Pressing Ahead

To understand the government commitment to put Japan in first place in science, industry, business and finance in the 1990s and beyond, one must realize that MITI is not the only agency pressing ahead in the 1980s. The Science and Technology Agency (STA) and the Ministry of Posts and Telecommunications (MPT) have pursued their own joint-research venture. One of the more ambitious projects involves automated language translation phone systems and artificial intelligence.

Needless to say, Japanese companies are rushing to take advantage of the results of these projects.

Otto Silha, *Minneapolis Star and Tribune*, January 13, 1987.

Fifth, and finally, through a rigorous system of capital controls, Japan prevented any substantial capital flight, thereby adding to the pool for domestic investment.

With such savings devices in place, Japan could accumulate the capital investment funds they needed to acquire the technology that would be the driving engine of the export-weighted economy. Japan decided to acquire its technology through a combination of four principal means.

Gaining Technology

First, Japan would "grow" its own technology by erecting a first-class educational infrastructure and through concerted and government facilitated R&D programs and a host of other "technology friendly" macro- and micro-economic means.

Second, they would "import" technology through joint ventures with high-tech American firms.

Third, they would buy the technology through licensing arrangements and royalty payments.

And, fourth, Japanese companies would establish a practice wherein they would purchase an American high-tech product, dismantle it, analyze it, re-engineer it and finally replicate it— that is they would "reverse engineer" our technology.

As I said, they undertook all four methods, but as you may have suspected, the Japanese relied more on the last two means for the relatively quick acquisition of expertise they sought and in fact achieved; and they depended upon the former two as long-range acquisition avenues.

The success of Japan's reverse engineering and technology-importation methods are patently evident and well-known—we see examples of it in our homes, in our jobs, in the cars we drive, etc.

However, the full effects of Japan's decision to grow their own technology are just now beginning to dawn upon us. One way they decided to do this was, of course, through a strong education system. . . .

While we should all be cognizant of the sometimes creativity-stanching rigidities of their system—shortcomings many Japanese recognize—we must still admit that we have much to learn from their example. I suggest that our educational community stop dismissing it as irrelevant to our culture and start focusing on those features that ask only that which could be asked of all humans everywhere—*like good hard work.*

Another aspect of Japan's choice to grow their own technology was the decision to make a national commitment—a truly strategic commitment involving government, universities and industry—to a research and development capability geared to keep Japan at the head of the pack.

Now I could go on all day providing you with examples illustrative of the commitment that has been made in this respect, but I will instance only three which I believe bring home the point most forcefully.

Examples

The first is Japan's "technopolis" plan, which is an attempt to create 19 high technology industrial centers—essentially 19 "silicon valleys" by the early 1990s.

Each technopolis will boast a high technology industry and a university or research institute geared to advance the state of the art in that industry. The government is facilitating and encouraging these efforts through a variety of mechanisms including tax-depreciation allowances, business financing and construction of critical infrastructure.

The second example of Japanese commitment to the long term deals with research into the sort of advanced materials upon which the futures of our automobile and aerospace industries—to name only two—increasingly rely. . . .

At one Japanese company alone, Nippon Steel, over 700 scientists and engineers are engaged in forefront research on a variety of advanced composite materials. Seven hundred—such magnitude is astounding. Approximately 763 scientists are engaged in advanced materials research for the entire U.S. steel industry. Thus the efforts of only one Japanese company are effectively at parity with the efforts of an entire American industry.

The third and final example concerns the Japanese commitment to carving out a lasting position of dominance in the field of semiconductor microchip technology—chips being the very stuff which make modern computers—well, modern.

Their commitment in this field has been impressive, involving university and government consortia, close corporate communications and collaboration between R&D functions and marketing functions, and a clear sense that the nation is in it for the long term.

For example, the Ministry of International Trade and Industry, the muchly-touted if often oversold MITI, has designated a number of projects in microelectronics requiring a decade or more of research before the products are even brought to the marketplace.

Technological Nationalism

As a result of Japan's industrial concentration and strong government industrial policy, the country's industrial behavior is subject to a degree of strategic control unthinkable in the United States or Western Europe. The protectionism, prevention of direct foreign investment, obstructionism in trade negotiations, unidirectional technology flows, and industrial targeting displayed by Japanese industry and government are not accidental or marginal. Rather, economic and technological nationalism is an enduring feature of the postwar Japanese system, an uncomfortable fact infrequently acknowledged in American policy deliberations concerning economic security.

Charles H. Ferguson, *Foreign Policy*, Spring 1989.

American chipmakers, for one, are still reeling from the results of these and *other efforts*. So are some 65,000 American workers who lost their jobs because of loss of market share. In less than five years, Japan has wrested top market share from the U.S. in the vital integrated chip business.

Japanese R&D and *other efforts* have also positioned them for a leadership position in this industry into the future.

In fact, a study for the National Research Council found that Japan now leads in several emerging technological areas which are absolutely key to future electronic and optical device development.

Recalling what I said about Japan's national commitment to R&D, you will rightly infer that those first two points listed on the American side—that is, basic research and breakthroughs and inventions—are characteristics that can now be added to Japan's side of the ledger.

Twice now, I've mentioned "other efforts" from which we are

reeling and which are positioning Japan for future positions of leadership. I am, of course, merely using discretion in describing some of the more unfair aspects of Japan's infamous "targeting strategy." Other nations are using targeting strategies now; Japan is simply the leader.

A Targeting Strategy

Bruce Merrifield, the Assistant Secretary for Productivity, Technology and Innovation in the Department of Commerce enumerates seven steps in the Japanese targeting strategy.

The first is to do just that, that is, target an industry for which there is a bright future—like semiconductor chips.

The second step is to concentrate the businesses through unreconstructed Darwinian tactics—that's my term—which tactics effectively fertilize the strong through government aid and let the weak die off.

In the third step, R&D objectives based on manufacturing engineering improvements are, in Merrifield's words, "parceled out to avoid redundant effort and the new systems are leveraged 80 to 90 percent with low cost capital."

Fourth, imports are closed off to further base-load economies of scale in the home market.

In the fifth step, a two-tier pricing system is established whereby incremental pricing puts all the costs into the first eight-hour shift for the home market, and the next two shifts are for export at substantially less. The next time you hear that the Japanese pay substantially more than we for the products they make, you'll know why.

Sixth, the product is forward priced below the existing costs of American companies.

And as a seventh and final step, the Japanese in some instances make use of export subsidies to cost way below our market cost. In the case of the 256k ram chip, they priced for export at about a third of our costs—the catch is—their costs are roughly equal to ours. Such practices are known in the vernacular as "flooding the market."

The downside of this approach is that in the long-term this is a very risky and potentially destructive game. Today, Japanese companies are operating under incredible debt loads that the owners of American companies would never put up with. This then is not really a good example to follow.

The upside of this approach, both theoretically and thus far in practice, is that market share is gained very rapidly until economies of scale catch up with the prices. And once market share is lost, it is very hard to regain.

Such predatory pricing constitutes a form of economic warfare as people familiar with industries like electronics can attest. It must be ended.

VIEWPOINT

"It has . . . been difficult for the Japanese government to take major overt steps to aid any of its industries other than agriculture."

Government Support for Technology Has Been Limited

Gary R. Saxonhouse

Gary R. Saxonhouse is an economics professor at the University of Michigan and has written extensively on the Japanese economy. In the following viewpoint, he argues that Japanese government assistance to its high technology industries, whether in the form of protectionism, research support, or tax subsidies, has not been significant. Japanese industries, he argues, have succeeded in developing technology without the government's help.

As you read, consider the following questions:

1. What different types of government aid to industry does Saxonhouse examine?
2. How does Japanese government support of scientific research compare with other countries, according to the author?
3. According to Saxonhouse, what are the real reasons behind Japan's industrial development?

Reprinted by permission from Gary R. Saxonhouse, "Why Japan Is Winning," *Issues in Science and Technology,* Volume IV, Number 3, Spring 1986. Copyright 1986 by the National Academy of Sciences, Washington, DC.

There is now widespread concern in both the United States and Western Europe that the Japanese government is unfairly acquiring for itself the few "most promising" high-technology tickets to prosperity in the twenty-first century. It is widely alleged that a number of knowledge-intensive Japanese industries have received extraordinary amounts of Japanese government assistance and that the triangular relationship between government, business, and education in Japan is now carefully structured to thrust the country ahead of other advanced industrialized nations in the development of sophisticated technology.

The obvious policy instruments that the Japanese government could use to give aid and comfort to a prospective strategic high-tech industry include direct protection from foreign competition through tariffs and quotas and other nontariff barriers; direct subsidies and grants; subsidies given through the tax code, including special tax credits and special accelerated depreciation; preferred access to credit and/or preferred terms for credit; and special aid through government procurement, the regulation of industry competition policy, and educational policy.

However, despite the preoccupation of U.S. and West European officials with problems of access to the Japanese market and concerns about Japanese industrial targeting practices, in recent years it has actually been difficult for the Japanese government to take major overt steps to aid any of its industries other than agriculture. The few steps that the Japanese government has taken to guide high-tech industries—such as biotechnology, high-speed computers, fine ceramics, and flexible manufacturing systems—are best understood as limited compensation for the absence in Japan of American-style financial markets and American-style markets for experienced scientific and engineering personnel, both of which are thought of in Japan as having particular benefits for Japan's U.S. competitors. This does not necessarily mean that Japan is handicapped in high-tech competition with the United States. The same asymmetries in U.S. and Japanese science and technology policy, which make for too little diffusion of information among Japanese firms, allow Japanese companies to benefit greatly from U.S. experience.

Trade Barriers

It is widely believed that foreign access to the Japenese home market remains tightly controlled. Yet, by most conventional indices, the Japanese market is among the most open of the advanced industrialized economies. The Japanese government no longer makes much use of such instruments of direct protection as tariffs and quotas to protect newly promising sectors of its economy.

On average, Japanese tariffs on manufactured products are now well below U.S. levels. Whatever tariff protection is given to

Japan's high-tech industries is almost entirely comparable to U.S. practice and well below European levels. What is true for tariffs is also true for quotas and other nontariff barriers, such as export restraints imposed on trading partners, variable levies, minimum price systems, tariff quotas, and similar restrictive techniques. Compared to other advanced nations, including the United States, Japan makes relatively little use of such protective barriers. For example, rather than protecting high-tech products, Japan presently keeps under quota nothing more exciting than silk, coal briquettes, and several types of leather products.

Limited Role of Government

MITI's [Ministry of International Trade and Industry] role in the research system is often cited as an example of "indicative planning," in which the government suggests to industry directions for economic growth and technological change. This is an exaggeration. Although government plays an active role in the formation and funding of research assocations, it works very closely with industry in this regard; in fact, it often takes action in response to industry suggestions rather than vice versa. Once an association has been organized, industry certainly has the dominant voice. Government officials function more as conveners, mediators, record-keepers, and administrators than as planners of the industrial agenda.

George R. Heaton Jr., *Issues in Science and Technology*, Fall 1988.

In striking contrast with the policies of some European countries, where large sectors of the economy are publicly owned and where large subsidies may maintain employment in otherwise unprofitable public enterprises, Japanese policy is to give few direct subsidies and grants to manufacturing industries. In the late 1970s, for example, among 13 major manufacturing sectors in Japan, only the food processing industry received direct subsidies greater than 0.1 percent of the gross domestic product in that sector.

What is true about direct subsidies, in general, is also true specifically about government research and development grants. In 1984 the Japanese government funded no more than 1.8 percent of all R&D undertaken by private sector industry. This contrasts with West Germany funding 16.9 percent of private sector R&D, France funding 24.5 percent, Great Britain funding 29.2 percent, and the United States funding 32.3 percent.

These aggregate R&D figures are consistent with Japanese government policies toward most sectors conventionally thought to have strategic economic value. The communications and electronics manufacturing industry receives R&D contracts, grants, and subsidies equal to no more than 1.1 percent of its total R&D

expenditures. Sectors such as pharmaceuticals, machinery, and precision equipment receive Japanese government aid equivalent only to 0.1 percent, 1 percent, and 0.2 percent, respectively, of their total R&D expenditures.

Limited Support

At a more disaggregated level the same findings hold for such potentially strategic sectors as biotechnology, machine tools, semiconductors, and computers. In all these high-tech cases, direct Japanese government support of R&D is a trivial proportion of the total R&D undertaken by the private sector. Invariably such government support is modest by comparison with the scale of research grants and contracts given by the U.S. government to its own industries where, for example, almost 40 percent of R&D undertaken by the electrical machinery industry is funded by the government.

[Former] Prime Minister Yasuhiro Nakasone himself has emphasized the importance of biotechnology to the future of the Japanese economy, but total Japanese government direct R&D expenditures for projects in this technology in 1985 totaled only an estimated $55 million. Although this is equal to the combined biotechnology R&D spending of the French and West Germans, it is just about what is being spent by the British government alone, and it is only 7 to 8 percent of what the U.S. government is spending.

Japanese government programs to aid the computer and semiconductor industries have drawn special criticism from opponents of Japanese strategic sector promotion practices. Yet the $73 million in Japanese government contracts, grants, and subsidies given to these industries in fiscal year 1984 is small relative to the total Japanese R&D spending on these technologies and compared to government programs in other countries. This Japanese government aid is no more than 6 percent of total R&D expenditures on computers and semiconductors in Japan in 1984. In the United States, government funding for semiconductor R&D alone averaged $70 million in the early 1980s, with another $310 million being spent annually on computer-related research by the Defense Department, the National Science Foundation, and the National Aeronautics and Space Administration.

Tax Policy

The Japanese government is equally tightfisted when it comes to providing direct aid for its manufacturing industries through tax policy. In the 1950s, 50 percent of the cost of a new Japanese automobile factory could be written off in the first year of operation. Today, such industry-specific largess is much less common. Japanese effective sectoral tax rates were already highly uniform as long ago as 1973, particularly when compared with U.S. and

British rates. In 1973 the effective incidence of capital income taxation in the United States ranged from a low of 19.7 percent on petroleum and related products to 131.2 percent on electrical machinery and a high of 144.7 percent on rubber products. By comparison, Japan's effective capital taxation ranged from a low of 34.7 percent on nonferrous metals to a high of more than 49 percent on electrical machinery.

Since the early 1970s Japan's effective tax policy has continued to be more concerned with removing distortions between sectors than with giving special help to any particular sector. Nonetheless, potentially strategic high-tech sectors in Japan do benefit from an R&D tax credit and a number of special depreciation allowances in the Japanese tax code. These incentives, however, appear to be less generous than incentives to stimulate high-tech industries in other major market-oriented industrialized countries, particularly the United States. For example, a National Science Foundation study finds that the U.S. R&D tax credit results in a tax expenditure of $1.5 billion annually. By contrast, Japan's Ministry of Finance estimates the Japanese R&D tax credit, on which the U.S. tax credit was originally modeled, provides incentives of no more than one-tenth this amount. . . .

Targeting Is Inappropriate

As for MITI's [Ministry of International Trade and Industry] infamous industrial targeting, many Japanese (as well as foreigners) have long doubted its effectiveness and believe it is now wholly inappropriate anyway. All technologies have started moving simply too fast to wait upon the whim of bickering bureaucrats. It is not as though Japanese civil servants have shown themselves any better at picking industrial winners than officials elsewhere; and none has bettered the invisible hand of the marketplace.

The Economist, August 23, 1986.

Taken together, all these industry-specific tax expenditures are estimated to provide no more than $37 million in special incentives to presumptive strategic sector industries. These incentives seem modest when it is remembered that the Japanese tax code has no provisions analogous to the beneficial treatment of limited R&D partnerships, which allows investment in R&D partnerships to be written off against current income while royalty income from ensuing patents may be treated as a capital gain. This is just one of the tax incentives that have allowed limited R&D partnerships to become a major vehicle for financing high-tech ventures in the United States, to the great envy of Japanese competitors.

Given the heavily regulated character of the Japanese financial system and the important role of government financial institutions, the Japanese government does have the means to pursue strategic sector policy through the manipulation of the availability of and terms of access to industrial finance.

In practice, the largest portion of the resources of government financial institutions is not used for promising new industries, and the loans that are made to new industries such as machine tools, robotics, and biotechnology are granted on terms hardly different from those available from private banks. The one high-tech sector that has attracted the attention of the Japan Development Bank and its counterpart institution, the Small Business Finance Corporation, has been the Japanese computer industry. Since the early 1970s this industry has received priority funding; in the early 1980s it was the beneficiary of more than $300 million in public funds. Much of this funding went to the Japan Electronic Computer Company (JECC), which finances the leasing of Japanese computers, but other loans went to fund R&D for fifth-generation computers and for the development of new software.

Although such special financing particularly facilitates the leasing of Japanese computers, the role of this financing cannot be critical, given the Japanese computer industry's annual sales (excluding IBM Japan) of $7 billion. Moreover, the terms offered by JECC are not so much more liberal than what is offered by private leasing companies that major Japanese computer manufacturers have not felt free to forgo JECC financing. Hitachi, one of the three major computer manufacturers, no longer uses JECC financing.

Supporting Farmers Instead of Technology

It is not that the Japanese government is allergic to using highly overt policy instruments when they suit its interests. Japan gives all manner of protection and aid to its economically backward agricultural sector. It employs stiff tariffs, numerous quotas, and overscrupulous health and safety inspection to protect Japanese farmers from international competition. Moreover, although manufacturing receives a trivial level of subsidies, agriculture receives direct aid equal to 13 percent of its gross domestic product. As may be expected, the effective tax rate on agriculture is much lower than the largely uniform rate levied on Japan's manufacturing sector. Japan's heavy protection of agriculture comes at the expense of its manufacturing industries. In this sense, both the overt Japanese and U.S. trade policies of recent years have had the same impact. Knowingly or not, they both reinforce the interests of Japanese farmers and U.S. manufacturers at the expense of U.S. farmers and Japanese manufacturers. Japan is a success at exporting manufactures in spite of its overt trade policy. . . .

If the Japanese government makes little use of the conventional instruments of strategic sector promotion policy and if much of the high-profile but largely informal government involvement in private resource allocation and R&D is a substitute for (not a complement to) market institutions that work successfully overseas, why is Japanese industrial and trade structure so distinctive by international standards? And why has Japanese economic growth been so rapid?

Both these questions can be answered on the basis of economic considerations that have little to do with a distinctively successful Japanese industrial policy. What is distinctive about the Japanese trade structure is its low share of manufactured product imports as a proportion of GNP [gross national product] and total imports. Japan does have a distinctive trade structure compared to other advanced industrialized nations, but only because the Japanese economy's other attributes are also distinctive. No other advanced industrialized economy of its large size combines such high-quality labor with such poor natural resources at such a great distance from its trading partners. It is these distinctive characteristics and not, for example, a strategic sector policy that other countries may or may not wish to emulate that gives Japan a robust comparative advantage in so many manufactured products.

Distinguishing Between Fact and Opinion

This activity is designed to help develop the basic reading and critical thinking skill of distinguishing between fact and opinion. Consider the following statement: "The US trade deficit with Japan for the month of April 1989 was eleven billion dollars." This is a factual statement which can be checked by looking up trade statistics. But the statement, "US exporters are not treated fairly in Japan," is an opinion. Whether Japan treats foreign competition unfairly (thus creating its trade surplus) is a debatable issue on which many people disagree.

When investigating controversial issues it is important that one be able to distinguish between statements of fact and statements of opinion. It is also important to recognize that not all statements of fact are true. They may appear to be true, but some are based on inaccurate or false information. For this activity, however, we are concerned with understanding the difference between those statements which appear to be factual and those which appear to be based primarily on opinion.

Most of the following statements are taken from the viewpoints in this chapter. Consider each statement carefully. *Mark O for any statement you believe is an opinion or interpretation of facts. Mark F for any statement you believe is a fact. Mark I for any statement you believe is impossible to judge.*

If you are doing this activity as a member of a class or group, compare your answers with those of other class or group members. Be able to defend your answers. You may discover that others come to different conclusions than you. Listening to the reasons others present for their answers may give you valuable insights in distinguishing between fact and opinion.

O = opinion
F = fact
I = impossible to judge

1. Japan is an island about the size of California.

2. The Japanese market is among the most open of advanced industrial countries.

3. In 1984 less than 2 percent of research and development undertaken by Japanese private industry was funded by the government.

4. On average, Japanese tariffs on manufactured products are below US levels.

5. The assumption that what sells in New York or Los Angeles will sell in Tokyo, without any alterations, is doomed to fail.

6. Many Japanese products are more expensive to purchase in Japan than in the United States.

7. All of Japan's domestic policies serve the goal of building its industrial strength.

8. The Japanese Ministry of Trade and Industry (MITI) often sets standards for industrial products that differ from the standards of other nations.

9. MITI has not had any real power over Japanese industry since the early 1970s.

10. Automobiles and consumer electronics were never selected by the Japanese government as priority industries.

11. Japan is a major importer of fossil fuels, raw materials, and foodstuffs.

12. Japan's economic success is not due to industrial policy.

13. For more than a decade Japan has been promising to open its markets to US products.

14. If the Japanese do not intend to let us sell them our products, we can no longer afford to keep our doors wide open to them.

15. One of Japan's informal trade barriers is "administrative guidance," in which the government uses veiled threats to get local businesses to avoid buying imports.

16. Selling to the Japanese market takes patience.

17. US companies should reconsider their preoccupation with short-term profits.

Periodical Bibliography

The following articles have been selected to supplement the diverse views presented in this chapter.

Robert F. Black	"Trade's Most Wanted List," *U.S. News & World Report*, May 22, 1989.
James Fallows	"Playing By Different Rules," *The Atlantic Monthly*, September 1987.
David Frum	"Neomercantilism," *Commentary*, May 1989.
Richard A. Gephardt	"US-Japan Trade Relations," *Vital Speeches of the Day*, May 15, 1989.
George Gilder	"IBM-TV?" *Forbes*, February 20, 1989.
David Halberstam	"Reflections on Japan Inc.," *Business Month*, February 1989.
Fred Hiatt	"Getting Less Fun for Their Money," *The Washington Post National Weekly Edition*, May 8/14, 1989.
Jim Impoco	"A Land of Papa-Mama Shops," *U.S. News & World Report*, April 24, 1989.
Chalmers Johnson	"The Japanese Political Economy: A Crisis in Theory," *Ethics and International Affairs*, vol. 2, 1988.
Tetsuya Kataoka	"Stop Bashing Japan for US Deficits," *USA Today*, January 1989.
Robert Kuttner	"Zen and the Art of Trade Negotiation," *The New Republic*, August 12/19, 1985.
Carla Rapoport	"Great Japanese Mistakes," *Fortune*, February 13, 1989.
Robert J. Samuelson	"What Makes Japan Tick," *Newsweek*, July 25, 1988.
Adam Smith	"Putting the Byte on Japan," *Esquire*, September 1988.
Lee Smith	"Can Consortiums Defeat Japan?" *Fortune*, June 5, 1989.
Robert Chapman Wood	"Japan's Economic Mess," *National Review*, July 8, 1988.

Is Japan an Internally Troubled Society?

Chapter Preface

A central value of Japanese culture, derived partly from the Japanese Shinto religion, is *wa*, or social harmony. Japanese society is structured to avoid open conflict and aggression, and to promote harmony.

Social harmony is reflected in many aspects of Japanese society. Crime and divorce rates are low; life expectancy is high. Japanese businesses promote cooperation between management and labor, and Japanese schools have a low dropout rate and high student achievement. Riots, strikes, and other forms of social unrest are much less common in Japan than in other countries.

Yet, according to observers such as Dutch journalist Karel G. van Wolferen, underneath the veneer of social harmony lies a people who are coerced and intimidated into accepting their place in Japan's rigid social system. Japan's critics point to several social problems. Japanese businesses have been criticized for exploiting workers. Japanese schools, with their emphasis on tests, have been criticized for creating stress and failing to teach creativity. And, many argue, Japanese society is highly racist and sexist because women, minorities, and foreigners seem to be excluded from the benefits of Japanese society.

As more countries in the world look to Japan as a model society, the debate on how this once obscure country copes with social issues becomes more important. The viewpoints in the following chapter examine the successes and problems of life in Japan.

"Democracy in Japan is thriving in its own way and in its own style."

Japan Is a Democratic Society

Ellen L. Frost

One of the United States' primary goals during its occupation of Japan following World War II was the establishment of a Japanese democracy. Today Japan has a constitution and an elected Diet, or parliament, but some observers continue to question the strength of Japan's commitment to democracy. In the following viewpoint, Ellen L. Frost argues that although Japan's system of government differs from the US in several ways, Japan is a free and democratic society. Frost works for Westinghouse Electric Corporation as director of government programs for US-Japan relations, and has held several positions in the US government.

As you read, consider the following questions:

1. What are some of the differences between the Japanese and American governments, according to Frost?
2. According to the author, how has the role of Japan's governmental bureaucracy changed over time?
3. What evidence does Frost use to argue that Japan truly supports democracy?

Ellen Frost, *For Richer, For Poorer.* New York: Council on Foreign Relations, 1987. Reprinted with permission.

The structure and process of Japanese politics are quite different from those in the United States. In America, two major parties take turns in the White House; in Japan, the LDP [Liberal Democratic Party] has ruled almost without interruption for forty years. The spectrum of political representation in Japan is more extreme, owing to the presence of sizable and active Socialist and Communist parties. Yet Japan's political parties, compared with political parties in the United States, are organized more around personalities than issues. Hence the prevalance of factions and personal support organizations and the relative weakness of local party organization. Party discipline is also much stronger than in the United States.

Japan has what is sometimes called a "one-and-a-half party system" because all of the opposition parties combined cannot seem to break the LDP's long-running majority. (As of 1987, the LDP held 304 seats out of 512 in the Lower House.) Although voters have signaled dissatisfaction with LDP policies by voting for candidates from other parties, they seem to stop short of actually wanting them to take power.

The legislative process presents another contrast. In Japan, emphasis is always given to building a consensus between the government and the Diet, among the parties, and within parties before draft legislation is submitted. Absent are such features of American politics as filibustering, up-and-down votes, bolting ranks, and public criticism of individuals in authority. Although showdowns are sometimes inevitable, the LDP takes great pains to avoid the appearance of exercising the tyranny of the majority. . . .

Demographics

Another difference between the two systems lies in the demographic make-up of political constituencies. Whereas large parts of America are still rural, a fact reflected in political representation, very few rural districts as such are left in Japan. Depending on the yardstick used, only 22 to 24 out of 130 Lower House districts (electing 76 to 91 out of 512 members) now qualify as "rural." It is true that the reapportionment of Diet seats lags way behind the urban sprawl of the 1950s and 1960s, but Japan's over-represented districts are no longer primarily agrarian; they are more like suburbs or provincial towns, or perhaps like America's northeastern districts. As a result of the decline of rural representation, the agricultural lobby in Japan, which has acted to restrict the sale of a number of products from abroad and maintain high price supports, has gotten weaker.

As the number of full-time farmers and agricultural laborers has shrunk, a new class of provincial businessmen and related interest groups has sprung up, spawned by the spread of industrialization in general and the extension of vast public works projects to rural and suburban areas. The construction industry has become particularly powerful. Its open resistance to foreign participation in the construction of the planned Kansai International Airport on the outskirts of Osaka is an ongoing source of U.S.-Japan tension. These dissimilarities tend to obscure a number of commonalities between the two political systems, including a drift toward centrism, a shift in the balance of power from the bureaucracy to the legislature, and—above all—a flourishing democracy.

Until the mid-1960s, postwar Japan's political life was marked by ideological polarization and conflict. The major opposition parties—the Socialists and the Communists—often took extreme positions and employed obstreperous tactics.

A True Democracy

Japanese intellectuals are given to shaking their heads in despair and complaining that their country is not a real democracy. That is rubbish. The electorate is regularly presented with a choice similar to that which exists in most Western countries—between being governed by conservatives, or socialists, or in-betweens. The result that emerges with such consistency may not be pleasing to the intellectuals, but there are no grounds for supposing that it is not a fair reflection of public opinion.

Peter Tasker, *Inside Japan*, 1987.

In the following decade, a more ideologically pluralistic, democratically mature, multiparty system emerged, with middle-of-the-road parties—notably the Komeito (Clean Government Party) and the Democratic Socialist Party—enjoying a rise of support. This development, along with the ongoing strength of the Socialists, obliged the LDP to respect what became known as "parity between conservatives and progressives." The handling of disagreements evolved from heated arguments and occasional fisticuffs to backroom compromises over drinks.

The 1980s have witnessed a further decline of political extremism and a corresponding shift toward moderate/centrist positions. Fewer voters in Japan now call themselves either "progressive" or "conservative"; more voters—especially those in their twenties—call themselves "independent." Annual polls have registered an increase in the percentage of voters who believe that "national policy corresponds to the people's will," which seems to be another way of saying that the Japanese are satisfied with the status quo. . . .

Another point of similarity is the increasingly complex maneuvering between the legislative body and the executive branch. Over time, Diet members as well as members of Congress have acquired real expertise in particular issue areas. There is, for example, a "defense *zoku*," which acts as an oversight group. Like their Congressional counterparts, some of these watchdogs have been around for years and wield considerable influence.

The enhanced political power of the Diet corresponds to a gradual erosion in the power of the government bureaucracy in favor of elected politicians. Several factors have contributed to this shift. One such factor transcends the political process as such: the bureaucracy has lost power because the gradual deregulation of the economy has reduced the number of available bureaucratic levers, such as postwar controls over the allocation of foreign exchange. The sheer size and vitality of the private sector has dwarfed government-funded industrial projects. New economic actors have grown out of infancy and are chafing at protective regulations. Although the government still enjoys great prestige and attracts some of the country's most elite graduates, it has lost much of its grip on Japanese society and hence on the country's elected leaders. . . .

History of Japanese Democracy

The single most important commonality of the two political systems is democracy. To a great extent, democracy is what the U.S.-Japan alliance is all about.

Democracy is not an alien concept grafted onto the skin of Japanese society by the American Occupation authorities after World War II. For almost sixty years following the Meiji Restoration of 1868, Japan nurtured its own democratic seedlings, adopting a form of limited parliamentary democracy patterned largely on German and French models. In the late nineteenth century, there was lively debate between advocates of constitutional monarchy and those favoring more direct forms of democracy. Although fragile, these seedlings sprouted further between 1910 and 1925, during the period of "Taisho democracy."

Throughout those sixty years, however, anti-democratic weeds sprouted as well. For some Meiji-era reformers, democracy in the sense of genuine pluralism and debate was wasteful, debilitating, and unfocused. Japan, like China, had no time for such political luxuries; catching up with the West required too much work. Democracy was rowdy and chaotic, a waste of the national spirit.

This attitude gained ground in the 1920s; the introduction of universal male suffrage in 1924 was overshadowed by the Peace Preservation Act, which aimed to intimidate political candidates and stifle opposition. The hardship of the Depression strengthened the anti-democratic forces. As Japan edged toward war, the seedlings were crushed and their cultivators imprisoned or silenced.

The imposition of democracy on postwar Japan was, to say the least, a contradiction in terms. Democracy was thrust upon it, sincerely but heavy-handedly. While Americans believed deeply in democracy, they also had other motives—notably winning the Cold War and repelling the Communists. In 1948, the then Secretary of the Army asserted that the purpose of building democracy in Japan was to deter "other totalitarian threats which might hereafter arise in the Far East." Takeshi Watanabe, then in charge of liaison between the Finance Ministry and the Occupation authorities, later said that America's "foremost preoccupation" was to keep Japan in the American camp without paying much in the way of economic aid.

How Democracy Operates in Japan

A major reason why outside observers often fail to appreciate what has happened in Japan is that its democracy operates in ways unfamiliar to Westerners. Many elements elsewhere considered essential to democracy, such as public debate in electioneering and in the Diet, are almost entirely absent. Few Japanese rally around party labels. Many prominent features of the Japanese political system, such as mass demonstrations of protest, inflamed public rhetoric, and confrontations in the Diet, are unattractive. Yet outside observers do not realize that these distasteful features are offset by extensive personalized electioneering, vast amounts of behind-the-scenes negotiations among political allies and with opponents, and reams of political commentary in the mass media, which most foreigners cannot read. Nor are most observers aware that, despite the popular skepticism shown toward political parties, Japanese in fact turn out to vote in far greater numbers than Americans and are personally as active in local political issues as people anywhere. All these factors make the Japanese democratic political process a very lively one, however obscure or deficient it may seem to foreign observers.

Edwin O. Reischauer, *The Japanese Today*, 1988.

In these circumstances, it is hardly surprising that many Japanese became somewhat ambivalent about democracy. Some critics faulted the Occupation authorities for being arbitrary and high-handed in their purge of the rightists; on the other hand, they asserted that the Americans did not go far enough. Although democracy became a cherished idea, the understanding of it left something to be desired. Intellectuals frequently contrasted democracy with feudalism, which was presumed to be its opposite; for a while, they debunked everything traditional. The voices touting *demokurashii* became self-righteous and shrill; far from promoting democratic styles of thought, they found comfort in Marxist slogans and rejected pragmatism as chaotic and wasteful. Instead of reason and logic, one found ideology and extremism. Instead of loyal opposition, one found pitched battles. These tremors came to a head in Japan's radical student movement of the 1960s. Although student leaders called their demonstrations "democratic action," they were inspired less by a spirit of genuine democracy than by a much-admired Japanese ideal: the doomed hero futilely defying authority and dying a noble death. A MITI [Ministry of International Trade and Industry] official who was a student with politically moderate views in those days confesses that it took him ten years to come to respect and appreciate the true meaning of the word "democracy."

Attitudes Today

Today, liberals and progressives in the universities and the press recoil from symbols reminiscent of Japan's militarist past. Many criticized Prime Minister Nakasone's official visit in 1985 to the Yasukuni Shrine and the revival of Founder's Day—commemorating, respectively, soldiers killed in action and the establishment of the imperial institution by Emperor Jimmu in 660 B.C. For similar reasons, many also opposed the lifting of the ceiling on defense spending, wondering why Americans seem so unconcerned about renewed militarism and so confident about the future of democracy in Japan. Some even suspect a double standard: "I often ask my American friends why they are so sensitive to signs of a Nazi revival in West Germany yet so willing to forgive former military collaborators and their protégés in Japan," complains journalist Yukio Matsuyama.

Others doubt that militarism poses even a potential danger. They acknowledge that Japan has a right-wing "lunatic fringe," complete with noisy sound trucks and occasionally nasty incidents. But the population at large, and the younger generation in particular, seems to have little attachment to the symbols of militarism. Like the "Me Generation" in America, Japan's young people are said to favor easy, eye-catching options and the pursuit of personal pleasure. Their attitude is hardly conducive to the patriotic self-sacrifice evoked by militarism. . . .

As poll results are variable, a more meaningful index of democracy is the strength of democratic institutions. One of these institutional safeguards, a multiparty system with free elections, has already been mentioned. Another is a free press or, more generally, the freedom of expression. In this respect, too, Japan seems to have come of age as a functioning democracy. . . .

At what point is a country judged to be truly democratic? More than forty years after World War II, many Americans and not a few Japanese still doubt the sturdiness of democracy in Japan. They note that in the postwar period, democracy has coincided with economic growth, and wonder how it would fare in the face of adversity.

On the worrisome side, Japan still lacks a system of checks and balances. In a society bathed in consensus and residual hierarchy, there are few cultural valves to shut off the flow of pressure to conform. Resistance to the abuse of power is often weak or non-existent. "A big tree protects you in the presence of authority," runs a Japanese saying. Another one goes, "If something long tries to coil around you, resign yourself and let it happen." Japanese society gathers momentum slowly, but once it embarks on a course of action it has difficulty stopping or reversing course. Japan's new arrogance seems to typify a kind of industrial nationalism, not particularly compatible with militarism but not particularly sympathetic to liberal and democratic values either.

On the other hand, key democratic institutions are not only well-rooted but blooming. It is less clear that democracy has been fully internalized at the level of the individual, but the trends seem healthy and appear to give no cause for concern. Democracy in Japan may not exactly resemble democracy as practiced in the model New England town meeting, but neither does democracy as it is practiced in most other societies. If democracy means making decisions through the free and public exchange of different points of view, then democracy in Japan is thriving in its own way and in its own style. Professor Gerald Curtis of Columbia University puts it this way:

> The truth is that Japan like the United States has woven the threads of democratic political life—civil liberties, open elections, competitive politics, and responsible government—into the fabric of the nation's social structure to create a stable political system that echoes universal values and behavior while at the same time being utterly unique.

"Turning the [Japanese] System into a modern constitutional state would require ... a genuine revolution."

Japan Is a Class-Based Society

Karel G. van Wolferen

Karel G. van Wolferen is a reporter for the *NRC Handelsblad*, a Dutch newspaper, and has lived in Japan since 1962. In the following viewpoint, van Wolferen argues that Westerners have misunderstood Japan's system of government. Japan's elected Diet, he states, is ineffectual, and Japan is actually ruled by an elite of bureaucrats, government ministers, and business executives. He concludes that Japan is not a true democracy as understood by the US and other Western nations.

As you read, consider the following questions:

1. What single institution holds ultimate authority in Japan, according to van Wolferen?
2. What is the significance of *kone*, according to the author?
3. How does van Wolferen believe Japanese society should be changed?

Japan perplexes the world. For almost two decades the Japanese have advised Westerners to have patience with them. But an awareness is gradually taking hold in the West that long-promised changes are not forthcoming, and that the explanations on which expectations of change have been based may have been wrong all along. For most Westerners, the Japan Problem is summed up by the country's record-breaking annual trade surplus: some $77 billion in 1988. The essence of the problem lies beyond such figures. Not only does Japan export more than it imports, but those exports in combination with the country's inhospitality to foreign products also undermine Western industries.

A straightforward desire to make money would be easy to understand. Japan's conquest of foreign markets, however, does not translate into more comforts at home. Urban housing is cramped and extraordinarily costly. Only about one-third of Japanese homes are connected to sewers. Commuter trains are overcrowded. The road system is ridiculously inadequate. The standard of living for average Japanese city dwellers is lower than that enjoyed by counterparts in less wealthy European countries.

What drives the Japanese? For what ultimate purpose do they deprive themselves of comfort while risking the enmity of the world? The usual explanation is that they are motivated by collective concerns. Indeed, Japan appears to be organized in a genuinely communal manner. As far as outsiders can tell, most Japanese accept with equanimity all the daily demands that they subordinate individual desires to those of the community. This striking communalism is, however, the result of political arrangements consciously inserted into society more than three centuries ago by a ruling elite. Japanese today have little or no choice in the matter. They are treated as a landscape gardener treats a hedge; protruding bits of personality are snipped off.

No Central Authority

Yet the power that systematically suppresses individualism in Japan does not emanate from a harsh central regime. For centuries, statecraft in Japan has resulted from a balance between semiautonomous groups that share power. The most powerful groups today include certain ministry officials, some political cliques, and clusters of bureaucrat-businessmen. There are many lesser ones, such as the agricultural cooperatives, the police, the press, and the gangsters. All are components of what we may call the System in order to distinguish it from the state.

We are dealing not with lobbies, but with a unique structural phenomenon. There is a hierarchy, or more accurately a complex of overlapping hierarchies. But it has no peak; it is a truncated pyramid. There is no supreme institution with ultimate authority to make policy. There is no place where, as Harry Truman would have said, the buck stops. In Japan, the buck keeps circulating. No one is ultimately in charge.

The Japan Problem appears less mysterious when we understand the way Japanese political power functions. We see things we would otherwise miss. One is that the System is in better shape than at any time in this century. We see that Japan's World War II defeat and occupation was less of a political watershed than has been thought. The prewar and wartime bureaucratic system—minus its military components—consolidated power after the war and is in the process of consolidating it even further.

Misleading Labels

At the most basic level of political life Japan is no different from any country. The Japanese have laws, legislators, a parliament, political parties, labor unions, a prime minister. But don't be misled by these familiar labels. The Japanese prime minister is not expected to show much leadership; labor unions organize strikes to be held during lunch breaks; the legislature does not in fact legislate (bureaucrats in ministries write the laws); laws are enforced only if they don't conflict too much with the interests of the powerful. The ruling Liberal Democratic Party (LDP) is conservative and authoritarian. It is not really a party, just a collection of factions, and it does not in fact rule. Since the late 1940s, the same relatively small group of politicians has played musical chairs with ministerial seats, making room only for protégés, with no demonstrable public influence on political decisions.

MOIR
Sydney Morning Herald
Sydney
AUSTRALIA

JAPAN DESERVES THE BEST PRIME MINISTER MONEY CAN BUY...

Moir (Australia) © 1989 Cartoonists and Writers Syndicate.

Seated above a weak parliament, the prime minister, who is invariably president of the LDP, in theory has opportunities to exercise great power. In fact, he cannot do things that foreigners, including foreign governments, expect a prime minister to be able to do. His power is less than that of any other head of government in the West or Asia. Proof of this was the recent experience of Yasuhiro Nakasone. As prime minister, Nakasone left no doubt about his ambition to rule. He tried harder than any of his postwar predecessors to strengthen the office. In the end, he failed to bring about the policy adjustments he championed—except for privatization of the company running what are probably the largest losses in the world, Japan National Railways. . . .

Truth and Law

Understanding Japan is made all the more difficult because of the country's penchant for what might be called management of reality. Japanese in positions of control show great agility in moving from one reality to another as they seek to explain facts and motives to other Japanese or to foreigners. When a Western businessman or government representative appeals to a contract, law, or international agreement, he may be told by his Japanese counterpart that Japan is guided not so much by cold rules as by warm human feelings. Yet should the foreigner, at the next opportunity, appeal to this extra-legal tradition by, for example, urging bureaucratic intervention in a trade problem, he may well hear that such a thing is impossible in democratic Japan, which, he should understand, is governed by laws.

The tolerance of contradiction is closely connected with another characteristic: the near absence of any idea that there can be truths, rules, principles, or morals that always apply, no matter what the circumstances. Bred into Japanese intellectual life over centuries of political suppression, this factor has been the most crucial in determining Japan's sociopolitical reality. To grasp the essence of a political culture that does not recognize the possibility of transcendental truths demands an unusual intellectual effort for Westerners, an effort that is rarely made even in serious assessments of Japan. . . .

The Ruling Class

Japan has a clearly discernible ruling class. Its members—mainly bureaucrats, top businessmen, and one section of the LDP—are all basically administrators. There is no room among them for an aspiring statesman. Strictly speaking it is not a hereditary class, but sons of administrators can join with ease. It is fairly open, though less so today than during the first decade after the war. And it is exclusively male.

Success in Japan depends almost entirely on who one knows. *Kone* (a Japanized abbreviation of the English word "connections") often provide the key to admission to the most desirable schools and jobs. For the best medical treatment, a special introduction to busy doctors is indispensable. Most Japanese are thoroughly indebted in this sense to numerous other Japanese, and others in turn are indebted to them; one of the main characteristics of Japanese life is an unremitting trade in favors. Politicians reinforce their positions by marrying the daughters of older, influential leaders in the LDP. Then they match up their sons and daughters with the children of prosperous and influential politicians and businessmen. Prime Minister Takeshita's eldest daughter married the eldest son of Shin Kanemaru, a pivotal member of the Diet. Takeshita's third daughter married the second son of the former president of Takenaka Komuten, one of Japan's better-known construction firms. The resulting networks are known as *keibatsu*, or family groupings through marriage.

Graduating from the University of Tokyo (Todai), especially its law department, means being automatically hooked up to a huge network of *kone*. The academic qualities of the Todai law school are not what make it the undisputed summit of the Japanese education system. More important is the fact that its graduates almost by tradition fill the highest administrative ranks. Of all the section chiefs and bureaucrats of higher rank in the ministry of finance, 88.6% are from Todai. For the foreign ministry the figure is 76%.

One-Party Rule

Even under the most extreme conditions, Japan operates as a country with one-party rule. Voters can choose any candidate they like, but the Liberal Democrats will always emerge as the ruling party. And that leaves a big unanswered question: What kind of democracy is that?

Alan M. Webber, *Los Angeles Times*, April 20, 1989.

The unregulated flow of money from business to politicians is a longstanding tradition in Japan. Contemporary LDP politicians can be very open about their extra income. Accompanying them on routine trips through their constituencies, I have seen them accept tens of millions of yen in brown paper bags . . . .

The country I describe does not resemble the common portrait of Japan as a society in which human relationships are based on consensus. This is because the much vaunted consensus is a myth. What is mislabeled consensus in Japan is a situation in which one thinks it worthwhile to challenge someone stronger. Parties to a Japanese consensus may, in fact, have very negative feelings about what they have agreed to. Conformity is to a large extent enforced by intimidation. Far from being abhorred, intimidation is accepted by Japanese as an inevitable aspect of social and political life, inevitable because the informal, nonlegal relations that characterize the System depend on informal coercion. Until a recent outcry, teachers in many schools encouraged their pupils in bullying practices. . . .

It is difficult to argue with success, and Japan's postwar economic record has drawn much admiration from the rest of the world. I do not mean to detract from the admirable accomplishments of the Japanese people. They have created a relatively safe society in which no one goes hungry and only a few thousand are homeless. But the System's successes have been so much admired and applauded that foreigners and the Japanese alike tend to overlook its inherent defects and deficiencies, the major one being that it has no control over itself. . . .

The Future

Can the situation change? Theoretically, the answer is yes. The System's character is ultimately determined by political relationships. Nothing that is political is irreversible in the long run, especially if the political dimension is recognized for what it is. For a start, you would have to abolish Tokyo University. The legal and party systems need basic changes. Law courses would have to be instituted in a large number of universities, and lawyers trained to give individual Japanese the means to protect themselves against the arbitrariness of bureaucrats. At the moment, the law does not regulate power in Japan; it is simply a tool administrators use to maintain control. The schools and the media would have to work to foster individual political awareness and a sense of individual responsibility while de-emphasizing the importance of membership in companies and other organizations. All this would encourage the substitution of legal regulations for *jinmyaku* [informal] relationships, and the legally safeguarded processes for the System's informality.

Unfortunately, experience so far gives no reason for optimism. If the System is guided by any overriding, sacrosanct aim, it is its own survival, which means the survival of the present constellation of administrators. This aim is mistakenly identified with the survival of Japan. It is possible that the Japanese System may yet go through a convulsion caused by an acute sense of confrontation with a hostile world. The more likely possibility, though, is that the System will muddle on, after having come to some accommodation with the Western world and the U.S. in particular. That will require wise policies in Western capitals. The wonderful alternative of turning the System into a modern constitutional state would require realignments of power akin to a genuine revolution.

"*Japanese companies treat employees as if they were family members.*"

Japanese Business Is Humane

Hiroshi Takeuchi

In the following viewpoint, Hiroshi Takeuchi writes that Japanese business reflects the positive values of Japanese society. Employers and employees alike, he argues, maintain respect for equality, teamwork, and achievement. Takeuchi is managing director and chief economist of the Long-Term Credit Bank of Japan, Ltd. and the author of many books on the Japanese economy.

As you read, consider the following questions:

1. According to Takeuchi, how does Japanese business motivate its employees?
2. How do Japanese companies treat employees, according to Takeuchi?
3. What kind of company president does the author believe employees are more likely to obey?

Hiroshi Takeuchi, "Motivation and Productivity," in *The Management Challenge*, Lester Thurow, ed. Cambridge, MA: The MIT Press, 1985. Copyright © 1985 by The Massachusetts Institute of Technology.

J apanese business organizations paradoxically use the principle of equality to motivate employees to compete and simultaneously to cooperate with one another.

There is in fact hardly any difference in starting salary between newly recruited blue- and white-collar workers. For instance, the pay for senior high school graduates who have served in the same company for four years is almost the same as the starting salary for newly recruited university graduates (who are all paid equally). And often the starting salaries for graduates with advanced degrees are lower than the salaries of university graduates with bachelor's degrees who have served in the company for two to five years.

Small Pay Differentials

In some companies salary differentials may expand for employees who have served for more than ten years and widen over time with the success or failure of the firms. But differentials among employees of such companies are smaller, far smaller than those in other countries. The pre-tax income of the president of a leading Japanese company is four to five times more than that of the average blue-collar worker of his age and even smaller once progressive taxes are taken into account. . . .

Japanese businesses start with the belief that all people have about the same ability. Let us suppose that a Mr. Suzuki has developed an innovative technology. Other employees of the firm recognize his achievement, but this does not necessarily mean that they assess his ability particularly highly. They will probably say: "Messrs. Sato, Yamada, and others worked hard at the factory and earned profits to provide ample funds for Mr. Suzuki's research work. If Messrs. Sato, Yamada, and others had been assigned to the same job as Mr. Suzuki, they would have produced the same achievement. They were engaged in harder and thankless work instead." Suzuki was able to develop the technology because of the efforts of many other researchers working under him and also because of research work undertaken by his seniors and fellow workers. It is usually judged that Suzuki was able to produce the achievement with the support of the entire staff including the blue-collar workers, not by his ability alone. The credit should go not to Suzuki but to the personnel department, which assigned him to the laboratory, and also to the head of the laboratory who gave the research project to him. Therefore his achievement belongs to the company, not to himself, and therefore he is not a special person.

If Suzuki concludes that his achievement was made possible by his ability alone and openly says so, he will provoke antipathy from all other workers and will be unable to stay in the firm. Another company will not employ him, however talented he may be, because he cannot cooperate with others. Major businesses will probably worry that employing such a person will sour their relations with his former employers. And even if Suzuki wants to go into business on his own account, his old company would not cooperate with him, and no other researchers would help him. Therefore Suzuki would be better off concluding not that he has an outstanding ability but that other people are equally capable and that he was simply fortunate to get that job.

Principle of Equality

Thus the principle of equality prevails in business. Few are chosen for special promotion; there can be no heroes and elite employees. Most people are promoted simultaneously through the same route, and some people are dropped from the race each year. But the dropouts can enter the race again in several years. Equality and competition coexist in the system for everyone. . . .

Sharing Risk

Rather than avoid risk, [the Japanese] manage it by sharing the unanticipated costs of economic change. In one large steel company that I visited, production workers whose jobs were eliminated at one mill were quickly placed by management in new jobs—either elsewhere in the corporation, or at a subcontractor's shop, or with a local government agency such as the public works authority.

Bennett Harrison, *Technology Review*, January 1989.

In Japan the most important task for supervisors is to forge a team among subordinates and help develop their confidence and abilities. If a competent subsection chief works hard, his section chief is well regarded for having trained him, and the section chief's position rises. Therefore section chiefs readily teach subsection chiefs how to handle work, who in turn eagerly teach it to their subordinates. No section chiefs refuse to teach subsection chiefs how to handle jobs for fear that they will lose their posts to capable subsection chiefs or that the subsection chief will be promoted over them. It simply isn't going to happen. Any manager who acted in such an antisocial way would be disqualified to hold a supervisory post and would be assigned work that could be performed alone. . . .

Thoughtful consideration of others is needed in business management and of course can be expected of those versed in the ways of the Japanese people. Old people provide the knowledge on the conduct of ceremonies of coming of age, marriage, funeral, and ancestral worship and on the proper way to make gifts. Thus there is a strong sense of unity among the elderly, middle-aged, and young, and this social bond is carried over to employees in

Japanese corporations. In this respect the Japanese seniority system is a product of a social climate that evolved over several hundred years. . . .

Employees as Family

Japanese companies treat employees as if they were family members. An employee who becomes crippled from an automobile accident after several years of service with the firm will continue to be employed and will not be discharged even if his work efficiency has fallen. If he dies in an automobile accident and his wife and children are unable to make a living, his company will probably give his wife an office job, hire her as a caretaker of a company dormitory for unmarried employees, or give her a job with a company-operated recreation facility. It will probably lend money interest free to pay for his children's school expenses.

Even a company in financial difficulty will not lay off employees unless it is on the verge of bankruptcy. If it suffers a loss, its president will cut his own pay; if he cuts his by half, the pay for other executives will be cut by 40 percent and that for middle-level management by 20 percent. Only after the firm's performance has failed to improve despite the pay cuts will it cut the pay for rank and file. As a last resource, if all these measures fail, the firm will lay off employees. And when the president decides on a personnel reduction, he must be prepared to resign. . . .

When in a poll presidents of leading companies were asked: "As the chief executive, for whom are you responsible?" 85 percent of the respondents answered "the employees." Although Japanese joint-stock enterprises are similar in structure to their Western counterparts, they still epitomize a very Japanese view. The employees are bound together as trusted comrades, not merely by the pursuit of financial interests.

In large part this trust stems from the fact that Japanese people know their roles in work. Even a person holding a high position will not make a decision independently. First, he must order his subordinates or organization to study a matter and consider the conclusion reached before he makes a decision. If the president makes decisions by himself all the time on his own authority, he will soon lose the support of his subordinates and become unable to exercise his ability. His subordinates will feel hurt, turn their backs on him, and, in effect, ignore his orders, although they may pretend to obey them. . . .

Japanese tend to define themselves by their work. When people are asked, "Who are you?" almost all will give their names and the names of their companies or organizations. Even a university professor will probably answer, "I am a professor at the University of Tokyo," instead of "I am an economist." Almost all people consider themselves members of corporate society and fulfill themselves through their companies.

Being members of a corporate society, employees work overtime for their companies, sacrificing their personal affairs when necessary. When business earnings are poor, they are content with small wage increases because they know that if their companies fail to achieve sustained growth due to high wages, their incomes will fall in the long run. . . .

Equal Rewards

In large American manufacturing companies, the chief executive is likely to earn up to 40 times more than a low-level employee; in comparable Japanese companies, the ratio is 15 to one. Also, a substantial portion of Japanese compensation is through bonuses that are proportionately equal for everyone. If the company does well, everyone does well. In this regard, a poll asked both American and Japanese workers whom they thought would profit from an increase in worker productivity in their plant. Only 9 per cent of the American workers felt they would benefit, as compared to 93 per cent of the Japanese. And if the company does badly, the bonuses fall proportionately, cushioning the company against the need to lay off workers.

Robert S. Bachelder, *The Christian Century*, August 26/September 2, 1987.

I believe that the productivity of the Japanese economy has been so high because of the delicate sense of balance inherent in the Japanese people. Employees compete with one another while cooperating among themselves. The president and others holding supervisory posts listen to the opinions of their subordinates and take these positions into consideration when giving orders. High Japanese productivity seems closely related to those relationships.

The Japanese sense of morality is based on long traditions, and Japanese business organizations are based on such traditional senses of morality.

"All those studies on Japanese management overlook the one ingredient that makes it all work: fear."

Japanese Business Is Inhumane

Doug Henwood

In the following viewpoint, Doug Henwood argues that many of Japan's much-hailed worker benefits, such as lifetime employment, are actually limited to a minority of workers. He states that Japanese management practices rely on instilling fear in their workers, who know that if they lose their jobs they have little chance of finding other employment, and Japan's limited welfare programs will be of little help. Henwood is editor of *Left Business Observer*.

As you read, consider the following questions:

1. In the author's opinion, what is wrong with idealizing Japanese businesses?
2. What anxieties does Henwood believe Japanese workers face?
3. Given current trends, what will be the future of labor in Japan, according to Henwood?

Doug Henwood, "Playing the *Zaiteku* Game," *The Nation*, October 3, 1988. Reprinted by permission of *The Nation* magazine/The Nation Company, Inc., copyright © 1988.

There's something about Japan that makes Americans lose their critical faculties, provoking extremes of hatred or admiration. Among the bashers, the language can get very ugly. For example, these words come from Texas Congressman Jack Brooks: "God bless Harry Truman. He dropped two of them. He should have dropped four." Or Senator John Danforth of Missouri, heir to the Purina Critter Chow fortune, who says the Japanese are "leeches." Howard Baker, Theodore White and Jack Anderson all say the Japanese are pursuing their dream of empire-building by peaceful means, having failed at military conquest. Anderson says he has access to secret information proving Japan's trade surplus is all part of a hundred-year plan to drive the white barbarians out—though it's hard to imagine who will buy all those Hondas and Sonys once the Japanese have crushed the White Peril.

This nonsense, though dangerous, is largely beneath serious comment. Of more subtle danger is the neoliberal prescription that we should emulate Japan, a line of thinking that has caught the attention of Michael Dukakis and other Democratic pragmatists as well as some of the more enlightened business intellectuals, from Felix Rohatyn to Robert Reich. In this technocratic view, Japan represents capitalism with a human face, where efficiency and equity travel hand in hand. Sounding not unlike a contemporary Calvin ("the business of America is business") Coolidge, Reich admires the way the Japanese "draw no sharp distinction between their business and civic cultures." Management, government and labor all cooperate to promote growth, since economic growth is acknowledged as the supreme good. Unemployment is virtually nonexistent, and workers, guaranteed a job for life, cheerfully cooperate with management. This equity promotes productivity. Unlike the United States, the productive economy is nurtured, and speculation—what Reich calls "paper entrepreneurialism"—is avoided.

Dulling Particular Circumstances

Much of this image is a myth and, like all myths, "deals in false universals, to dull the pain of particular circumstances," in Angela Carter's phrase. In this case, corporatist neoliberals are dulling particular circumstances in order to promote docility and a spirit of self-sacrifice among U.S. workers. Whether they know better or not is a matter for their own consciences. But a closer look at the reality hidden behind the shiny images of the Japanese "miracle" would be the best way to evaluate their prescriptions. Such a look reveals the following:

• Lifetime employment applies to only a shrinking minority of workers—and it's a luxury subsidized by a reserve army of the "dependently" employed.

• Even lifetime employees are forced into early retirement.

• If hidden unemployment is included, Japanese joblessness rates are not all that different from those of the United States.

• The welfare system is the chintziest of the big five economies—that is, behind West Germany, France, Britain and the United States.

• Japanese firms are moving production abroad at a rapid pace, on the model of U.S. multinationals.

• Financial and real estate speculation is the most intense anywhere in the developed world.

In other words, capitalism with a human face is suffering from ailments quite similar to those plaguing capitalism of a less benign countenance.

Women Out of Luck

If you happen to be female or a minority group member, you are out of luck in the workplace. Women enjoy little opportunity to enter lifetime positions and are often expected to leave the workplace after marriage or childbirth. Astoundingly few exercise senior responsibility or climb the corporate ladder. Not one of the companies interviewed had even one woman serving in the top positions of general manager or director.

Alice Tepper Marlin, *CEP Research Report*, September 1987.

"Lifetime employment" is the myth most in need of demystification. The Japanese were pioneers of a strategy now gaining wide appeal in the United States and Europe—dividing the work force into a minority of core workers supplemented by a majority of contingent or "dependent" workers, the term used by the Japanese Ministry of Labor. Core workers have the plum jobs. They are highly skilled, well paid, often company-housed (in a country where housing is very expensive) and guaranteed a job for most of their lives. When business changes, they are retrained or redeployed. But they account for only about a third of the work force, and that proportion is shrinking with every passing day, because new employees are far less likely to be offered lifetime security.

Tenuous Employment

Unskilled, dull, seasonal or unpleasant labor is reserved for contingent workers, who can be part-time or temporary employees of big firms, or employees of the innumerable subcontractors supplying parts and services to big firms. (Part-timers are characterized more by the tenuousness of their employment and the absence of fringe benefits than the length of their week, which can be as long as forty-eight hours.) The subcontractors range from medium-sized, relatively sophisticated firms to tiny family enterprises

131

operating in garages and basements. Contingent workers, in-house or out, are expected to bear the brunt of the business cycle: When business is slow, big firms reduce their supply of temporary workers and cut back on orders and payments to subcontractors. This forces the subcontractors to cut costs at their operations, already none too plush, by laying off workers or cutting their pay.

Redundant workers often just drop out of the labor force by going home to the family. Consequently, their plight doesn't show up in the unemployment statistics. As in the United States, Japanese workers are not considered unemployed if they have given up the job search or if they are working part time despite wanting a full-time job. Were such people counted as jobless, the U.S. unemployment rate would be sharply higher—about 8.3 percent rather than the official 5.6 percent. According to U.S. Labor Department estimates, counting hidden joblessness would raise the Japanese unemployment rate from the 2.5 to 3 percent that has prevailed in recent years to more than 8 percent.

As might be expected, Japanese women are especially "contingent." Their pay is about 53 percent of men's, as compared with 64 percent in the United States. They are found disproportionately in part-time and temporary work and in family businesses. Higher education for women is relatively rare, and careers are rarer still; a 1985 survey of Japan's bigger firms found that 80 percent planned to interview no women university graduates that year. "Instead," noted the March 4, 1985, *Business Week*, "they will look for high school and junior college graduates who . . . must be younger than 24, cute, well-mannered, and unambitious," whose "main function is to support and motivate male workers" for a few years before snagging a man. Women not young or cute enough to become "office flowers" work menial jobs at low pay with little chance of promotion.

Fear Makes It Work

Not that the life of core employees, white- and blue-collar, is anxiety free. Though layoffs of core workers are rare, they do happen. And short of a layoff, core workers live in fear of a humiliating transfer to an obscure or distant subsidiary as punishment for failure. All are forced to retire from the core at 55 to take a lower-paying contingent job. As *Inc.* magazine, which celebrates the entrepreneurial culture, put it in its April 1986 issue, "All those studies on Japanese management overlook the one ingredient that makes it all work: fear."

To fans of the Japanese labor market, this fear is a wondrous thing. In an article celebrating the entrepreneurial virtues of small-scale family enterprises and self-employment, Hugh T. Patrick and Thomas P. Rohlen note the following less-than-humane stimuli: "Welfare and employment policies that increase insecurity about old age also play a role by (1) encouraging self-help, (2) inducing workers to work even for low wages, and (3) causing people to view entrepreneurship as a means to greater security in retirement. Big businesses do not hire mid-career changers, and their early retirement programs throw out many people who wish to continue to work. The still limited level of government as well as private retirement benefits have, thus far at least, offered relatively little income security even for the retired employees of large firms." Consequently, many Japanese must continue working into their 70s.

Lifetime Employment for an Elite

So much has been made of "lifetime employment" in Japan, seen as the cornerstone of the management system, that many foreigners assume this phenomenon pervades the labor force. They are therefore amazed to learn that there is some turnover, workers are dismissed and yet others quit. How can this happen?

The primary reason is quite simple. "Lifetime employment" does not apply to all workers by any means. It only applies to a minority of workers who are in a particularly fortunate position, so much so that they are often referred to as the "labor aristocracy."

Jon Woronof, *The Japan Syndrome*, 1986.

Management by fear couldn't work if the social welfare system weren't so tightfisted. Although it pays out enough to keep the poor, handicapped and unemployed from starving, Japan spends the smallest portion of G.N.P. [Gross National Product] on social welfare programs of the big five economies, and the country lacks a system comparable to the United States' Aid to Families with Dependent Children. Though unemployment benefits are payable for 300 days to those over 55, job-losers under 30 get only ninety days' benefits; after that, they're at the mercy of an intrusive and skeptical welfare system. (Only 1.2 percent of the population gets benefits from the Ministry of Welfare, compared with about 4.6 percent on A.F.D.C. in the United States.) Public hospitals are overcrowded, private facilities are beyond the reach of the poor, and the handicapped constitute a "semi-underclass," in the words of economists Martin Bronfenbrenner and Yasukichi Yasuba. Japanese cities have their roving homeless (*furōsha*), just like ours; in Tokyo, patrols urge merchants not to feed the *furōsha* and spread water or wet sawdust on the ground where the homeless might sleep or sit. . . .

Japan could face some rough spots over the next few years. The export-led, high-growth era is over. It's not clear whether the domestic economy can avoid slipping into Western-style stagnation without the export stimulus. Japanese companies are becoming more like Western multinationals, relying on overseas suppliers and plants. High-wage industrial jobs are disappearing to automation and to new factories in Taiwan, South Korea and Thailand. This "hollowing out" of the economy promises that more core workers will be cast into the lake of contingency, driving the unemployment rate—visible and invisible—upward. Young workers are the most likely to find contingent jobs at cafés and oxygen bars than core jobs at Toyota or Nippon Steel. Regional income disparities are widening, as finance-led Tokyo throbs and steel towns sag. Japanese income distribution is now one of the most even in the world—though the distribution of wealth and power is another matter. But this is bound to change as the middle class is fragmented by the emergence of a free-spending upper class. Until recently, Japan's rich were quite inconspicuous consumers, and class distinctions were less visibly dramatic than in the United States. All these developments threaten to undermine Japanese social harmony.

Harsh Labor

This look at the reality of the Japanese political economy is not intended as another round in the popular sport of Japan-bashing. Americans were spoiled for years by the absence of serious competition; now, the Japanese have beaten us at our own game. But given the harshness of Japanese labor markets, the sacrifice of comfort and security to the totem of growth, and the wildness of speculation in stocks and real estate, should we really emulate the Japanese—even if that were possible?

"Japan can be said to have an elite system [of education] for the mass of students."

Japan's Education System Is Successful

Herbert J. Walberg

In the following viewpoint, Herbert J. Walberg writes that Japan's economic success can be attributed to the superior education of its youth. Each student, regardless of social class, he argues, has an equal chance to advance via objective testing and evaluation. Walberg is an educational psychologist and professor at the University of Illinois in Chicago.

As you read, consider the following questions:

1. How are national prosperity and education linked, according to Walberg?
2. Why does the author believe that Japan's education system is so successful?
3. According to Walberg, how is merit objectively measured in Japan's educational system?

Herbert J. Walberg, "What Can We Learn from Japanese Education?" This article appeared in the March 1988 issue and is reprinted with permission of *The World & I*, a publication of The Washington Times Corporation. Copyright © 1988.

Substantial reforms of U.S. schools resulted from American alarm over the first Russian space launch in 1958. Today, an impetus for rethinking our education system is provided by the astonishing growth of the Japanese economy.

Starting with a per-person income of $188 in 1953—less than that of Brazil and Malaysia—Japan grew faster in industrial productivity and real income than any other large modern country, while maintaining low rates of unemployment. Because of the recent appreciation of its currency, Japan's per-person income now exceeds that of the United States and most other countries.

By other comparisons, the Japanese also do very well: They have very low rates of infant mortality, youth delinquency, and adult crime; and exceedingly high standards of health, life expectancy, and other indexes of the quality of life. Known as the manufacturers of shoddy trinkets after World War II, the Japanese have since become world-renowned for the quality and reliability of their goods and services. How do the Japanese do it? Superior education provides part of the answer.

Human Capital

In 1776, Adam Smith speculated in *The Wealth of Nations* that prosperity depends on "human capital," the abilities of people. Research on industrialized countries indeed suggests that economic growth and general welfare depend on national abilities. When various nations' students are compared in knowledge and skills, Japan's usually rank at the top. . . .

In large national samples of students from many countries, the Japanese clearly exceeded in hypothesis testing, problem formulation, and other high-level skills more than in factual mastery. It is true that Japanese students are required to memorize, just as American students are asked to commit Shakespeare sonnets, physical constants, and historical dates to memory. It is misleading to believe, however, that those who can recite the facts cannot also think conceptually; in most fields, facts and concepts are inextricably intertwined.

Mathematics and science can be most validly compared, but it appears that Japanese students also do extremely well in other subjects such as geography, history, art, and music. Nearly all Japanese students study English, and most can read it reasonably well (but few speak it fluently).

Not only do Japanese students attain very high scores by objective standards, but about 96 percent graduate from high school with twelve years of education. This rate is considerably higher than the 76 percent graduated in the United States, where the goal has been to provide a high school education for all; the Japanese rate is also much higher than that of Europe, which has a more elite system with relatively fewer students attending school a full twelve years. Japan can be said to have an elite system for the mass of students—perhaps unique in the world, although such Asian countries as Hong Kong, Korea, Singapore, and Taiwan are gaining rapidly according to both quantitative and qualitative standards.

The efficiency of Japanese educational practices should provoke American legislators, parents, and educators to reevaluate their own standards and policies. Japanese teachers, for example, are

"The A on my report card means excellent. The M next to it is what it would be in Japan—mediocre."

highly honored and well paid, yet education costs no more than it does in the United States. Per-student costs are kept low by maintaining large classes—often three times the current U.S. average of about seventeen students per class. American educators, sometimes in their own interest, tend to equate educational quality with high spending and small classes; but extensive research shows little linkage between either dollars spent or class size and how much students learn.

More Work for Teachers

Japanese teachers work more hours per week and substantially more weeks per year than do U.S. teachers. This time includes lesson preparation and paper grading before children arrive and after they leave, and regular Saturday classes. More class time for students, as well as more teacher time spent on preparation and grading, helps students learn and improves teachers' performance. A longer workweek, comparable to business hours, and a long school year justify Japanese teachers' high pay; high pay gives education authorities a good pick of candidates from college graduates.

Japanese students also work hard and long. The numbers of hours spent in class and on homework, as well as the number of school days per year, are all much higher than in the United States. My observations in Japan indicate that time spent in class and in outside study are also used more efficiently. Japanese students appear to be getting twice as much study time as our own; and a Japanese high school diploma may be roughly equivalent to an American baccalaureate. . . .

In addition to expending long hours on academic subjects taken in regular school, many Japanese students attend *juku*—special tutoring schools with afternoon, evening, and weekend hours. *Juku* attendance increases as children get older, about 6 percent of the first graders and half the ninth graders participate. *Juku* offer general enrichment and supplementary programs in a wide variety of subjects including piano, flower arrangement, fencing, use of the abacus, and calligraphy.

Older children more often attend academic *juku* to help them keep pace with the demanding school curriculum and to prepare for the tough entrance examinations for the best senior high schools and universities. Those who do well on the exams are admitted to the famous institutions that channel their graduates to the best jobs in business and government. Of those, for example, who recently passed the civil service examinations for high government positions, some 60 percent were graduates of the University of Tokyo or Kyoto University.

Some American parents and educators worry about hard work leading to stress, but Japanese suicide rates among youth are half the U.S. rates and have been declining as educational standards have been raised. In contrast, youth-suicide rates in the United States have risen dramatically since about 1965. If anything, it appears that study and other constructive pursuits may work to solve rather than cause youth anxiety and other psychological problems. . . .

Japan maintains a rigorous, agreed-upon national curriculum—no course in driver education is taught in the Japanese school. All Japanese children study the same subject matter in the same grades, and they all learn science, mathematics, geography, history, and civics. Instead of music "appreciation," they gain proficiency in actually playing Bach and Mozart on one or two Western instruments. In addition to mastering their own difficult language, they acquire a reading knowledge of English and often other languages. Japanese schools deliver reliable, quality-controlled human capital to industry and society.

Educational Meritocracy

The Japanese strive for equality—not of results but of opportunity. They frankly recognize that students vary in how much effort they can put forth at learning and the rates at which they can acquire knowledge. At several points during their education, particularly in the ninth and twelfth grades, students may take tests for admission to a graded system of senior secondary schools and universities. Bright, hard-working students from poor families have an excellent chance of being admitted to elite schools by virtue of objectively measured merit.

Japanese Universities

Like the elite senior high schools, the elite universities are meritocratic. The great majority of universities are public institutions, receiving substantial government subsidies. Again, as with the senior high schools, fees are quite low, and loans are available to defray expenses. In principle and to a considerable extent in practice, any young Japanese can get into the University of Tokyo, or one of the other elite universities, provided only that he or she is talented enough and is prepared to do the work necessary to pass the entrance examinations.

Richard Lynn, *National Review*, October 28, 1988.

Because of finely graded selection, students are fairly similar in their achievement within schools. Such similarity minimizes invidious daily comparisons of students of unlike accomplishments; it allows fine-tuning of the pace and depth of instruction within schools to a narrow range of students. Students can proceed with their peers at their maximum rates.

Western observers have noted that many aspects of Japanese accomplishment are rigorously graded or ranked. For example, similar to the various colors of belts that signify the ranks of judo, degrees of expertise in flower arrangement are given at schools of various levels of prestige. These ranking systems reveal the Japanese fastidiousness about quality, which is also evident in their schools.

Yet a middle or low rank stings less than might be expected. Grouping students with similar levels of achievement makes differences less conspicuous. Students, moreover, cooperate closely with one another in learning; their main competition is against external examinations, not their classmates. Japanese students, parents, and educators believe that success is attributable to hard work rather than ability; a student who fails may be regarded as insufficiently hard working—not inherently unlucky or stupid. Finally, while high achievers are rewarded with higher pay in later life, the compensation is justified by early effort; and the spread of income within occupational ranks and the entire society is smaller than in most countries.

Japanese Families

In contrast to the pattern of rising divorce rates, child abuse, and other indicators of family problems in the United States, Japanese family members make permanent investments in one another. Pensions are small, and adults care for their aging parents in return for the care they received as children. Mothers rarely work before their children reach school age; they devote themselves instead to their children's education and character development. In turn, children who do well in school honor their families and nation.

Mothers warmly encourage their children, but they also give them practical help. They ensure, for example, that children have a quiet place for study—often a desk surrounded by partitions to encourage concentration and equipped with a bell to request assistance or a snack. Mothers often study along with their children from a duplicate set of textbooks. They visit their children's class to understand the teacher's methods, and invite teachers to their homes for meals—both of which manifest the close alliance of two chief agents of the child's development.

Education works well in Japan; it is undoubtedly one reason for the country's expanding income, the highest life expectancy in the world, and other indicators of national welfare. Japan's example also shows that educational excellence can be explained by productive choices and effort—rather than by cultural or genetic superiority.

"Reforms in the basic structure of the school and educational system are clearly needed."

Japan's Education System Is Flawed

Amano Ikuo

Amano Ikuo is a professor of the sociology of education at the University of Tokyo. In the following viewpoint, Amano argues that Japan's education system is in need of reform. Japanese education, Amano contends, is dominated by tests and leads to fierce competition among students vying for limited space in the top high schools and universities. Amano argues that this emphasis on competitive testing increases student stress, leads to school violence, and distorts Japanese education.

As you read, consider the following questions:

1. According to Amano, what factors are responsible for the increasingly competitive entrance examination system in Japan's schools?
2. Why does Amano think that students are less likely to compete for entrance to prestigious schools?
3. Why is there violence and other problems in the schools, according to the author?

Amano Ikuo, "The Dilemma of Japanese Education," *The Japan Foundation Newsletter,* Vol. XIII/No. 5, March 1986. Reprinted with permission.

The recovery and rapid growth of Japan's economy [after World War II] was partly responsible for the sharp increase of the numbers of students going on to senior high school or college. Japan's industrial structure underwent enormous changes during the process of rapid economic growth and these were accompanied by great strides in technological innovation. Private enterprises, especially in the secondary sector, experienced remarkable growth and the demand for university graduates increased rapidly. Opportunities to enter the upper strata of society were abundant. Defeated in World War II and in the throes of revolutionary changes in the educational system and other aspects of its society, Japan once again became a "land of opportunity," and there were many success stories, just as there had been after the Meiji Restoration. Higher wages and more equal distribution of income encouraged people to seek better education at better schools in pursuit of the academic credentials that served as the passport to success in society.

This new wave of rising aspirations made the competition in the entrance examinations even more intense than before the war. First of all, the number of competitors tremendously increased. In 1935, 19 percent of those who had completed compulsory education (six years of schooling) went on to secondary school. Only 3 percent of those who had completed compulsory schooling went on to college. The competition then was among a very small elite. After the war, the scale expanded tremendously; the corresponding figures for 1960 were 58 percent and 10 percent and for 1980, 94 percent and 37 percent.

Unavoidable Ordeal

Even when nearly 95 percent of junior high school graduates go on to senior high school, they must take entrance exams, and this means an unavoidable ordeal for virtually every 15-year-old. The same may be said for almost all of the 70 percent of students at general high schools (those schools which emphasize academic subjects, as opposed to commercial and technical ones). The curriculum offered at general high schools, moreover, is designed in such a way that the main emphasis is on preparation for university entrance examinations. Passing the university entrance exams is the chief educational concern of most senior high schools. . . .

After the war, all universities, old and new, were officially ranked equally. Corporations, too, abolished the practice of starting-pay differentials determined by the rank of the school or university of the new employee. Nevertheless, the ranking of universities has not disappeared. A small group of prestigious universities with traditions going back to before the war, including the former Imperial universities, continue to occupy the top of the hierarchy. Most of the institutions established after the war,

142

therefore, suffer from very low social regard.

The personnel policy of businesses—the most important employers of university graduates after the war—has contributed largely to maintaining and expanding the stratification of higher education. The starting-pay differentials may have been dropped, but corporations adopted the policy of preferring graduates of certain first-class or prestige universities in hiring new workers. This forged an explicit connection between first-class universities and top-ranking corporations.

In Japan there is a very close correlation between the size of a corporation and the wages its employees receive, as well as their career stability and social prestige. It is natural, then, that people seek employment at large corporations. Moreover, thanks to the connection just mentioned, the competition for jobs at these large

companies begins with the race to enter the prestigious universities at the top of the educational hierarchy. The entrance exams of the universities, then, are part, a kind of first phase, of the scramble to secure a stable career.

Rapid Growth Ends

Even after the end of the postwar period of rapid economic growth, the structure of inter-relationships between the overheated "examination hell," stratified educational institutions and educational credentialism has not fundamentally changed. But the attitudes of the children and young people who are being educated and who take part in the examination competition have changed greatly. In particular, it would seem that their aspirations to receive a good education and climb the ladder of success are weakening. Paradoxically, it was the remarkable economic growth that began in the 1960s that is responsible for this change.

Rapid economic growth brought to Japan affluence such as it had never before experienced. Moreover, this prosperity was enjoyed not just by a few but by all the people. It is well known that of the advanced nations Japan is among the top in terms of equality in the areas of income, consumption, and education. Egalitarianism pervades the popular consciousness, so much so that today by far the majority of Japanese people believe they are members of the middle class. . . .

Fewer Opportunities

The more affluent and egalitarian a society becomes—one might say the less hungry the people are—the weaker its motivation for success becomes. After the oil crisis of 1973, it became apparent that rapid economic growth was coming to an end, and that Japan was in the process of becoming a mature society. This meant that opportunities to move into higher social classes would grow fewer. It gradually became clear that hard work was not always sure to gain the expected reward. For the first time in its one-hundred-year history of modernization, Japan is ceasing to be a land of opportunity and success stories, and young Japanese keenly feel this change.

In the past, a university diploma ensured its holder prestige, power, and very high wages (although the degree of these benefits differed according to the university in question). Now that nearly 40 percent of young people go on to college, prestige and privilege are no longer at the disposal of every university graduate. Already there is a growing number of very well-educated college graduates who will not receive promotion to managerial positions, or who cannot even find white-collar jobs.

A university education, particularly at a prominent university, is still an effective passport to employment in a large corporation, of course, but having entered such a corporation no longer necessarily ensures a stable career with lifetime employment and promotion and wage increases by seniority. With the economy in a phase of slow growth, competition among corporations has become fierce both domestically and internationally. The struggle for survival is intensifying not only among corporations but also within them. The white-collar employees and engineers of large corporations, who by now are almost all college graduates, face a severe battle for a few managerial posts, and the chances of winning are getting slimmer.

In other words, the rewards promised by academic credentials are no longer certain. As it is becoming clear that higher wages, greater prestige and power do not necessasrily follow from academic credentials, young people's aspirations to aim for the upper rungs of society or to undergo the grueling competition for academic credentials are naturally cooling down.

Cooling Down

Despite weakening aspirations, no basic change has occurred in the educational structure so far. With few exceptions, students still have to pass entrance exams to enter senior high schools or universities. Because of the stratification of senior high schools and universities, moreover, the schools cannot revamp their curriculums, which are designed to prepare students for entrance exams and to put as many students into good senior high schools or universities as possible. Parents will not let the schools do that. But children and young people are of another mind.

Social Darwinism

Japanese education is social Darwinism developed to its fullest. Eighth graders who fail to keep up with the curriculum are often relegated to second-class citizenship for life. They are often forced out of college-preparatory programs, and makeup opportunities are virtually nonexistent. At 13 years of age, they have sealed their future in a menial job.

For those who go on, there are only four universities (Tokyo Daigaku, Meiji, Waseda and Keio) that can provide entry into the management of Japan's large corporations. Graduates from other universities are never considered executive material and will spend their working lives as low-paid "salarymen."

Russell Shor, *The New York Times*, January 23, 1987.

Of course, there are still many children who will study very hard to pass the entrance exam of a prestigious school in hopes of gaining a high position in society. And school education takes it for granted that children are strongly oriented to upward mobility.

As a whole, however, such children are becoming a minority.

The existence of a pyramid, the top of which is occupied by a handful of first-rate, prestigious universities, is a fact of life. But the number of places at the top is limited, and the race to gain one of them is harsh. Many children enter the competition with alacrity, and many parents encourage them every step of the way. But as they proceed through each stage, battling their way from elementary school to junior high school, and then to senior high school, the aspirations of many young people and their parents as well may suddenly cool, for the toll they must pay is heavy.

In order to enter a first-rate university, it is most advantageous to enter a six-year private secondary school. Such schools are something like prep schools in the United States or public schools in Britain. The competition to enter them is severe. Another option is to attend one of the few high schools, run by local governments or privately, that are well known for producing graduates who pass the entrance exams to the top universities. The competition to enter these schools is also fierce.

The children who attend such schools not only study very hard exclusively to prepare for entrance exams; they also repeatedly take mock exams prepared by exam-preparation companies. The results of these tests are scored by computer and sent to the children and their parents. Like it or not, the computer data tell them exactly where the child's level of academic ability stands in comparison with other children. Many students give up the idea of going to a good university if their showing in such exams is poor.

Lower Aspirations

The examination system, which once greatly encouraged the aspirations of children and parents, has begun to play the role of "cooling down" their hopes. Ironically, the more emphasis the teachers and the schools place on examination-centered curriculums and the harder they push children to study to beat the competition for entrance to better schools, the lower the children's aspirations are becoming.

As long as children want to go to a senior high school or college, they cannot avoid taking part in the entrance examination competition. Not only do their teachers and parents expect them to participate, the school education system itself gives top priority to that eventuality. Students who have little desire to gain better marks or acquire higher academic credentials suffer a serious dilemma at school, and this is the source of the problems that are endemic in junior and senior high schools today, especially the former. Well over 90 percent of junior high school graduates go on to senior high school today, which means almost every junior high school graduate is on track to take entrance exams.

One of the reasons, and probably the greatest reason, for the pathological phenomena occurring in the schools today, including violence and "bullying," is the gap between the changed values and attitudes of young people and the unchanged orientation of the older generation. The educational system and institutions, which are maintained and run by the latter, have changed little.

Children's aspirations are no longer directed solely at gaining academic credentials and higher ranks in the social hierarchy. What the schools must do now is to establish new objectives for education that will nurture and encourage other aspirations. Reforms in the basic structure of the school and educational system are clearly needed, for without them, little improvement can be made in the examination system centered on entrance exams.

Recognizing Ethnocentrism

Ethnocentrism is the attitude or tendency of people to view their own race, religion, culture, group, or nation as superior to others, and to judge others on that basis. An American, whose custom is to eat with a fork or spoon, would be making an ethnocentric statement when saying, "The Chinese custom of eating with chopsticks is stupid."

Ethnocentrism has promoted much misunderstanding and conflict. It emphasizes cultural and religious differences and the notion that one's national institutions or group customs are superior.

Ethnocentrism limits people's ability to be objective and to learn from others. Education in the truest sense stresses the similarities of the human condition throughout the world and the basic equality and dignity of all people.

Several of the following statements are derived from the viewpoints in this chapter. Consider each statement carefully. *Mark E for any statement you think is ethnocentric. Mark N for any statement you think is not ethnocentric. Mark U if you are undecided about any statement.*

If you are doing this activity as a member of a class or group, compare your answers with those of other class or group members. Be able to defend your answers. You may discover that others will come to different conclusions. Listening to the reasons others present for their answers may give you valuable insights in recognizing ethnocentric statements.

1. The structures and processes of Japanese politics are quite different from those in the United States.

2. Despite America's help after World War II, Japan is still backward when it comes to achieving a truly democratic society.

3. Foreigners can never understand what it truly means to be Japanese.

4. Deep down, every person in the world wants to be an American.

5. Japan has created a relatively safe society in which no one goes hungry and only a few thousand are homeless.

6. American society is superior to Japan's because it permits more freedom.

7. Democracy in Japan began in the nineteenth century. It is not an alien concept grafted onto the skin of Japanese society by the US after World War II.

8. Japan has the world's strongest economy because of the delicate sense of balance between cooperation and competition inherent in the Japanese people.

9. In American companies, a chief executive often earns forty times more than a low-level employee. In Japan, the ratio is fifteen to one.

10. Japanese superiority is shown by how management, labor, and government cooperate harmoniously for economic growth.

11. The Japanese model of lifetime employment is reserved for a minority of workers.

12. Japan succeeds economically because its business executives are less greedy and its workers less lazy than American managers and workers.

13. Japanese students rank highest in the world on standardized math tests.

14. Japanese schools are superior to American schools.

15. Japanese schools are cruel in how they treat students— they make students do janitorial work.

16. Japan's example shows that educational excellence can be attained by productive choices and effort, rather than cultural or genetic superiority.

Periodical Bibliography

The following articles have been selected to supplement the diverse views presented in this chapter.

Barbara Beull and Neil Gross
"The Myth of the Japanese Middle Class," *Business Week*, September 12, 1988.

John Burgess
"Is It a Nerd? Is It a Brain? No, It's Salaryman!" *The Washington Post National Weekly Edition*, September 7, 1987.

Ian Buruma
"What Remains Sacred," *The New York Times Magazine*, May 28, 1989.

James Fallows
"The Other Japan," *The Atlantic Monthly*, April 1988.

Jim Impoco
"Who Runs Japan? Not Its Politicians," *U.S. News & World Report*, August 29/September 5, 1988.

Charles Shiro Inouye
"Do Non-Japanese Fear the Flame?" *The Nation*, January 30, 1989.

Richard Lynn
"Why Johnny Can't Read, but Yoshio Can," *National Review*, October 28, 1988.

Diane Ravitch
"Japan's Smart Schools," *The New Republic*, January 6/13, 1986.

Jonathan Rowe
"Zen and the Art of Cultural Misappropriation," *The Washington Monthly*, May 1987.

Murray Sayle
"Playing Sneaks and Leaders," *The Spectator*, January 21, 1989.

Carol Simons
"Secret of Japan's Schools," *Reader's Digest*, July 1987.

Takahiro Suzuki
"A Hollow Future for Japan?" *The Futurist*, May/June 1988.

Karel G. van Wolferen
"The Recruit Scandal: Business as Usual for Japan," *The Washington Post National Weekly Edition*, May 8/14, 1989.

Philip Yancey
"The Message the Japanese Have Missed," *Christianity Today*, March 17, 1989.

Should Japan Increase Its International Role?

JAPAN

Chapter Preface

In the decades following its defeat in World War II, Japan has played only a small role in world politics. While the US, for example, took on such causes as containing communism, providing aid to poorer nations, and promoting democracy and open markets, Japan was content to leave such concerns to larger nations and focus its energies on rebuilding its own economy and developing its own export markets. In this endeavor Japan was enormously successful and accumulated a great deal of wealth.

It is Japan's economic success, in fact, which has made its international relations increasingly controversial. As Japan has grown richer and more powerful, more and more nations have called on it to assume greater responsibilities in the world community.

Exactly what Japan's obligations are—and how it should fulfill them—is a continuing source of debate both within and outside of Japan. The viewpoints in the following chapter examine different opinions on Japan's proper role in the world.

"Japan can, and should, do much more in its own defense."

Japan Should Contribute More to Its Defense

Edward A. Olsen

Japan spends roughly 1 percent of its gross national product (GNP) on its military. In the following viewpoint, Edward A. Olsen argues that because Japan has become a major economic power, it should spend more resources on its own defense and be responsible for protecting its own national interests. Olsen, a former State Department official, is a professor of national security affairs and Asian studies at the Naval Postgraduate School in Monterey, California.

As you read, consider the following questions:

1. Why does Olsen call Japan an unsympathetic ally?
2. In what areas of the world should Japan play a more active security role, according to the author?
3. Why does Olsen believe that Japan's increasing economic aid to other countries is an inadequate substitute for its spending on defense?

Reprinted by permission of the publisher, from Collective Defense or Strategic Independence?, edited by Ted Galen Carpenter. Lexington, MA: Lexington Books, D.C. Heath and Company, copyright 1989, D.C. Heath and Company.

Japan is the only Asian country with economic and technological power, and political and military potential, capable of being a regional equal of the United States. Japan could become another superpower; in economic terms it already is. None of that can safely be jeopardized by the United States's making Japan vulnerable to setbacks, intimidation, or co-option by the Soviet Union. However, U.S. interests in preventing those possibilities do not equate with an interest in perpetuating the status quo. It is not necessary for the United States to remain a perennial benefactor of Japan, protecting it from common threats. Japan can, and should, do much more in its own defense. . . .

A Cheap Rider

Tokyo and Washington know Japan is not a free rider, but neither does it pay a full fare. I tried to explain that difference to a Japanese audience by coining the expression *chiipu raida* ("cheap rider"). Japan's annual defense expenditures are sizable in absolute amounts—about $26 billion in recent years. Tokyo also contributes greatly to the cost of keeping U.S. forces in Japan. Moreover, Japan is a major supplier of invaluable high-technology components in various weapons systems that are essential to the defense of the entire West. No one should discount any of these assets. They pale, however, in comparison to what Japan could—and should—do on its own, and the West's, behalf. Japan's defense contributions remain decidedly minimalist, parsimonious, and inordinately cautious. Japan is indeed getting a cheap ride. It benefits from an international security system predicated on collective security but refuses to pay its fair share of the costs or bear a fair share of the risks.

The U.S.-Japan defense burden-sharing issue is frustrating to many Americans, who consider it virtually insoluble in the short run. On the contrary, the free or cheap rider issue is eminently soluble if both sides treat each other with respect and seek to share burdens by sharing power and decision making. The United States cannot mandate Japan's future strategy any more than Japan can shirk its responsibilities indefinitely. Neither should the United States subsidize a prosperous ally's economy, providing funds for Japan's defense so that Tokyo does not need to spend from its own resources on Japan's defense and can allocate them to economic purposes. These amount to an opportunity cost for Japan, increasing its ability to compete with the United States. . . .

An Unsympathetic Ally

Allies that do not sense a palpable threat, imminent or on the horizon, do not show much sympathy with U.S. desires to maintain a resilient economy capable of being the foundation of greater Western security. Despite a somewhat improved sense of strategic

154

Dick Locher. Reprinted by permission: Tribune Media Services.

realism in recent years, Japan is the prime example of an unsympathetic ally. It remains essentially unconcerned about the threat of external aggression. Tokyo's threat perceptions are highly abstract and not really in sync with Washington's. Actually, compared to what is widely considered by the Japanese to be a remote possibility of Soviet military aggression against Japan, the Japanese often see the pressures from the United States on trade and burden sharing as a more tangible threat, prompting Tokyo to pursue its "appeasement" policies regarding U.S. pressures without being sufficiently motivated by the Soviet threat. Consequently Japan is not well disposed to listening to what it considers parochial U.S. security-based arguments for greater fairness in economic and defense relations. To remedy this situation and explain its case to all allies not sufficiently sympathetic to U.S. needs, there is a clear need for a U.S. strategic doctrine that encompasses fairness in trade and defense.

Such prospective burden sharing should not be seen as a panacea automatically rectifying U.S.-Japan trade problems or necessarily saving the United States money for Asian defenses. Japan, militarily weak or strong, will likely remain a competitive economic partner. As a strong ally with a strong economy, Japan can undertake tasks that permit the United States to spend its defense dollars more efficiently. Such a Japanese role, however, might not guarantee overall savings because dollars not expended

155

by the United States in Japan's defense may well be allocated to other defense priorities. It would, however, ensure crucial improvements in the superpower balance in Asia, serving Japanese as well as U.S. interests.

Japan's Security Interests

Americans need to understand the nature of Japan's stake in the Pacific, the Indian Ocean, and adjacent countries. Throughout the region, the United States is committed in varying degrees to defend countries whose security benefits Japan as much as the United States, and often more. In neighboring Korea, the United States expends major resources and faces great risks to defend the Republic of Korea against North Korea. Although this is in the United State's interests, too, in certain respects it is overwhelmingly beneficial to Japan. The United States is a de facto surrogate for Japan in Korea, doing what the Japanese do not want to do (and what South Koreans are not ready to accept from Japan) in defense of Japanese security interests on the Korean peninsula. In many ways the Korean demilitarized zone is Japan's front line. In nearby China, the United States, in pursuit of what Washington considers converging U.S. and Japanese interests versus the Soviet Union, has shaped an alignment of U.S.-PRC [People's Republic of China] security interests that benefit the United States and Japan equally. But it is the United States that takes the lead in these matters, not Japan. In Southeast Asia, the United States projects its armed power from Philippine bases for the benefit of regional freedom of the seas. Though this is valuable to the United States and all its friends and allies in the area that rely extensively on the oceans for trade, the country benefiting the most is, again, Japan. Going east or west in the Pacific, the United States bears the brunt of the responsibility for protecting freedom of the seas near the Panama Canal and in the Persian Gulf, two more areas strategically crucial to Japan's economic security.

In all of these cases and several lesser ones, the United States is in the front lines while Japan remains far behind in relative safety, taking advantage of U.S. strategic largesse. Except for Panama, where the United States exerts a unique presence, these are examples of the United States doing more than its share and Japan doing far less than a fair share. Japan contributes very little to Korean security, except for allowing the United States the privilege of access to bases in Japan so that Americans might defend militarily interests that Japan refuses to accept. Similarly in China and Southeast Asia, Japan is reluctant to accept a fair share of the responsibility and risks in defense of its strategic interests. While one can sympathize with Japanese, and other Asian, reluctance to avoid Japanese reinvolvement militarily in the region less than half a century after Pearl Harbor, where is it written that

Americans must perennially pay an onerous price for having won World War II? Are we to be stuck with these security responsibilities and risks forever? Most egregious, perhaps, was the situation in the Persian Gulf where the United States speedily provided naval assistance to friendly oil-producing states so that the flow of oil to the West would not be impeded by the Iran-Iraq War. U.S. complaints about lack of help from the Western European and Japanese recipients of nearly all those Middle Eastern oil exports motivated several NATO [North Atlantic Treaty Organization] allies to dispatch naval vessels to help maintain freedom of the seas. In stark contrast, Japan, with much wringing of hands, fell back upon its no-war constitutional inhibitions and popular domestic opposition to its getting involved in collective security. This was but the most glaring example of Japan's sanctimoniously evading responsibility for defending its own interests and relying on the United States to pull its chestnuts out of the fire. This is grossly unfair when one remembers that Japan's interests in the region's security are comparable to those of the United States and often are greater.

The Free Ride

We should mention the central fact of Japanese existence: They are our wards. They live in a very dangerous neighborhood, close to some big bad countries who don't like the Japanese—Russia and China. The Japanese do little to protect themselves—spending just over 1 percent of their gross national product on defense, the lowest rate of any modern nation.

The big reason they spend so little on defense, they say, is because their voters are afraid of resurgent militarism. Japan, after all, almost destroyed all of Asia, including itself, in World War II. So now the Japanese are the ultimate double free riders: They spend stingily on defense and yet feel secure because the United States guarantees their security. The American guarantee is worth something because we spend 6 percent of our GNP for defense.

Ben Wattenberg, *The Washington Times*, June 18, 1987.

Considering Japan's great indigenous stake in Asian-Pacific security, Americans should not be more willing than the Japanese to maintain regional strategic well-being. The United States has a right to expect Japan to behave in a militarily responsible manner and act to prompt such behavior. The United States should not accept all the responsibilities from which it and Japan receive approximately equal benefits. In some parts of the world, Americans may still echo President Kennedy's inaugural remarks about paying any price and bearing any burden, but these words ring hollow in Northeast Asia, where both U.S. allies (South Korea is the other) can pay a full share of the price and bear a full share of the burden for our mutual security. If a moderate French politician can ask, "Do you think 320 million Europeans can continue forever to ask 240 million Americans to defend us against 280 million Soviets?" surely the Asian version of such a query would be far more portentous. Americans have a right to expect the Japanese to ask such questions too and to help devise answers more appropriate to circumstances that are far different from those prevailing when Washington committed the United States to Japan's security in the 1950s.

Moreover, the United States has good reasons to seek strategic integration with Japan as a major partner and a regional equal in an asymmetrical global strategic system because of what Japan, alone in Asia, can do for U.S. security. Japanese advanced technology probably will become an even more integral portion of the strategic hardware and software systems that enable the United States to survive in the nuclear age. Although the United States long has relied on dual-use Japanese technology, in June 1985 the first formal request for transfer of Japanese military high technology was made under the terms of a 1983 agreement. In cooperative circumstances, this may flourish and dramatically underscore Ambassador Mike Mansfield's frequently repeated admonition that U.S.-Japan ties are the most important bilateral relationships of the United States. The possibilities of Japanese participation in SDI [Strategic Defense Initiative] and other high-tech defense research are extremely encouraging and would intensify bilateral interdependency.

Sharing the Costs

On a regional level, Japan could offer the United States much to ease financial burden sharing. Until the major revaluation of the yen versus the dollar in the mid-1980s, Japan's defense budget and the amount it reimbursed the United States to maintain its forces in Japan in recent years totaled about $12 billion annually, about twice the amount North and South Korea combined (countries with a radically different military image than Japan's) spend on defense. Because of the greatly increased value of the yen coupled with small actual increases, Japan now appears to be spending close to $26 billion per year, but such a figure is somewhat artificial and illusory because the actual amount of yen involved in yearly expenditures has not changed nearly as much as the dollar-denominated figures suggest. The much-vaunted surpassing by the Nakasone government in 1987 of Japan's self-imposed 1 percent of GNP defense spending limit was largely symbolic. Defense expenditures went from a tiny fraction under 1 percent to an equally tiny fraction over it. Though Japan's percentage of yearly defense budget increases often exceeds that of other U.S. allies, there is no sign that cracking that barrier means Japan will move quickly to match the proportions of GNP spent on defense by other Western powers. It stands in dramatic contrast to neighboring South Korea's 6 percent of GNP spent on defense. Furthermore, most of those Japanese funds are not ordinarily spent abroad, so their actual purchasing power has not increased appreciably. In sharp contrasts, the United States spends over $40 billion per year on Asian defense. And U.S. dollars spent in the Japanese security environment today buy markedly less than in prerevaluation days. U.S. bases in Japan, albeit partially under-written by Tokyo, still cost the United States a great deal to maintain in a high-cost environment. Were Japan to expend a portion of its GNP equivalent to the 6 to 7 percent share spent by the United States, it would have available an additional $60 billion to $72 billion in prerevaluation terms or a contemporary (but artificial) figure of about $125 billion to $150 billion. That is more than double the defense expenditures of all other Asian states combined. Japan clearly could become once more a major military power, perhaps a nuclear power, if it decides to do so.

Japan's Security

No one expects Japan to spend close to that amount in the near future. This is especially true if the United States continues to spend so much on Japan's security that Tokyo lacks any incentive to expand seriously its responsibilities or expenditures. Yet with an increase to half the U.S. percentage spent on defense, Japan could readily meet all its current and future needs and pay for about half of what the United States spends on the Asia-Pacific region, largely to protect Japanese interests. If this happens (and it should), it must not be seen by China, the Republic of Korea, or other Asian states as an attempt by the United States to make Japan a U.S. proxy or surrogate, for the reverse is true. The United States has acted on Japan's behalf for four decades. It is time for a change. A new, improved security scheme for Northeast Asia is long overdue. Washington should explain its effort to get Tokyo to share burdens throughout Asia, which are more properly Japanese, in terms of a reduction in its acting as a proxy for Japan, which should shoulder its own burdens. Japan can do much more in defense of its security in the Asia-Pacific region and in more distant areas of concern such as the Persian Gulf. Despite the legitimacy of U.S. intentions to stop being a surrogate for Japan, some Japanese and other Asians will interpret any such move as an effort by the United States to dump its responsibilities on the Japanese and force Japan into a level of cooperation it does not want. These perceptions should not be ignored—they are hot political issues in Japanese domestic politics—but they must not be permitted to obstruct what is necessary for the United States to meet the changing needs of its national interests. . . .

Unfair Measures

Japan may never be willing to do as much as Americans might like, but it is clear that it is capable of doing much more to defend itself. The current pressures on it to become defensively self-reliant are inadequate. Furthermore, this approach allows Japan to drag its feet in pursuit of limited objectives. Japan should expand its objectives and do something concrete, beyond economic measures, to help the United States and other allies with regional security. Japan's renowned comprehensive security doctrine, which stresses the economic and political components of augmenting stability as crucial ways to preserve security and minimize the need for armed defensive measures, is an admirable concept. Unfortunately the Japanese use that doctrine as a rationale for contributing minimally to armed security while emphasizing its unarmed (economic and political) contributions to global peace and security. This approach leaves the United States responsible for military security. If Washington allows the situation to persist, Japan will be able to play a benign role in international affairs while the United States plays the "heavy." It is an unfair division of labor, responsibility, and risk that should not be perpetuated. . . .

There is something terribly wrong with a strategic relationship in which one economic giant does so much more than the other economic giant. Japan's attitude is reminiscent of selfish individuals who say, "What's mine is mine; what's yours let's negotiate." Such self-centered behavior is intolerable and should be rejected by Americans.

"Japan is playing a significant defense role today. . . . It is not enjoying a free ride."

Japan Contributes Enough to Its Defense

James E. Auer

James E. Auer is the director of the Center for US-Japan Studies and Cooperation at Vanderbilt Institute for Public Policy Studies at Vanderbilt University in Nashville, Tennessee. In the following viewpoint, he argues that Japan has greatly increased its spending on defense, and has cooperated effectively with the United States in sharing defense technology.

As you read, consider the following questions:

1. How does Japanese defense spending compare with other countries, according to Auer?
2. Does the author believe Japan's increasing military power poses an offensive threat to Asia?
3. What significance does the author attach to Japan's foreign aid?

James E. Auer, "Japan Spends Well on Defense." This article appeared in the January 1989 issue and is reprinted with permission of *The World & I*, a publication of The Washington Times Corporation. Copyright © 1989.

To give a simplistic answer to the question, What does Japan spend on defense? could cause considerable misunderstanding. There are some in the United States who believe that Japan, which spends only about 1 percent of its gross national product (GNP) on defense while the United States spends almost 6 percent, is enjoying a free ride. Others, in Japan, believe that, rather than contributing to Japan's security and safety, Japanese defense cooperation with the United States results only in making Japan a target for Soviet aggression. Some critics say that Japan is entrapped in U.S. global strategy.

Close examination shows neither of these extreme views to be correct. For although Japan does spend only slightly more than 1 percent of its GNP for defense, its economy is enormous. Japan's $2.5 trillion economy in 1987 is now clearly larger than the Soviet Union's $2.2 trillion. And Japan's economy will almost certainly continue to grow rapidly far into the foreseeable future. In 1988, Japan [spent] about $30 billion for defense, making Japan's defense budget almost third in the world, drawing abreast or ahead of the United Kingdom, France, and West Germany. . . . Japan's budget may soon be as high as 1.5 percent of its GNP.

The idea of Japan becoming the world's third largest military power frightens some Japanese and some of the populace of Japan's noncommunist trading partners in Asia as well as some Americans. However, third largest is still far, far removed from Japan's becoming a major military power; at third largest GNP, Japan is still only ahead of all the other countries except the two military superpowers, whose military spending dwarfs the others. Japan as No. 3 could double defense expenditures without assuming any threatening offensive capability.

Quality, Not Quantity

What is really important about Japan as No. 3 is that Japan is spending its limited defense resources extremely well in constructing a high-technology anti-invasion air-defense and antisubmarine network around its territory in the Northwest Pacific. This capability, backed up with U.S. strategic power in the Pacific that removes the threat of Soviet nuclear blackmail vis-à-vis Japan, significantly complicates Soviet military planning in the Pacific. Because of Japan's complement to U.S. power, Pacific deterrence is well maintained at present and could be further strengthened in the 1990s.

This is of enormous benefit to the United States, which not only profits immensely from its economic activities in the Pacific Basin, the newly emerged economic center of the world, but also is able to more flexibly operate its military forces in other theaters, given the favorable environment in the Pacific. Japan's benefit is equal to or greater than that of the United States, benefiting economically in a similar fashion vis-à-vis the integrity of the Pacific Basin economy and enjoying a high degree of national security despite its vulnerable location in close proximity to the Soviet Far East. Rather than being entrapped in U.S. global strategy, Japan, which has few natural resources and needs to import in order to survive and prosper, can afford to safely go about its business while devoting a minimal percentage of its national wealth to military expenditures. If Japan is not satisfied with the situation, it has the right, unexercised since the law came into effect in 1970, to ask the Americans to leave. Japan has wisely not asked them to go.

Americans Are Misinformed

The reason most Americans still subscribe to the view that Japan is getting a free ride under the mutual security treaty is because they are largely uninformed. Depending on the method of analysis, Japan's defense expenditure is ranked from the sixth to the third highest in the world. The quality of Japan's defense force places it among the best in the world, and Japan is one of the most open-handed American allies in terms of the amount it spends to support U.S. troops on its soil.

Chūma Kiyofuku, *Japan Quarterly*, January/March 1989.

The military relevance of Japanese defense efforts is a recent phenomenon that came about slowly and gradually and, as a result, has not been given wide notice in the United States or even in Japan. Also, with the size of the Japanese trade surplus vis-à-vis the United States, some in the U.S. Congress have been unwilling to concede any positive action from Tokyo and have chosen to use the free-ride argument as a means to vent frustrations resulting from the trade imbalance.

The Reagan-Nakasone Years

Defense cooperation between Washington and Tokyo became extremely smooth during the Reagan and Nakasone administrations. It is perhaps going too far to say that what transpired under the so-called Ron-Yasu relationship would not have occurred without their administrations' actions, but the pace and quality of the defense relationship were almost certainly speeded up and enhanced during their tenures. . . .

In March 1981, Secretary of Defense Caspar Weinberger told the Senate Armed Services Committee that a division of defense responsibilities among the United States, its NATO allies, and Japan would be a central thrust of the new administration's defense policy.

Later the same month Weinberger proposed such role sharing to Japan's foreign minister and promised that, if Japan were willing, the United States was prepared to extend offensive protection to Japan, both by providing a nuclear umbrella to remove the threat of blackmail and by providing other offensive capability, such as basing the aircraft carrier *Midway* in Yokosuka (the only aircraft carrier the United States has ever based outside of the United States). Weinberger said that if it were necessary, for example, to strike Vladivostok, the headquarters of the Soviet Far Eastern navy, the United States would undertake that type of mission, which by its own constitution, Japan is prohibited from doing. He also stated that the defense of Japan could not be limited to Japan's four islands and their immediate surroundings since Japan had to import virtually all of its oil, a majority of which comes from the Persian Gulf. Weinberger said the United States would be willing to protect Japan's vital sea-lanes in the Southwest Pacific and Indian oceans.

The Postwar Period

His proposal was accepted during the visit of Prime Minister Suzuki two months later. The Reagan-Suzuki joint communiqué stated, for the first time in the postwar period, that a U.S.-Japan division of defense responsibilities was appropriate. While still in Washington, Suzuki, at a press conference at the National Press Club, proclaimed that Japan's national policy was to defend its own territory, the surrounding seas and skies, and its sea-lanes to a distance of 1,000 miles. This was a much clearer statement of Japan's intentions than had been provided previously and was a perfect complement to Weinberger's statement of March to Japan's foreign minister. The problem was that Japan's capability to carry out those defense missions was seriously lacking.

Nakasone became prime minister in November 1982. He clearly understood the implications of the 1981 communiqué and stepped up efforts to obtain the capability required to meet Japan's responsibilities. While freezing or reducing virtually all government spending in the 1983-85 national budgets, he allowed defense spending to grow by 5 percent annually in real terms, in stark contrast to spending in the politically popular areas of education, public works, and social welfare. In 1985, Nakasone permitted the Japan Defense Agency (JDA) to formulate an ambitious 1986-1990 defense program designed to achieve the capability necessary to meet the 1981 defense goals. He also changed the status of the five-year plan from a JDA-only wish list—which for the previous six years had been funded annually at only 60 percent of the requested level—to a cabinet-approved plan that thus far, from 1986 to 1988, has been fully funded. Full funding is even more significant in that, in 1987, it was necessary to exceed the politically sensitive barrier of 1 percent of GNP in defense spending to keep the program on track.

At the end of the 1986-1990 program, Japan will have 13 combat divisions in Hokkaido. These are ground forces, five of which are forward deployed and reinforced with heavy equipment, with improved sustainability (ammunition supply, and so forth). For antisubmarine warfare (ASW), the JDA will have 60 destroyer-type vessels and 100 P3C aircraft, about three and four times, respectively, the number of the U.S. Seventh Fleet, which has responsibility for the entire Western Pacific and Indian oceans. Air defense will be provided by the state of the art Patriot and Aegis missile systems and by 200 F15 and 100 F4 aircraft, about the same number and types of modern tactical aircraft the United States has defending the continental United States, and more than the U.S. Air Force has in Japan, Korea, and the Philippines combined.

Japan's Defenses

Japan's defense budget is already the world's third largest—about $40 billion compared to the Federal Republic of Germany's $31.7 billion, France's $32.4 billion, and the United Kingdom's $35.7 billion. . . . Moreover, Japan's defense expenditures have been growing over the last decade at the rate of 5% real growth per year—substantially better than the United States or our other allies.

William Clark Jr., *Department of State Bulletin*, December 1988.

All of these Japanese forces are deployed on and around Japanese territory, which extends out like a picket fence to 500 miles on either side of the key Soviet strategic Far East bastion of Vladivostok. Given the fact that the Soviets must now and for the foreseeable future prioritize their military efforts—first, in Eastern Europe, and second, along their long and disputed land border with China—and that 90 percent or more of the support for the USSR's other two Pacific sanctuaries at Petropavlovsk on the Kamchatka Peninsula and in Vietnam come by sea from Vladivostok, Japan's high-technology anti-invasion air-defense and ASW network, complemented by U.S. strategic power, very significantly complicates Soviet military planning for the Pacific, the essence of deterrence. The resulting favorable Pacific security environment allows the United States flexibility in utilizing forces in other theaters, thereby strengthening deterrence elsewhere. Japan's 1 percent of GNP defense budget thus not only achieves local self-defense, but at least indirectly contributes to both regional and global deterrence.

Financial Support

Since 1981 Japan also significantly increased its financial support for the upkeep of U.S. forces stationed in Japan. Although, under the U.S.-Japan Security Treaty, Japan is only required to provide rent-free bases for American use, Japan has increasingly provided new facilities, particularly housing units, on a voluntary basis. As a result, the morale and efficiency of the approximately 55,000 U.S. personnel and their families stationed in Japan is extremely high, a contrast to the condition of U.S. forces in some other overseas locations. Also, in 1986, Tokyo responded to a U.S. request, occasioned by a steep rise in the value of the yen, and passed a special law authorizing the JDA to assume a significant share of the costs of Japanese laborers who work on the U.S. bases. Less than a year after this special Japanese legislation had been passed, Prime Minister Noboru Takeshita, Nakasone's successor, decided on a revision, further increasing Japan's share of U.S. labor costs in 1989 and 1990. In 1988 Japan budgeted more than $2.5 billion on behalf of U.S. servicemen, more than $45,000 per capita, the most generous arrangement the United States enjoys anywhere in the world. In 1989 Japan will spend more than $1 billion for U.S. facilities and labor costs alone. As a result of these generous, voluntary Japanese expenditures, keeping the same forces in the United States or at any other foreign location outside Japan would cost more money. Thus, unless the forces are to be demobilized, stationing them in Japan saves the United States significant funds as well as keeps troops forward deployed.

Sharing Technology

In 1981 Secretary Weinberger also asked his Japanese counterpart if Japan could find a legal way to share its defense technology with the United States. Shortly after Nakasone became prime minister, he exempted the United States alone from restrictions on the export of defense technology. Although it took more than two years to arrange procedures under which transfers could actually take place, Japan's new support fighter for 1990, the FSX, and the Strategic Defense Initiative (SDI) provide two avenues toward making this program a practical reality. Japan is adding much of its own state of the art technology to improving a U.S. fighter aircraft, and some U.S. SDI scientists believe that Japan has more capability to contribute to SDI than any other country. [Former] Secretary of Defense Frank Carlucci believes that until glasnost and perestroika result in actual reductions of Soviet force levels. . . .Western technological superiority will be absolutely necessary to deter numerically superior Soviet force levels. He also has stated that technology transfer could be Japan's most significant contribution to Western security. Carlucci's predecessor, Weinberger, stated, "In the age of high-technology defense, there are few opportunities for deterring Soviet power more promising than combining U.S. and Japanese technological capabilities."

For the 1990s Japan is considering improvements that will make its already meaningful defense capability more effective by adding components such as broad-area surveillance (Over the Horizon Radar), aerial tankers, and long-range early-warning aircraft. These enhancements would make undetected Soviet access to the Pacific by ship, submarine, or aircraft virtually impossible, further complicating Soviet Pacific planning. Japan is almost certainly able to do this as well as to increase its financial support for U.S. forces within a defense budget only slightly larger than 1 percent of GNP. Since the United States will continue to spend in excess of 5 percent of GNP, many in the United States will say this is unfair and/or politically unacceptable, even to a Republican president. Since expenditures above 2 percent of GNP would bring Japan close to military superpower status within a decade, a status neither Japan nor its Asian trading partners desire, a case can be made for additional Japanese endeavors, relevant to peace and security, above and beyond its exclusive self-defense efforts.

The Free Ride Delusion

America's biggest delusion about Japan is that the "free ride" on defense that we give Japan is the key to the two countries' problems. If we can only make the Japanese pay for their own protection, many Americans feel, our economic difficulties will work themselves out. . . .

I think this concept has things exactly the wrong way around. The military relationship between Japan and America, "free ride" and all, is much better for each party than any alternative I've heard suggested so far. The division of labor is complicated and obviously unequal—even if Japan is paying more and more of the cost of defending its own home territory, it has nothing like America's worldwide military costs. Still, it sounds easier to correct the imbalance, by "making" Japan pay its way, than it turns out to be when you look at the details. We can do ourselves a favor if we concentrate on our real disagreements with Japan, about trade policy, and forget about the "free ride."

James Fallows, *The Atlantic Monthly*, April 1989.

In 1988, for the first time, Japan's budget for economic aid—overseas development assistance (ODA)—exceeded that of the United States, although it still constitutes only 0.3 percent of GNP. Increasing this aid to the 0.7 percent of the GNP minimum level recommended for developed countries, or even more so to 1 or 2 percent of GNP, could make a tremendous difference over a decade in providing stability to important countries throughout the world.

To make such an enhanced aid program effective, qualitative as well as quantitative improvements would be necessary, untying

Japanese aid from the mere promotion of Japanese industries to really develop the economies of recipient countries. Such a program, if extremely well managed, could significantly aid regional and global peace and security and help counterbalance the jealousies built up by Japanese trade surpluses in many countries. To carry out such a program would be extremely difficult, but there could hardly be a nobler goal for Japan to pursue in seeking a meaningful but peace-loving world role.

In sum, Japan is playing a significant defense role today and is likely to do even more in the future. It is not enjoying a free ride nor is it dangerously trapped in an alliance with the United States. Japan can do even more in defense: for itself, for the well-being of U.S. forces in Japan, and for worldwide technology sharing. But if very significant increases in Japanese spending are to take place in the future, areas outside the pure defense sector, such as ODA, should be carefully examined.

"The great majority of the people endorse a larger role for Japan in foreign aid."

Japan Should Increase Its Foreign Aid

Koichiro Matsuura

Koichiro Matsuura is director-general of the Economic Cooperation Bureau, a department of the Japanese Foreign Ministry which administers many of Japan's foreign aid programs. In the following viewpoint, excerpted from an interview in the Japanese publication *Ekonomisutu*, Matsuura states Japan's foreign assistance has helped poorer countries and promoted good relations between Japan and the world. He argues that Japan should increase its foreign aid budget to a level consistent with its position as the world's second largest economic power.

As you read, consider the following questions:

1. What should be the primary goal of foreign aid, according to Matsuura?
2. What obstacles has Japan faced in administering its foreign aid programs, according to the author?
3. Why does Matsuura believe Japan's foreign aid budget is still too small?

Koichiro Matsuura, "Administering Foreign Aid: The View from the Top," *Economic Eye*, Spring 1989. Reprinted by permission of the Keizai Koho Center.

Interviewer: Japan today is moving into the position of the world's biggest foreign aid donor. Thanks to steadily increasing allocations and the yen's appreciation, the dollar value of Japan's aid has snowballed. The taxpayers who ultimately pick up the tab support this use of their funds, but they are beginning to grumble about what they perceive as inefficiencies in the aid program. From your standpoint as one of the top administrators, what do you see as the goals of Japan's aid program?

Benefiting Both Recipients and Taxpayers

Koichiro Matsuura: Japan offers aid with two goals in mind. The first is to foster economic and social development in the third world, and the second is to promote the relations between developing countries and Japan. The second motive follows from the fact that we're spending Japanese taxpayers' money. Naturally taxpayers want their money to benefit them in one way or another.

There have been shifts in the thinking about the first goal. In the United States, the country most active in foreign aid since World War II, aid in the 1950s and 1960s was inspired by a hope to contain communism by fostering healthy growth in the developing world. Over time, however, many Americans came to doubt whether this generosity was doing much good in keeping the communists at bay.

People then began to rethink aid, and a new philosophy was spelled out in the 1969 Pearson report of the Commission on International Development [chaired by former Canadian Prime Minister Lester Pearson]. It states our contemporary view that aid should be given as a humanitarian gesture. In other words, rich countries should help poor countries for no other reason than a desire to rescue impoverished people. I agree with this premise. Essentially what it means is that aid programs are part of a global welfare system designed to assist people until their country's development has gone far enough to do without external support.

But we shouldn't simply throw money around in random directions. Aid must be steered to places where it will bring long-term benefits back to its donor. Here the second goal is relevant.

Focus on Asia

Sub-Saharan Africa is undoubtedly one of the poorest areas in the world today, and it receives a major share of North American and European aid. But this doesn't mean that Japan should concentrate on this area. As an Asian country, Japan's ties with its neighbors are naturally of central importance. Our foreign aid policy reflects this reality, the bulk of Japanese aid being channeled to other Asian countries. There's no pressing reason to alter that policy now.

Within Asia, the three top recipients of Japanese aid are China, Indonesia, and Thailand. Even more so than the United States, Japan needs good relations with China for strategic and other reasons. The other two countries are central members of the Association of Southeast Asian Nations with whom Japan has historically been on good terms. The Philippines, another ASEAN member, is also important to Japan, and we must continue to assist it in the years to come. In this way our decisions on whom we extend help to should not fail to take Japan's national interests into account.

Interviewer: The recipients of aid from Western nations express profound gratitude for the assistance, perhaps because of the efficiency with which their aid is applied toward its intended goals. But the recipients of Japan's aid don't seem overjoyed.

Matsuura: I can't agree with that assessment. Take our aid to China. I accompanied Prime Minister Noboru Takeshita on his visit there and know for a fact that Chinese leader Deng Xiaoping personally and repeatedly thanked him for this aid. I also heard much praise of Japan at every project site I inspected. I'd say that Japanese assistance is definitely appreciated and that it has built the foundation of strong bonds of good will that now exist between our two countries.

The US Position on Japanese Aid

Burdensharing is not limited purely to defense expenditures, just as our cooperation with Japan is not limited only to the defense relationship. One of the areas in which we cooperate very closely is overseas development aid. Japan now has the second largest foreign aid program in the world, and if current trends continue, Japan will overtake the United States in 1991 as the world's largest aid donor.

Increasingly, Japan provides foreign aid to countries of strategic importance to the West. Japan has substantial development assistance programs in countries like the Philippines, Pakistan, Egypt, Jordan, Oman, Turkey, and Jamaica, which are of special importance to us. Still, we believe Japan could do more in this regard.

Gaston J. Sigur, *Current Reflections on US–Japan Relations*, 1988.

Interviewer: But what about the complaint of inefficiency? Aren't there problems here?

Matsuura: On this point, let me first explain that every donor's aid is intended only to help the recipient help itself. If a nation is already well on the road to industrialization, it should be able to provide 90 percent of development costs on its own, and we need only furnish 10 percent. If a country is less developed, aid will have to cover a larger share. The success or failure of development depends not just on our efforts but on the efforts made by the recipients themselves.

For the past eight years or so, we've been subjecting our aid projects to a fairly thorough review. Though the assessments are conducted after the projects are complete, we spend money to remedy any serious defects that turn up. The projects that are found to be less than satisfactory teach us valuable lessons about how things should be done differently the next time around. Thus far, we've evaluated nearly a thousand projects.

All in all, I believe our projects have been successful; only 10 percent to 15 percent have required serious rethinking. We've made some big mistakes, certainly, but they've been very few. I'd say our track record is better than those of most other donor nations.

Interviewer: When a project goes awry, Japan is partly to blame, isn't it?

Matsuura: Yes, although the recipient country is often more to blame. Some of our mistakes have occurred in the planning stage. For instance, we've designed projects that were too sophisticated to do the recipient much good. We've also understimated how fast parts would wear down, leading to delays in parts supplies. But let's remember that Japan is a latecomer in the field of foreign aid, and we're still feeling our way forward.

Administering Aid

The biggest obstacle to an efficient program is the size of our staff. The official development assistance budget has grown threefold over the past ten years in yen terms despite the overall fiscal belt-tightening. And it's swelled fivefold in dollar terms, putting Japan in a position to displace the United States as the world's largest ODA [official development assistance] donor. Because of a government policy to cut back on the number of civil servants, however, we've only been able to increase our staff size by 50 percent. This means that each administrator now handles much more aid than a decade earlier.

Today there are roughly 1,600 Japanese civil servants involved in administering foreign aid. They work for government ministries, the Japan International Cooperation Agency, the Overseas Economic Cooperation Fund, and the related sections of Japanese diplomatic offices overseas. Britain has about the same number of people in its aid administration, but they're responsible for an ODA budget only about one-fourth the size of Japan's. In short, each ODA staff member in Japan must handle four times more aid than his or her British counterpart.

Interviewer: The Japanese program is also criticized for its disunity, being administered jointly by the Foreign and Finance ministries, the Ministry of International Trade and Industry, the

Share of Development Assistance*

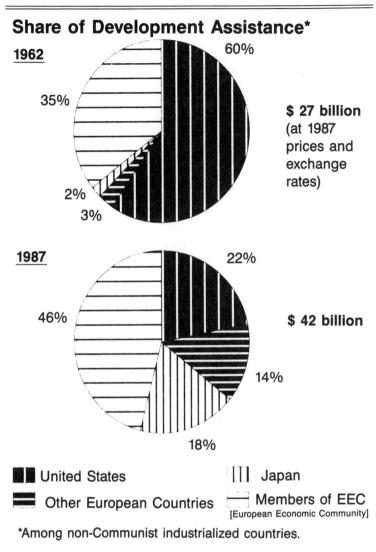

1962

60%

35%

$ 27 billion
(at 1987
prices and
exchange
rates)

2%

3%

1987

22%

46%

$ 42 billion

14%

18%

■■ United States |‖| Japan

▬▬ Other European Countries   ⌐¬ Members of EEC
[European Economic Community]

*Among non-Communist industrialized countries.

Economic Planning Agency, and other government bodies.

Matsuura: In most countries you'll find that foreign aid is administered by a single agency within or under the foreign ministry. Few countries, if any, employ a system as complex as Japan's. The merit of this arrangement is that we can tap the resources of various ministries and agencies. For agricultural projects we seek the counsel and participation of specialists in the Ministry of

Agriculture, Forestry, and Fisheries; for medical assistance we turn to the Ministry of Health and Welfare.

I therefore have my doubts as to whether we need to reorganize our operations under a single ministry. Of course, some unity is essential. We can't expect aid-seeking countries to go directly to the Ministry of Transport for help with port and airport projects or to the Ministry of Construction for help building roads, and that's why we at the Ministry of Foreign Affairs mediate all contact between the recipients and the relevant government organs. True, the aid bureaucracy is a bit more complicated than is necessary, and we're going to have to work to streamline and simplify things.

Keeping Politicians Out

Interviewer: The ruling Liberal Democratic Party and the government have indicated they want to form a cabinet-level committee on ODA. This would give politicians a greater say over what has been the exclusive domain of the bureaucracy.

Matsuura: I understand their viewpoint. It used to be the opposition parties that were most critical of our efforts, but now that the ODA budget is so big, the LDP wants to get into the act. People have suggested, for instance, that we follow the U.S. example of drawing up aid programs by recipient and submitting them separately to the National Diet for its approval. But the United States is the only donor that employs this practice. It hardly seems an appropriate arrangement for a country like Japan with a parliamentary form of government.

One thing we've tried to make clear to members of both the ruling and opposition parties is that once ODA appropriations in the budget have gained Diet approval, as required under the Constitution, decisions on their use properly fall in the sphere of diplomatic—or administrative—authority. Quite frankly, the forms of aid have become far too diverse to permit decision making by anyone but experts in the aid administration and the recipient country.

To begin with, aid can be extended in the form of loans, grants, or technical assistance. In the case of a yen loan or grant, we must further decide whether its use will be tied to a specific project or whether it will be "nonproject" assistance, which finances developing countries' structural adjustment programs. Technical assistance, meanwhile, can involve sending specialists abroad, inviting trainees to Japan, dispatching Japan Overseas Cooperation Volunteers, implementing development projects, and so forth. . . .

The Big Donor's Small Burden

Interviewer: Some say Japan is spending too lavishly on aid at a time when the national budget is already shackled by a huge deficit.

Matsuura: The people should have the final say on how much money is spent on aid. If their feeling is that they don't want to foot as high a bill as people in other donor countries are footing, then we would be justified in taking a low profile. But Japan is heavily dependent on ties with other countries. In the absence of brisk exchange with other countries, today's level of development wouldn't have been possible. We've profited from the rest of the world, and now it's our turn to help others prosper.

Japan is the second biggest economic power in the world. It's the largest creditor and is running up the biggest trade surplus. It depends heavily on external supplies of energy and food. Because Japan has chosen not to contribute to world peace through military power, it needs to make extra contributions in other areas. With all these factors in mind, it's not hard to see why all recent administrations and the great majority of the people endorse a larger role for Japan in foreign aid. We can't back down from this role just because of fiscal restraints.

In fact, we should do much more. The ODA funds in the general account, which comes directly out of the taxpayer's pocket, amount to roughly 700 billion yen, or about 1.5 percent of the 50 trillion yen budget. The ratio in West Germany is much higher, at 2.5 percent. In per capita terms, the Scandinavians and the Dutch pay 20,000 to 30,000 yen on aid each year, all in the form of grants, but the Japanese pay only 5,000 yen. To be sure, I am excluding from these figures Japan's ODA contributions from special accounts and the fiscal investment and loan program, but for the most part these are loans that the recipients return to Japan with interest. And even if we add them in, Japan's ODA per person still comes to only 10,000 yen. By international standards, the aid burden we're shouldering is still small.

"We can no longer hide behind our contributions in foreign aid to escape from other responsibilities."

Japan Should Not Increase Its Foreign Aid

Abe Motoo

Abe Motoo is an economist and a member of Japan's House of Representatives. In the following viewpoint, he opposes significant increases in Japan's foreign aid. Abe argues that Japan's level of foreign aid already compares favorably with that of other developed nations, and that many foreign aid programs are wasteful and counterproductive.

As you read, consider the following questions:

1. How are foreign aid statistics for Japan and other countries distorted, according to Abe?
2. According to the author, how has Japan's international reputation been affected by increases in its foreign aid program?
3. What ulterior motives lie behind foreign aid, according to Abe?

Abe Motoo, "Foreign Aid: A Dissenter's View," *Japan Echo*, Vol. XVI, No. 1, 1989. Reprinted with permission.

I first began to question the ever-growing foreign aid budget around 1985. A famine in Africa was in the news then, and the media were giving a lot of coverage to Japanese good-will donations of blankets and other emergency supplies. People were saying that Japan should spend more on foreign aid, especially on official development assistance, but I could not agree. On May 21, 1985, I went on record in the Finance Committee of the House of Representatives with words to the effect that Japan was behaving like a person with a loan shark on his heels who continued running around handing out useless gifts to other people. At the time, Japan was awash in surplus funds, but they were in the hands of the private sector. I would have had no problem with a plan to recycle some of these private funds to developing countries, but I saw no reason for the public sector, which was already up to its ears in debt, to go any deeper into the red with ODA [offical development assistance] spending.

Lonely Opposition

Even in those days, when "administrative reform" was on everybody's lips and the government was valiantly holding down expenditures, generosity prevailed in foreign aid. The aid budget had become a sacred cow, and year after year we watched it grow fatter without a single protest. When I eventually raised my voice on the matter in the National Diet, the official from the Ministry of Foreign Affairs who fielded my query brushed it off lightly, saying that *nobody*—either ruling party or opposition—had ever opposed ODA. He even warned me that to do so might damage my reelection prospects.

True, virtually no one has ever spoken out directly against the annual increments to the ODA budget. Given the consensus that the time is right for newly wealthy Japan to take on greater international responsibilities, to argue otherwise would only give one a reputation for international insensitivity and a lack of awareness of Japan's status. The opposition parties may fight the government on other matters, especially increases in defense spending, but when it comes to foreign aid they have always been even more gung-ho than the ruling Liberal Democratic Party. Perhaps, then, to oppose something so sacrosanct is to call one's sanity into question. Still, the very absence of any opposition makes me suspicious. Might people not be overlooking something? . . .

Generous Japanese Aid Funding

In the interest of justifying my solitary rebellion, let me lay out my arguments.

The first point to note is that the dollar value of Japan's aid has skyrocketed over the past few years to the point where Japan is the world's largest donor. On a per capita basis, we Japanese spend more than twice as much as Americans on aid. How did spending manage to rise so fast? Quite simply, because the yen doubled in value against the dollar. Even if ODA appropriations had been held flat in yen, their dollar value would still have shot up. In 1986, when the ODA budget was hiked by 7% in yen, it jumped 52% in dollar terms; in 1987, similarly, a rise of just under 6% in yen became a 23% dollar hike.

Other Needs

The government in the years ahead will be asked to shoulder a multitude of new burdens. Washington is already urging Tokyo to assume a greater share of the expense of propping up the Philippines, a country of strategic importance to the Pentagon. Similar requests based on security considerations are bound to grow. Within Japan, meanwhile, many industries are likely to step up their demands for financial support to offset the adverse effects of market-opening measures. At such a time of multiplying demands, when the country must decide how best to allocate its public funds to meet its national and international commitments, it would be irresponsible to continue the expansion of aid handouts without first considering what other needs will have to be met.

Abe Motoo, *Japan Echo*, Spring 1989.

The dollar value of the budget is what counts. The aid recipients generally use dollars to procure materials. So if 1 billion yen was enough to build one hospital a few years ago, the same amount should pay for two today. In fact, the real problem in aid administration is said to be that ways of spending all the extra cash cannot be worked out fast enough.

Comparisons with Other Countries

Consider next the fallacy of the common belief that Western countries are miles ahead of Japan in their aid-giving largess. Admittedly some spend a higher percentage of gross national product on aid than Japan's 1986 level of 0.29%, but the point to note is where this aid goes. Look at the United States, for example. Its 1985 ODA was, at 0.23% of GNP, actually under the Japanese level. And this included massive outlays for strategic purposes to Israel and Egypt, which between them received one-third of the ODA budget. Excluding these, true American development assistance came to only 0.15% of GNP.

Britain at first glance seems slightly ahead of Japan, since its 1985 allocations came to 0.32% of GNP, but again one-third of the total had ulterior objectives. This is the aid to former colonies, which is aimed at maintaining bonds among members of the Commonwealth. Subtracting this portion from the British ODA program brings its share of GNP down to about 0.20%.

The French statistics change even more radically when subjected to this sort of analysis. France claims that it allocates a high 0.72% of GNP to ODA, but the figure quickly drops to 0.50% when we correctly discount the portion spent on overseas territories that are an integral part of France itself. Further excluding the portion its French-speaking former colonies receive, we arrive at a more realistic figure of 0.27%.

Comparisons of aid based on percentages of GNP cannot be taken at face value. The Japanese level of 0.29% is admittedly nothing to brag about, but neither is it unusually low. In absolute terms, moreover, Japanese aid is enormous in volume. The 1988 ODA budget came to $10 billion, against $8.8 billion for the United States. Each Japanese citizen was footing a bill of $82 to finance that aid, compared with $37 for each American.

Budgetary Constraints

My third point is that budgetary constraints must also be taken into account. West Germany stands out as a nation that devotes a larger slice of GNP to aid than Japan does and that does not spend this aid to promote special relationships, as the United States, Britain, and France do. But West Germany's budget is in a much healthier state than Japan's, which has to cover the cost of servicing a mammoth national debt. Outstanding government bonds in Japan amount to roughly $9,500 for each Japanese citizen, almost three times the German figure of $3,500. (The figures for Britain and France are $4,300 and $1,700, respectively.) Few nations need struggle as hard as Japan does to pay debt-servicing costs. And it must also spend heavily in other areas to upgrade the quality of life, which has not suddenly moved above Western living standards regardless of the appearance of affluence created by handsome export profits. . . .

Japan's emergence as an economic superpower means, everyone agrees, that it must step up its overseas assistance. But among those who so fervently support foreign aid, not all are aware that it comes out of the taxpayer's pocket. Almost nobody, moreover, takes into account the heavy burden that taxpayers are already shouldering to finance the national debt. . . .

My position is not that Japan has no obligations to the world community. To the contrary, it must offer cooperation on a level commensurate with its economic power. From the perspective of the Japanese taxpayer, however, every effort must be made to set appropriate priorities and ensure that the aid is used effectively. . . .

Aid Can Be Wasteful

Some aid grants may even be wasteful or counterproductive. As became apparent during the news coverage of the African famine, there has to be a good government, along with a solid infrastructure, to ensure that aid gets to where it is needed. Some of the food sent to Africa just piled up on docks, while other donations were cashed in to buy weapons to fight domestic insurgencies. And as some observers have noted, there have been instances when the provision of food has worked to undermine a country's agricultural base. Thus far the Japanese have rarely bothered to consider whether their money is being effectively spent; all they are interested in is the quantity of aid and generosity of the terms on which it is extended. The day may come when they can state proudly that aid has reached 0.40% of GNP, but this will be a meaningless boast if the money spent is doing little good.

Lessons, Not Money

The Japanese could make a real contribution to world development if they set about to raise the living standards in developing countries by applying methods derived from their own experience. Many developing countries wish to learn from Japan, which has transformed itself from a backward nation to a global economic leader in little over a century. Lessons from Japan's development cannot be conveyed simply by increasing the volume of aid or the share of the grant element. If we become too obsessed with such statistical measures, nobody will take much notice of what we have to offer.

Meru Kōichi, *Japan Echo*, Spring 1989.

People are apt to assume that more aid means greater bargaining power for Japan in international affairs, but this also needs further thought. Although Japan's ODA has more than doubled in dollar terms, and although Japan is now the world's top donor, have these developments in any way affected the strength of Japan's hand in its trade and market-opening negotiations with Western countries? If Japanese negotiators were to call attention to Japan's ODA record at the bargaining table, no doubt their Western counterparts would comment with approval but then go on to say that they were there to discuss something else. To be sure, being a star pupil in the foreign aid classroom is bound to work to Japan's advantage in one way or another, but it will not deflect the demands placed on Japan in other quarters. . . .

The sacrosanct status we have accorded ODA must be brought to an end. The time has arrived to treat it on an equal footing with other spending categories, be they for international commitments apart from foreign aid or for domestic programs to bolster industry and guarantee employment. We can no longer hide behind our contributions in foreign aid to escape from other responsibilities.

Even more so than today, tomorrow we will be called to make contributions in many areas other than aid.

Bringing ODA Down to Earth

Since Japan's opposition parties are always on the lookout for arguments to bolster their demand that defense spending be kept within 1% of GNP, it is not surprising that the Kōmeitō (Clean Government Party), taking note of the yen's rise, asked the government in Diet deliberations why cheaper imports had not significantly reduced the defense budget. This is indeed a valid reason for expecting cutbacks in defense spending, which at least in some areas has become cheaper, but it makes even more sense when applied to ODA, most of which has gained value as a result of the yen's climb. In the debate over ways to pass the benefits of the strong yen on to taxpayers, should we not give more attention to foreign aid than to military expenditures? Our stance of turning thumbs up on ODA and down on defense does not hold water.

To appreciate the extent to which the burden of ODA on taxpayers has grown, consider the following statistics: The 1988 budget allocated 1.5 trillion yen to overseas assistance projects, of which about 1 trillion yen is being financed with taxes (0.7 trillion yen directly from the general account and the rest indirectly from government bonds). This tax bill is substantial. It amounts to half or more of the money collected from people each year to pay the universally detested inheritance taxes. And even now, as taxpayers struggle under the burden of servicing the national debt, the ODA budget just keeps on growing. Surely we should not be so foolish as to make foreign commitments beyond what we can reasonably bear just so that politicians can brag about how Japan is meeting its international obligations. We must take a hard look at this spending and reassess its efficacy.

During Yasuhiro Nakasone's administration, the budget drafters always hiked ODA by more than they boosted military outlays. No doubt this was a ploy to make Japan appear less militaristic, but it combined with the currency realignment to thrust our country to the top of the list of donor nations. Rationally analyzed, both defense and aid are insurance payments guaranteeing a country's security in the world. From this perspective, it is their aggregate rate of increase that should be watched. Specifically, when we embark on a rapid military buildup, we should go slow on ODA expansion, and vice versa. But this sort of levelheaded rationalism does not appeal to the members of the ruling party, who place image ahead of substance and see foreign aid as an effective means of camouflaging their hawkish attitudes. Their aid policy is but the international edition of their domestic policy of spreading subsidies around to hold down discontent. . . .

181

I am not advocating chauvinism. I am simply stating that aid has come to be used as a means for Japan to flaunt its wealth. Western countries easily see through this affectation; they themselves take a more serious view of their assistance programs. Our aid has more than doubled in value in the space of a few years; instead of blindly piling on more money, we need to stop and scrutinize the contents of our assistance. We should make sure that we are spending on realistic projects that will truly help the recipients, not just inflate our egos.

"The United States and Japan have a crucial role to play, individually and collectively, in pulling the world economy forward."

Japan Should Share World Economic Leadership with the US

Toyoo Gyohten

Japan's position as the world's largest creditor has given it significant influence on the world economy. In the following viewpoint, Toyoo Gyohten argues that the United States and Japan should cooperate to guide the global economy and maintain world economic growth. To achieve these goals, Japan has taken steps to reduce its trade surplus by increasing domestic consumer spending and importing more foreign products, according to Gyohten. To further stabilize the global economy, he recommends that the Japanese yen be used more frequently as international currency, instead of the US dollar. Gyohten is vice-minister of finance for international affairs of Japan.

As you read, consider the following questions:

1. What are the three major economic issues facing the US and Japan, according to Gyohten?
2. How has Japan's role in world banking changed in the 1980s, according to the author?
3. According to Gyohten, how has Japan helped to reduce Third World debt?

Toyoo Gyohten, "Cooperating with Confidence," *Speaking of Japan*, August 1988. Reprinted by permission of the author and Keizai Koho Center.

It is obvious that the United States and Japan have a crucial role to play, individually and collectively, in pulling the world economy forward while curing whatever malaises it suffers. This is not only because the United States and Japan are now the largest and the second largest economies, with some 40 percent of total world gross national product [GNP] between them. It is also because the United States and Japan represent one of the most visible imbalances in the world economy, namely, that between the largest deficit country and the largest surplus country and the largest debtor and the largest creditor.

Because of the importance of their economies in the world and because of the highly interdependent structure of the world economy today, close cooperation between the United States and Japan is highly desirable. And cooperative efforts need to serve various objectives. First of all, both countries are expected to make their best efforts to correct the domestic and external imbalances of their own economies. Without the effort to put one's own house in order, no effective cooperation can be established. Second, both countries need to assist each other's self-help efforts. Third, joint efforts by the United States and Japan are required to deal with many economic problems of global importance.

Obviously, numerous areas exist where U.S.-Japan cooperation is called for. In my view, there are three major issues concerning the world economy for which close cooperation between the United States and Japan is critically important. The first is supporting the balanced growth of the world economy. The second is facilitating desirable world financial flows. And the third is fostering international financial stability.

US Distortions

The stimulative fiscal policy pursued in the United States in the early 1980s generated strong growth in domestic demand, and inflation was controlled by a tight monetary policy. Although this achievement was indeed remarkable as far as the domestic economic situation was concerned, the large budget and trade deficits, high interest rates, and the overvalued dollar have created a serious distortion in the world economy. Since 1985, there has emerged a growing recognition that the distortion needed to be corrected through coordinating the economic policy measures of major countries.

The first phase of coordination took place in the currency market. In September 1985, with the aim of weakening the overvalued dollar, monetary authorities of major currency countries launched a concerted intervention and exhortation in the market. The operation was a dramatic success, and the dollar fell quite adequately during the course of 1986. The substantial change in the terms of trade brought about by the exchange rate realignment has not failed to exert a favorable impact on the U.S. trade performance. However, the lead time was necessarily considerable, and meanwhile the large and rapid appreciation of the currencies of surplus countries dampened the business climate in those countries and discouraged the prospect of strong economic expansion, which would have helped increase their imports.

The Maekawa Report

Japan is today posting large current account surpluses, and there are signs of intensifying economic friction with other countries. This imbalance cannot be allowed to continue, either for the Japanese economy itself or for the harmonious development of the world economy. This situation having arisen in an interdependent world economy, Japanese policy responses alone cannot rectify this imbalance. International policy coordination is also needed, including reductions in the United States fiscal deficit. Nevertheless, as a country largely dependent upon free trade, a country accounting for one-tenth of the world GNP, and the world's largest creditor nation, Japan must take the initiative in rolling back protectionism and defending the free trade system by seeking to achieve an internationally harmonious external balance and to make a positive contribution to the international community.

Summary Report of the Economic Council's Special Committee on Economic Restructuring, April 23, 1987.

It has come to be recognized that exchange rate adjustment alone was not an adequate means or the most efficient means of rectifying the trade imbalance. Thus, the exercise in coordination among major countries developed into the new area of macroeconomic policies, and it was widely accepted that a large budget deficit, together with inadequate saving in the private sector, was the single most important cause of the U.S. trade deficit. The issue of highest priority in policy coordination, therefore, is the reduction of the U.S. budget deficit by cutting expenditures and thereby correcting the overspending character of the economy. . . .

Japan's Responsibilities

At the same time, countries with large trade surpluses need to absorb more exports from deficit countries. For that objective, they should undertake to maintain strong growth in domestic demand while keeping their markets open to foreign products. And Japan, being the largest surplus country, obviously has the biggest role to play in carrying out this undertaking. Since 1987, the government of Japan has implemented a series of stimulative fiscal measures, including inter alia additional public works expenditures of $40 billion, a tax cut of $10 billion, abolition of tax incentives for saving, etc. . . .

The combined impact of the strong yen and expansionary macroeconomic policies has started to be seen in the accelerated growth of domestic demand and rapidly increasing imports. The cyclical upturn of the economy also supported this favorable development. In 1987, compared with the previous year, Japanese domestic demand grew 5 percent, and Japanese imports increased 9.3 percent in volume terms and 18.3 percent in dollar terms.

Thus, correction of the overvalued dollar and the parallel efforts made in the United States and Japan have begun to produce encouraging results in the direction of fostering better balanced growth of the world economy. In 1987, for the first time in the 1980s, the net exports of the United States made a positive contribution to the country's economic growth, while, contrarily, the external sector of the Japanese economy has become a negative factor for economic growth. The shift of the growth patterns of the United States and Japan is a very significant event because it means that the destabilizing behavior of the world's two largest economies is now changing. . . .

World Financial Flows

The second important objective for U.S.-Japan cooperation is to facilitate desirable world financial flows. In spite of the progress we have been making, we still have major international financial disequilibrium in the world today. On the one hand, we have the large U.S. budget deficit, which at present needs to be financed by foreign savings. On the other hand, there are a number of developing countries that also need external financing for their economic development and debt servicing.

In the financing of the U.S. deficit, a major role is played by private investors and the monetary authorities of surplus countries. In the financing of the Third World debt and development, private banks, the governments of the industrialized countries, and various international financial institutions are major players. Although the United States as a country is the largest borrower today, American banks and the U.S. government are the largest providers of credit and assistance to the Third World.

Japan, on the other hand, is the largest capital exporter to the United States and plays the second largest role in the financial flow to the Third World. In other words, the United States and Japan, through their governments, banks and investors, are now two key figures in the global flow of financial resources, and New York and Tokyo are main arenas of activity. In all likelihood, we will have to live for some years to come with a considerable degree of international financial disequilibrium. Therefore, what is important is to provide the needed financial flow in a free, efficient, and productive way.

At this point, let me discuss just briefly the role being played by the Tokyo market and Japanese investors. Tokyo's role as an international financial center was remarkably enhanced in the 1980s. The huge amount of investable funds, the steady progress of financial deregulation, the strong hinterland economy, and the wider use of the yen as an international currency have all contributed to the increased eminence of the market. As a stock market, Tokyo has the largest capitalization in the world today.

Must Assume Responsibility

The Japanese are themselves now threatened by their longstanding national focus on exports and trade surpluses. While consumers must pay dearly for simple imported goods such as steak, huge piles of dollars have ballooned domestic prices of securities and real estate to levels that surely must be artificial and prone to bust. Japan has reached a stage where, in its own interest, it must broaden its ambitions. It must accept greater responsibility for the health of the interdependent world economy in which it sells its products by coordinating its policies more closely with those of its partners.

The Wall Street Journal, April 30, 1987.

In 1987, the net export of long-term capital from Japan amounted to $133 billion. Since Japan's current-account surplus was not larger than $87 billion during that period, the figures indicate that Tokyo is functioning not only as a producer of capital but also as an intermediary transforming short-term liabilities into long-term assets. Of the $133 billion in capital export, some $88 billion was portfolio investment in foreign bonds and stocks; $20 billion was various forms of direct investment, such as the building of factories offshore and merger and acquisition of foreign companies; and $17 billion was credit extended by both public and private financial institutions. . . .

Both the governments and private banks of the United States and Japan have to continue to play a major role in securing adequate financial flows to the developing world. Although some of the developing countries, particularly in Asia, have remarkably strengthened their economic capability, many countries still have sizable current-account deficits that need to be financed from external sources.

Furthermore, the debt accumulation in some countries, particularly middle-income developing countries in Latin America, is posing a serious burden on the international financial system. Of course, in dealing with this issue various international financial institutions and other developed countries also have to play their part. Yet the United States and Japan, because of the magnitude of their economic and political stake in the Third World, need to take a leading role in addressing this issue. . . .

Financial Stability

The third important objective for U.S.-Japan cooperation is to foster international financial stability. All of us were greatly alarmed by the stock market crash in October 1987 and the following turmoil in the currency market. Looking back, we managed the situation reasonably well in New York and Tokyo, and markets have regained most of the loss. Yet it was very important that the episode reminded us in a forceful way of the underlying uneasiness and instability in the market, which had been disguised by seeming buoyancy. The uneasiness could easily be exposed even by casual remarks by senior government officials, which made the market suspect that international policy coordination had been abandoned.

To maintain and strengthen international stability, it is therefore critically important for us to succeed in convincing the market that international disequilibrium is steadily being corrected. It is all the more important because recent events in the market have been clearly telling us that major financial markets in the world are so interdependent and that markets of different financial commodities, such as equities, bonds, and currencies, are so closely linked together that a crash in one market cannot possibly be isolated.

In addition to the need to improve the fundamentals, we should be aware that there is considerable room for improvement in the functioning of the financial markets and in the viability of financial institutions. While I am of the view that the average creditworthiness of Japanese financial institutions is adequately high and that Japanese financial markets have demonstrated their efficiency and resilience, I nevertheless believe that we should endeavor to improve the situation further. In view of the steady progress of the globalization of financial markets and financial institutions as well, it is desirable to have better international collaboration and harmonization on these issues, and in this respect we have been making considerable progress. . . .

Some Proposals

So far I have briefly described three broad areas where close cooperation between the United States and Japan is desirable and workable. Based on this general background, I would like to make to the United States and to Japan somewhat more specific proposals, which, in my view, are doable and would enhance the level of the financial cooperation between our two countries.

First, Japan should step up its economic assistance to the developing world. It is sometimes argued that since Japan's defense budget is considerably smaller than that of the United

States, Japan should spend more for economic aid in order to keep a balance. I am not convinced by this argument because military spending and economic aid do not have the same objectives and they are not interchangeable. Yet it is true that if economic aid succeeds in stabilizing the situation in developing countries, the chance for world peace could be enhanced. Japan, whose prosperity is so much dependent on world peace, does have a good reason to enlarge and improve its economic aid activities. . . .

My second proposal to Japan is that Japan should seek greater use of the yen in the international market. In spite of the progress made so far, the yen's share in the world's currency reserves is still less than 10 percent. The yen is used only for 35 percent of Japanese exports and 10 percent of imports. The excessive dependence on use of the dollar is one of the destabilizing factors in the international monetary system. I consider it would be desirable for Japan and for the world as a whole if the yen's share in the world's reserves were increased to 20 percent and if 50 percent of Japan's trade were settled in yen. In order to achieve such a goal, the availability and usability of the yen needs to be enhanced; the deregulation of interest rates and the improvement of the domestic short-term financial markets are two areas of high priority. Strong political will is called for to overcome institutional squabbles.

Joint Leadership for Economic Security

For Japan, the question is how to use our financial capability. For what purpose? Since the US is not capable of its previous leadership in economic areas, we should join together, along with Europe, in a constructive effort to revitalize the global economy. . . .

Most Japanese now realize that without contributing to an expanding world economy, our own development cannot advance. Without a prosperous world economy, Japan cannot prosper. We know that a prosperous island cannot exist in a depressed area.

Saburo Okita, *New Perspectives Quarterly*, Spring 1987.

Now for the United States, I would propose the issue of a yen-dominated Treasury bond. Although it is a matter for the United States to decide, from the Japanese point of view the step could have the following benefits. First, it will attract foreign investors. Second, it will improve the market perception about the dollar's stability. Third, it will inject additional discipline in the budget. Fourth, it will help reduce the excessive role of the dollar in the international monetary system. Fifth, if the issue helps stabilize the dollar, the Treasury may enjoy some financial benefit.

"Japan has earned its way to the top, but it has yet to demonstrate the leadership needed to stay there."

Japan Is Not Ready for World Economic Leadership

R. Taggart Murphy

R. Taggart Murphy is a managing director at Chase Manhattan Asia Limited in Tokyo, and an affiliate of the Program for US-Japan Relations at the Center for International Affairs at Harvard University in Cambridge, Massachusetts. In the following viewpoint, he argues that although Japan has enormous financial strength, it lacks the global vision and international understanding necessary to be an effective world economic leader. Japan, according to Murphy, still makes its economic policies with only itself in mind, while neglecting concerns of the world economy.

As you read, consider the following questions:

1. According to Murphy, what special traits did Great Britain and the United States have that Japan lacks?
2. What are the five fundamental obligations of world financial leadership, according to the author?

Reprinted by permission of *Harvard Business Review*. An excerpt from "Power Without Purpose: The Crisis of Japan's Global Financial Dominance" by R. Taggart Murphy, March/April 1989. Copyright © 1989 by the President and Fellows of Harvard College; all rights reserved.

Japan today sits on the largest cache of wealth ever assembled. It has the power to move markets anywhere in the world. Consider that:

The Tokyo Stock Exchange has now surpassed New York to become the world's largest on the basis of market capitalization. Osaka has bumped London to fourth place.

Of the world's ten largest banks, nine are Japanese. If deposit size is the unit of measurement, no U.S. bank makes it into the top 25.

Japanese investors' appetite is the key determinant of the price of U.S. Treasury bonds.

Japanese and Japanese-owned banks now supply more than 20% of all credit in the state of California.

The market value of Japan, as measured by an extrapolation of real estate prices, exceeds that of the United States. The market value of the Imperial Palace grounds in central Tokyo is said to exceed that of a number of entire U.S. states.

Japanese households save an average of 17% to 19% of their annual income; American households save less than 5%. . . .

A Disturbing Development

Clearly, Japan has replaced the United States as the world financial leader. That fact is disturbing, not because Japan is conspiring to rule the world or is creating unholy alliances to command the world economy; it is not. It is disturbing because Japan lacks certain qualities necessary to be the kind of financial leader that can maintain stability and openness in the world's financial and trading system.

In most respects, Japan is well qualified to take on the leadership role. Over the past generation, it has done a better job of managing and expanding its economy than any other industrialized nation, and it has shown much more self-discipline in its fiscal and monetary policies than has the United States. . . .

For all its success at managing its own economy, however, Japan lacks the ideology and political commitment necessary to fulfill the obligations that go with financial power. To turn sheer financial strength into leadership, a country must be able to think in global terms, to view itself as a world central banker, to sacrifice certain short-term gains to maintain stable financial and trading systems. Japan does not have this world view. It holds the rest of the world at arm's length, and that separateness prevents Japan from assuming some of the important mandates of world financial leadership.

It is no accident that Great Britain and the United States were the world financial leaders from the mid-nineteenth century to World War I and from the end of World War II until the collapse of Bretton Woods in 1971, two periods when the global economy was strong. The political elites in Great Britain and the United States were possessed of a sense of mission. The British elite in the last century fervently believed in their divinely appointed task of spreading Christian civilization and Anglo-Saxon concepts of the rule of law to the farthest corners of the globe. The U.S. "Atlanticist" elite of the immediate postwar world felt it their mission to spread U.S.-style democracy and to prevent the Western democracies from making economic mistakes like the Hawley-Smoot Tariff Act or geopolitical mistakes like Munich.

The Importance of Ideology

What was distinctive about U.S. and British leadership was the combination of ideological fervor and basic economic literacy. Both countries realized that the world they were striving for required stable and freely convertible currencies and open trading systems, and they were willing to sacrifice certain self-interested, short-term gains to achieve those goals. These sacrifices included giving foreigners access to domestic markets, relinquishing some measure of control over domestic fiscal and monetary policies, and ensuring that foreigners could earn the leader's domestic currency by selling goods and services in the domestic markets.

Japan Still Thinks It Is Poor

Ask any Japanese to describe his country and he will deliver the same stock phrases about tiny Japan's paucity of resources, using almost the same words in the same order. Anyone who has had to deal with the Japanese has heard it repeated countless times. . . .

Japan's classification of the world's countries is the natural outcome of its own self-image. Just mention Brazil and China and eyes light up, but talk about India and Argentina and you will elicit only shrugs. The Japanese divide the world into two types: resource-rich countries that promise to alleviate Japan's mineral poverty, and consumer countries that provide markets for manufactured products.

Japanese simply don't care about the rest of the world. Perhaps our single-minded and arrogant view would be understandable if Japan were truly a tiny nation, fighting against terrible odds just to survive. But it is not any longer. Tiny, weak Japan is a myth.

Kenichi Ohmae, *Beyond National Borders*, 1987.

As any student of Japanese civilization can attest, Japan vacillates between feelings of inferiority or deep insecurity vis-à-vis other nations and an overweening pride verging on arrogance. Whichever sentiment is ascendant in the national mood, however, the vast majority of Japanese—most emphatically, the political and business elite—do not believe for a moment that the country's way of doing things is applicable abroad or that Japanese social arrangements in the business, financial, or cultural spheres are at all analogous to what takes place in other countries.

The only real ideology Japan has is an overwhelming sense of its own uniqueness. The Japanese believe deeply that their people, language, social mores, and institutions are utterly different from anyone else's. They have an instinctive urge to keep the foreigner at arm's length. This is every bit as true of financial markets as of agriculture, refugees, telecommunications, lawyers, university professors, supercomputers, and aluminum baseball bats. . . .

Five Important Obligations

Lacking the ideology, Japan will not sacrifice its own interests for the interests of the global financial system. For all its financial prowess, then, Japan is unlikely to meet the five most important obligations of world financial leadership.

A financial leader must, first of all, be willing and able to maintain its currency as a store of value. Here Japan does very well, in part because this is fundamental to the prosperity of any country, big or small, financial leader or entrepôt city-state. Over the past 40 years, Japan has demonstrated both the will and the ability to maintain the yen as a store of value. Japanese monetary authorities have consistently avoided inflation as a "solution" to other pressing economic and political problems and have refused to engineer a devaluation of the currency as a cheap way of relieving balance of payments pressure. Japan's authorities have achieved not only the near-complete elimination of price inflation but also a currency that is now one of the world's hardest. . . .

Second, a financial leader must allow the country's currency to function as a global reserve currency. Otherwise, trade flows and capital movements are hampered. Realizing this, the leading central banks of Europe agreed in 1875 to fix their currencies in relation to gold, and the Bank of England ensured the convertibility of the pound and permitted outflows. Thus, until World War I, the world enjoyed an approximation of a universal currency that was simultaneously a store of value. In 1944 at Bretton Woods, the Allied powers agreed to make all currencies convertible into dollars, the dollar was fixed against gold, and the Federal Reserve permitted outflow of dollars. The world again had a global reserve currency.

Japan's Reluctance

Japan has yet to demonstrate such a willingness. It fears that encouraging substantial outflow of yen would reduce its ability to accomplish the twin jobs of low inflation and low-cost funds, which have been so important to the country's success. Due in part to the absence of a highly developed free money market in Japan, Japanese monetary authorities are unable to engage in the sophisticated open-market operations the Federal Reserve uses to control the money supply. They fear that large outflows of yen or the development of a Euroyen market as broad as the Eurodollar market would inhibit their ability to control the money supply and interest rates. They do not want, for instance, foreigners to be able to affect interest rates on Japanese government debt by dumping large volumes of yen securities (the United States provides a lesson here).

Sitting on the Bench

Japan has been reluctant to take on the responsibility commensurate with its status as a global economic power. It is like the power hitter in baseball who has been called up to the majors but is still sitting on the bench. The Japanese have simply not stepped up to the plate. On trade liberalization, the time has come to lead by doing, not by talking. Similarly, Japan must adopt measures to ensure strong growth in domestic demand. The Japanese must come to rely more and more on strong growth in domestic demand and less on exports as the engine of Japanese prosperity.

Douglas W. McMinn, *Department of State Bulletin*, October 1987.

Japan's reluctance to allow yen outflow and to encourage its use as a global reserve currency is a serious shortcoming. Ceding a certain amount of control over the domestic economy is part of the price for being a global central bank and meeting the obligation of financial leadership.

Third, a financial leader must act as lender of last resort and provide liquidity to the world's banking system. On this score, Japan is trying. Moves such as the agreement by a syndicate of Japanese banks to purchase $130 million of Bank of America's subordinated debt in August 1987 or Prime Minister Noboru Takeshita's suggestions at the June 1988 Toronto economic summit on resolving the Third World debt crisis show that Japan understands the need to protect global banking stability. Yet even here there is the sense that the Japanese are serving their own commercial interests. . . .

Trade and Banking

Fourth, a financial leader keeps the trading system open, even at some domestic political cost. If the leader does not permit foreigners the opportunity to earn its currency, that currency will continually appreciate and the global balance of payments will be thrown out of kilter. This is what has happened in Japan.

Here the distinction between finance and trade blurs. The debate over Japan's trading practices is both complicated and murky—in part because the Japanese keep it that way. It is enough to say that the issue has been touchy since the late 1950s, and that despite the removal of most of the formal rules protecting Japan's markets, the problem is getting worse. Japan's "us against them" mentality and its deep-seated reluctance to depend on foreigners means the trade problem will continue to fester. The world simply cannot look to Japan as an impartial guarantor of an open trading system.

Finally, a financial leader must ensure that its financial institutions, including its domestic financial markets, are both sound and innovative. Japan's record is mixed. . . .

Japanese financial institutions are much like their industrial counterparts: regulations exist for the benefit of the institutions, not for the domestic consumers. The institutions enjoy high earnings in a domestic market that is effectively protected not only from foreigners but also from "excessive" competition. Japanese banks compete bitterly with each other for retail deposits, for example, with small gifts to individual depositors and repeated visits to their homes, but there is no difference in the interest rates banks pay those individuals or the fees they charge them. Japanese commercial and investment bankers have succeeded overseas partly because of their diligence and attention to detail but also because they can offer lower spreads and lower fees to borrowers, thanks to the profits they enjoy from a cartel-like, protected market at home. Such a market is inconsistent with global financial leadership.

Being the world's financial leader is not the same as exercising financial world leadership. Japan has earned its way to the top, but it has yet to demonstrate the leadership needed to stay there.

Japan has command of the world's financial resources but lacks a global sense of purpose. The United States has the mission but can no longer finance it. This uncoupling of financial power and global vision poses a dilemma—for Japan, the United States, and the world.

Japanese authorities cannot invent an ideology overnight. They cannot suddenly change their attitudes and behave like thoughtful, magnanimous world leaders more concerned with global prosperity than with the immediate problems of their own constituents. Nor can the United States simply recapture its position. While Paul Volcker's Federal Reserve did stop inflation, the world will not soon forget the disastrous inflationary policies of the late 1960s and 1970s. . . .

Combining Countries Is Unrealistic

One way out of the dilemma is to combine America's and Japan's complementary strengths. In both Tokyo and Washington, one hears talk of Americans and Japanese sharing the burden of global financial leadership. Americans interpret burden sharing as an arrangement whereby they supply the leadership and the Japanese supply the money. This strains credulity. It is doubtful that U.S. and Japanese interests will become ever more congruent; that Washington can and will direct Japanese aid to the parts of the world that need it; that the Japanese will happily buy U.S. Treasury bonds and corporate debt but will politely back off from purchasing corporations and real estate; or that Japan will share the burdens of financial leadership as a junior partner and gracefully slip back into the shadows when the United States gets its fiscal house in order.

Avoiding Responsibility

When Japan was a relatively insignificant country, the international community granted the inevitability of social and economic institutions designed to promote outflows and restrict inflows. But now that Japan is one of the world's leading economic powers, such institutions are no longer acceptable. Japan may have the lowest tariff rates of any nation in the Organization for Economic Cooperation and Development, but Japan's systems taken together block the international movement of economic resources. If Japan does not redesign its social and economic systems to facilitate broad-based participation, the exchange rate will become the sole means of adjustment, perpetuating and even exacerbating international friction.

The 1986 Maekawa report's recommendations for bringing Japan's economic structure into harmony with the international economy indicated that the authorities recognize this problem. But reforming Japan's systems to match the internationalization of its economy entails conflict with various domestic vested interests. The people of Japan, bent on protecting these interests, are deliberately averting their eyes from their nation's responsibilities as an economic superpower.

Nakatani Iwao, *Japan Echo*, Fall 1987.

More likely is that Japan will continue to use its financial strength to further Japanese interests, which are not necessarily the same as the world's—especially given Japan's seeming compulsion to dominate every important value-added industry. The uncoupling of financial power and global vision could lead to a series of political, economic, and financial crises like the run on Continental [Bank of Illinois] or the stock market crash of October 1987. . . .

No Simple Solutions

Policymakers, businesspeople, and even bankers still think of New York and London as the financial centers of gravity, of the dollar as the ultimate standard of value, and of the venerable firms of Wall Street and "The City" in London as dominant. They are wrong. The world's economic well-being is in the hands of politicians and financiers in Tokyo. Since it took decades of declining educational standards, fiscal profligacy, bias toward consumption, insufficient spending on infrastructure, and willful ignorance of the Japanese industrial machine for the United States to lose its world leadership position, that standing will not be won back easily.

Appealingly simple solutions are actually counterproductive. Protectionist walls will lead to horrendous inflation, soaring interest rates, depression, and a precipitous drop in our standard of living. They will also cause severe problems for Japan, which needs the U.S. market for its exports and investment. No other market has the same combination of political stability, economic growth, size, and openness to investment. The United States and Japan depend on each other. We must therefore seek a middle ground between acquiescing to the Japanese takeover of the U.S. economy and building walls between the two countries. . . .

We should have no illusions about the stakes involved. We do not have the option of passing the baton of global financial and industrial leadership to Japan and settling down, as Great Britain did 40 years ago, to a dignified decline in the shadow of the world's new hegemonic power. The alternative to U.S. leadership is a series of escalating economic and political crises leading to a breakdown of the liberal economic and political order as we know it. If the United States is to champion that order, however, it cannot be a second-rate industrial power whose financial system is in shambles. We must strengthen our banking system, restore sobriety and prudence to our financial markets, begin the long climb out of indebtedness, and recapture leadership in high-value-added industries. Otherwise, we will forfeit the mandate of history.

Understanding Words in Context

Readers occasionally come across words which they do not recognize. And frequently, because they do not know a word or words, they will not fully understand the passage being read. Obviously, the reader can look up an unfamiliar word in a dictionary. However, by carefully examining the word in the context in which it is used, the word's meaning can often be determined. A careful reader may find clues to the meaning of the word in surrounding words, ideas, and attitudes.

Below are sentences from the viewpoints in this chapter. In each excerpt a word is printed in italics. Try to determine the meaning of each word by reading the excerpt. Under each excerpt you will find four definitions for the italicized word. Choose the one that is closest to your understanding of the word.

Finally, use a dictionary to see how well you have understood the words in context. It will be helpful to discuss with others the clues which helped you decide on each word's meaning.

1. Both the United States and Japan have a crucial role to play in pulling the world economy forward while curing whatever *MALAISE* it suffers.

   MALAISE means:
   a) expansion   c) illness
   b) alarm   d) achievement

2. Leaders of both countries agree that Japan's trade surplus (and America's trade deficit) should be reduced. But making American products cheaper by decreasing the dollar's value has not been an adequate means of *RECTIFYING* the trade imbalance.

   RECTIFYING means:
   a) increasing   c) buying
   b) correcting   d) electing

3. As its fortunes rise and fall, Japan remains indecisive. It *VACILLATES* between feelings of inferiority to other nations and looking down on them with smugness.

VACILLATES means:
a) wavers
b) abandons
c) demonstrates
d) compromises

4. In keeping with its goal of peace, Japan has banned military sales to other countries. However, it has *EXEMPTED* the United States from this restriction—it sells military technology to the US.

EXEMPTED means:
a) examined
b) excused
c) targeted
d) included

5. Thanks to the yen's *APPRECIATION*, the amount of Japan's foreign aid, measured in dollars, has grown enormously.

APPRECIATION means:
a) increase in value
b) decline
c) positive evaluation
d) shortage

6. In measuring Japan's contribution to its security, one should remember that defense spending by itself is important, and that foreign aid by itself is important, but it is their *AGGREGATE* rate of increase that should be watched.

AGGREGATE means:
a) separate
b) offsetting
c) increasing
d) total

7. Fairer military burden sharing should not be seen as a *PANACEA* that would automatically solve US-Japan trade problems.

PANACEA means:
a) problem
b) remedy
c) argument
d) attack

8. The US is a *SURROGATE* for Japan in Korea. Japan doesn't have to take responsibility for the security of South Korea, because the US does it for Japan.

SURROGATE means:
a) substitute
b) teacher
c) victim
d) enemy

Periodical Bibliography

The following articles have been selected to supplement the diverse views presented in this chapter.

Warren T. Brookes
"Time To End Japan's Free Defense Ride," *Conservative Chronicle*, December 21, 1988. Available from *Conservative Chronicle*, Box 29, Hampton, IA 50441.

Susan Chira
"Japan Ready To Share Burden, but Also the Power, with US," *The New York Times*, March 7, 1989.

William Clark Jr.
"Burdensharing and Japan," *Department of State Bulletin*, December 1988.

Peter F. Drucker
"Japan's Choices," *Foreign Affairs*, Summer 1987.

James Fallows
"Let Them Defend Themselves," *The Atlantic Monthly*, April 1989.

Hilary F. French
"Japan Becomes World's #1 Aid Giver," *Worldwatch*, March/April 1989.

Yasuke Kashiwagi
"Japan's Expanding Role," *Vital Speeches of the Day*, November 15, 1987.

Chuma Kiyofuku
"Whose Burden Is Shared Defense?" *Japan Quarterly*, January/March 1989. Available from Japan Publications Trading Co., Ltd., P.O.B. 5030 Tokyo International, Tokyo 101, Japan.

Flora Lewis
"Japan Glimpses the Light," *The New York Times*, April 13, 1988.

Oda Makato
"Sovereignty and Domination in East Asia and the Pacific," *Social Justice*, Spring 1989.

Hisatomo Matsukane
"Japan and Security of the Sea Lanes," *Global Affairs*, Spring 1989.

Saburo Okita
"Japan's Quiet Strength," *Foreign Policy*, Summer 1989.

Samantha Sparks
"Japanese Banks and the Third World," *Multinational Monitor*, November 1988.

W. Allen Wallis
"The US and Japan: Partners in Global Economic Leadership," *Department of State Bulletin*, July 1988.

Is Cooperation Between the US and Japan Beneficial?

Chapter Preface

US-Japan relations following World War II have been hailed as one of America's shining success stories in foreign policy. While it occupied Japan from 1945 to 1952, the US played a major role in transforming Japan from a bitter enemy into a strong ally. In subsequent years Japan, under US guidance and military protection, rebuilt its economy and became stronger than before. The US gained an important ally in East Asia. Starting in the 1970s, American consumers reaped many additional benefits from Japan's economic miracle in the form of high-quality, inexpensive consumer goods, ranging from cars to portable tape players. In short, both countries have gained much from what Mike Mansfield, former US ambassador to Japan, calls "the most important bilateral relationship in the world."

Yet this relationship is constantly fraught with tension and difficulty. One US poll found that almost half the people surveyed believed Japan was a greater threat to the United States than the Soviet Union. Complaints about Japan's trade and foreign policies often seem to resonate with the fear and distrust that linger from World War II. Anti-American sentiment also is rising in Japan, where books such as *Japan Is Not Bad, America Is Bad* have been bestsellers.

Observers have pointed out two reasons for these tensions. One is the ignorance many Americans and Japanese still have about each others' societies. The other is the changing status of Japan. For decades Japan has viewed itself as clearly the weaker of the two countries, and has cooperated with the US accordingly. Today, however, Japan seems the US's equal, especially in areas such as world finance and technology. Many people argue that the challenge the US faces now is how to treat Japan as an equal partner.

The following viewpoints examine the future of relations between the US and Japan.

"It could be argued that there is greater harmony between the United States and Japan on foreign policy issues than with any other country."

US-Japan Relations Benefit Both Countries

Mike Mansfield

Mike Mansfield served as US Ambassador to Japan from 1977 to 1989. In the following viewpoint, he argues that the US and Japan have developed and maintained successful diplomatic and economic ties. He states that cooperation between the US and Japan is increasing, and that the two countries are successfully working together on trade issues.

As you read, consider the following questions:

1. How much importance does trade have in relations between the US and Japan, according to Mansfield?
2. What examples docs Mansfield provide of cooperation between the US and Japan?
3. How do Japanese foreign policy objectives differ from American goals, according to the author?

Mike Mansfield, "The U.S. and Japan: Sharing Our Destinies." Reprinted by permission of *Foreign Affairs*, Spring 1989. Copyright 1989 by the Council on Foreign Relations, Inc.

The most important bilateral relationship in the world today is that between the United States and Japan. It was only 44 years ago that our two countries were at war. In the short span of time since 1945 we have constructed an enormously complex relationship that touches all aspects of both societies and much of international human endeavor. The victor and vanquished of World War II have become the cornerstones of the international economic system, together producing almost 40 percent of the world's GNP [gross national product]. That all this has been accomplished in only four decades helps to explain why we find that there are still details to work out in managing this critical relationship.

This relationship is of immense benefit to the peoples of both nations. The United States enjoys the support of a strong, loyal and democratic ally in the Pacific, which contributes greatly to regional peace and prosperity. Japan has the protection of the U.S. nuclear umbrella and enjoys great access to the U.S. market, the world's largest. The two countries' foreign policies and foreign aid programs complement and support each other. Our individual and cooperative scientific and technological achievements have brought about a new age of information, increased our knowledge of ourselves and of our world, and contributed to the welfare of all nations. The lives of both peoples are enriched by a vast and burgeoning network of educational and cultural exchanges.

Interdependence

In sum, two nations that historically have acted quite independently have become interdependent. Neither nation can survive at the current level of economic welfare and security without the active cooperation of the other.

This fundamental aspect of our relationship has been overshadowed in the media and in our bilateral dialogue by a seemingly endless series of disputes over market access and unfair trade practices. At times these frictions have spilled over and threatened to damage other areas of our economic partnership as well as our political, security and diplomatic cooperation.

I do not for a minute deny the importance of, and the need for, a fair and effective resolution of trade problems between the United States and Japan. But these frictions must be addressed in the context of an overall partnership that embraces all aspects of our relationship. . . .

Japan's postwar development owes much to the international free trade system, a system sustained primarily by the willingness of the United States to keep its market open, even at the cost of substantial dislocation in important U.S. industries such as steel and automobiles. The United States did not do this to be altruistic but rather out of the conviction that its economy would be strengthened through free trade and the laws of comparative advantage. Free trade has had and continues to have enormous benefits for the U.S. economy, but for too long Japan did not bear its fair share of the burden of maintaining the system by paying the short-term domestic political and economic costs of opening its own markets to foreign goods.

The Need To Cooperate

Despite frictions and divergent interests, Japan and the United States ought to cooperate to fulfill their joint obligation of taking the lead in working for the causes of world peace and development. There is no doubt about that. How to promote this cooperation is the more important issue.

Sumio Okahashi, *Speaking of Japan*, February 1989.

This is changing. In 1986 Japan established a framework for a major restructuring of its economy, prompted by altered exchange rates. It reduced the role of exports in stimulating economic growth by increasing domestic demand, thereby expanding manufactured imports and helping Japan to share the global economic burden. This has occurred at considerable political costs, resulting in some minor social and economic dislocations in Japan. But on the whole I believe that the Japanese economy and people have benefited.

Japan still has a considerable distance to go before its markets are as open as those of the United States, but the combination of the restructuring of Japan's economy, U.S. success in individual negotiations and the upward reevaluation of the yen are resulting in dramatic changes in the right direction. . . .

Progress on the serious issue of market access has also been impressive. Japan, on the prodding of the United States and other trading partners, has opened up to a significant extent its telecommunications, tobacco and pharmaceuticals markets, and reduced its tariffs to among the lowest in the world. In 1988 Japan acceded to the decision of a General Agreement on Tariffs and Trade panel, agreeing to allow freer trade in some categories of food products. Agreements providing for access to public works, and to beef and citrus markets, were also concluded. These market-opening measures are significant for the increased sales they will provide to U.S. suppliers—U.S. exports in these sectors are expected to increase by billions of dollars over the next few years—and also because they are concrete evidence of Japan's commitment to trade liberalization. . . .

At the end of 1987 the United States had direct holdings in Japan worth $14.3 billion, making the United States Japan's largest foreign investor. There are only five countries in the world that host more American investment: Canada ($57 billion), the United Kingdom ($45 billion), Germany ($24 billion), Switzerland ($20 billion) and Bermuda ($18 billion). Moreover, the average annual return on American direct investment in Japan since 1983 has been a striking 21 percent—more than U.S. investment in any other region and, in my opinion, solid evidence of the rewards that can be reaped by American firms that commit themselves to establishing operations in the Japanese market. Start-up has not been easy by any stretch of the imagination, or cheap, but it is clear that the rewards are well worth it.

Japan at the end of 1987 had direct investments worth $33 billion in the United States, much of them due to the increase in value of the yen. Media attention regarding Japanese investments has triggered a debate in some quarters of the United States. What has not been mentioned in this debate is the fact that the $33 billion in Japanese investment is far less than the $75 billion in British investment and the $47 billion in investment by the Netherlands. I welcome Japanese investment, as do the 47 U.S. state governors who came to Japan during my tenure to seek new jobs, new capital sources, new tax contributions and development opportunities.

Investment benefits both countries. Japanese direct investment in the United States creates jobs, expands the tax base, provides healthy competition for American firms on their home turf, and often brings new technology and innovative management techniques into the U.S. economy. Japanese portfolio investment in the United States, which totals $160 billion, helps to finance the U.S. fiscal deficit and to keep interest rates from rising, while it provides Japan with a safe and profitable haven for excess capital. . . .

Future Challenges

For all that the United States and Japan have achieved, both sides need to do more to achieve a better balance in their economic relationship. Japan must take further steps in its initiatives to remove impediments that hinder foreigners from doing business there or enjoying access to Japanese research and technology. It cannot afford to wait until foreign pressure builds up and a confrontation results. The Japanese government has already done much at the macroeconomic level to stimulate domestic demand and thus imports. The United States has also been successful in sectoral negotiations on such items as wood products, medical equipment, telecommunications, beef and citrus. Remaining barriers relate primarily to difficult, socially embedded areas such as Japan's labyrinthine distribution system, strong supplier-customer bonds and Japanese suspicions of the quality, safety and "after-service" associated with foreign products.

But old habits are crumbling under the impact of the high yen, with discount houses specializing in low-cost imports springing up all over Japan. Japan's leaders should work to continue removing these barriers until not a trace remains to support allegations of a closed Japanese market.

The United States, however, faces the greater challenge. As a nation we have become soft. We have allowed the technology and manufacturing base of our industries to languish, and we have neglected quality and service. This has allowed Japanese firms and others to capture much of our market. The emphasis in American industry has been on short-term profits rather than long-term market growth. This is the reverse of the Japanese approach. Thus, when the upward yen reevaluation created opportunities for U.S. manufacturers to gain back their markets at home and abroad, many companies took this opening to raise prices once again—a terrible waste of opportunity.

Diplomatic Progress

Trade issues have tended to overshadow a great deal of progress in the diplomatic and security areas in recent years. Defense cooperation and Japan's host nation support for U.S. Forces in Japan have never been greater. Japanese cooperation with the United States to promote global peace and political and economic stability is more active and extensive than ever, ranging from the Philippines and Afghanistan to the Persian Gulf and Angola/Namibia. In short, Japan's commitment to play a larger global role in sustaining the Western economic and security structure is increasingly tangible.

William Clark Jr., *Department of State Bulletin*, December 1988.

The United States must also confront its national budget deficit and its $140-billion global trade deficit, not only its $54-billion deficit with Japan. In an unsettlingly short time, the United States has gone from the world's greatest creditor nation to the world's biggest debtor. . . .

As the United States and Japan undertake these individual economic responsibilities it is equally important to reduce the rhetoric and political heat each directs toward the other. The United States, in particular, needs to find a less contentious mechanism to handle trade problems. . . .

Defense

Perhaps no other aspect of the U.S.-Japanese relationship is misunderstood as frequently as our security relations. What ought to be a source of pride for both nations as a brilliant achievement of international cooperation is sometimes dismissed as a "free ride" for the Japanese. Let us take a closer look.

Much of the debate focuses on Japan's defense spending. Some argue that Japan spends too little, yet the one percent of GNP that it spends on defense amounts to $30 billion. This is comparable to the $35 billion spent by the United Kingdom, the $32 billion spent by France and the $31 billion spent by the Federal Republic of Germany. Moreover, if one includes the additional $10-billion worth of pensions and survivors' benefits, which the Japanese handle in a separate budget (unlike the United States and European nations), Japan's defense spending considerably exceeds the expenditures of our European allies.

Japan uses this spending for the mutually agreed objectives of maintaining a defense capability to protect its home islands and two sea-lanes out to 1,000 miles, the first extending from the Bay of Tokyo southeast to the region of Guam, and the second from Osaka Bay southwest to the Bashi Channel.

This "small" defense budget buys Japan more destroyers and more antisubmarine aircraft than the United States deploys in the Western Pacific and more F-15s than the United States has for defending its homeland. The Japanese commitment to the joint development of the FSX fighter, to the production under license of 100 P3C antisubmarine aircraft, and to the purchase of such advanced warning systems as the Aegis ensures that its defense capability will be the best possible, that it will be compatible with American defense systems and that it will be developed in cooperation with U.S. defense industries.

This joint defense effort pays enormous dividends to both countries. The United States will defend Japan if the need ever arises. By the same token, the increased capabilities of Japan's own defense forces have allowed the United States to stretch its resources to other parts of the immense Pacific Basin area. . . .

Tangible Benefits

As we look at the many tangible benefits the United States derives from this fruitful security relationship, we should count our blessings to have as a close and loyal ally the strongest, most stable democracy and greatest economic superpower in the region. We need to remember that the U.S. forces in Japan are stationed there in America's interest as much as in Japan's. At a time when U.S. bases in other parts of Asia are under pressure, we must ask ourselves: If the United States were to lose its bases in Japan, where we would draw our new defense perimeter? How much would it cost to establish that new defense perimeter? And how could the United States maintain its strategic influence in the most dynamic region in the world?

In sum, the long-term benefits of the defense relationship must not be put at risk by shortsighted and ill-conceived demands for a greatly enhanced Japanese defense effort. Japan should and will do more to support joint defense efforts, but we must recognize what is already being done, how much the United States benefits from this relationship, and how much the United States will lose if cooperation is replaced by confrontation.

Cooperation

Cooperation between the United States and Japan, as the two largest economic powers in the world and as two important democracies, is essential to address development and political problems around the world. I do not mean to imply a U.S.-Japanese "condominium" in Asia or elsewhere, but these two countries by virtue of their economic strength will have to take a leading role along with like-minded states in creating and maintaining the kind of international environment that benefits everyone. Our current cooperation on trade . . . and on debt relief are examples. This aspect of the relationship is just beginning to be developed, but I believe that as the United States and Japan move into the next decade, global political and economic cooperation will replace bilateral trade confrontation as the watchword of the relationship.

A Key Ally

Japan is a key ally of the United States and has a vital role in the Western alliance. Japan is, obviously, very strong, very democratic, and very stable. Military cooperation has never been better. That is not very well understood, but it is the case.

The movement of people between the United States and Japan has never been greater or more active. Each of our countries is now engaged in a strenuous effort to better understand the other through special emphasis in the media and through special efforts at our universities. The interdependence of the two economies is extraordinary.

John D. Rockefeller IV, *Speaking of Japan*, July 1988.

Foreign economic assistance is one area for such cooperation. The United States has traditionally borne the greatest foreign assistance burden through its aid program and by keeping its market open to the agricultural and industrial products from the developing world, and it must continue to play a major role in this area. The United States must also acknowledge, however, that Japan's aid program will soon become the largest in the world. Japan already surpasses the United States in terms of the ratio of overseas development assistance to GNP (0.23 percent for the United States versus 0.31 percent for Japan) and aid per capita (the United States spends annually $39.60 per American and Japan spends $46.40 per Japanese citizen). . . .

Geographically, Japan's overseas development assistance remains strongly oriented toward the Asian Pacific region. There are obvious historical and political reasons for this orientation. Its assistance has been effective; the stable and prosperous environment in East Asia since 1975 owes much to Japanese aid and trade. But Japan is also currently one of the top benefactors of Pakistan, Turkey and Egypt, and has begun increasing assistance to Mexico, South and Central America, the Caribbean and sub-Saharan Africa. . . .

Similar Interests

It is fortunate that Japan's foreign policy interests coincide almost completely with those of the United States; the recipients that the Japanese government selects for such aid are generally those countries that the United States would like to see receive support. Since the U.S. aid budget is unlikely to increase in the near future and because so much of its aid is "earmarked" for special countries such as Israel and Egypt, Japan can play a critical role in promoting economic development and political stability in regions that are important to the United States and the West as a whole.

Japan is also making a significant contribution in absorbing an increasing share of manufactured products from developing countries. Japan has increased its imports from Asia's newly industrialized economies by over 70 percent since 1987, albeit from a very low level. Almost all of this represents manufactured goods such as textiles and electronics, making Japan an engine of growth for the region.

None of these developments should be regarded as an excuse for the United States to reduce its aid program further; diminishing aid means diminishing influence, and this is not in the U.S. interest, nor as the Japanese remind us, in the interest of Japan. But, in assessing our partnership, Japan's role in our mutual effort to promote economic security, well-being and development for less fortunate regions of the world deserves U.S. attention and acknowledgement.

Global cooperation between the United States and Japan extends beyond economic assistance. In the United Nations, the United States and Japan work as closely as any two allies in pursuit of shared interests. On regional issues, including Afghanistan, Cambodia, the Middle East and even Central America, Japan is an increasingly active player and contributor. Indeed, it could be argued that there is greater harmony between the United States and Japan on foreign policy issues than with any other country. In the years ahead Japan may take an active role in international peacekeeping activities and in finding other areas to contribute politically. I do not mean to suggest that a more active Japanese foreign policy will always produce initiatives to our liking, but as I noted, we share the same fundamental interests and objectives—a more secure, democratic and prosperous world. . . .

The relationship is sound. In most areas the relationship is exemplary, notably in the areas of security, foreign policy cooperation, foreign aid and cultural exchange, among others. In trade, we still have much to learn, but we can build on our recent successes, and we will find that a better mechanism exists for keeping our disagreements from being blown out of proportion. I am optimistic because neither the United States nor Japan has the option of going it alone anymore. The ocean that divided us now unites us. Every year more and more individuals on both sides of the Pacific understand the importance of and are working for the betterment of the U.S.-Japanese partnership—the most important relationship in the world, bar none.

"Close, friendly relations with Japan . . . could be tested and even discarded over the next decade."

US-Japan Relations May Harm the US

Edward J. Lincoln

In the following viewpoint, Edward J. Lincoln argues that the future of US-Japan relations is clouded by changing economic conditions. He argues that the US owes a significant amount of money to Japan, and Japan could use this creditor position against US interests. Lincoln is a research associate specializing in the Japanese economy in the foreign policy studies program at the Washington, DC-based Brookings Institution.

As you read, consider the following questions:

1. Why has Japan built such a large current-account surplus, according to Lincoln?
2. What stereotypes about Japan and the United Staes does the author believe are accurate?
3. According to the author, what differences do Japan and the US have concerning free trade?

Automobiles, VCRs, televisions, cameras, camcorders, calculators, and watches: Americans know Japan primarily through their purchases of products from Japan. They like Japan because Japanese products have developed a reputation for low price and superior quality. In fact, this attitude fits well with the traditional American distaste for its own manufacturing industry. We have been eager to criticize American manufacturers and vigorously demand redress for problems in product safety and pollution.

What Is the Problem?

Why then do we seem to have so many problems with Japan? Is it simply a failing American manufacturing sector lashing out against superior competition? Is it lazy American firms that cannot be bothered to learn enough about the Japanese market to penetrate it effectively, and unfairly blame their failure on Japanese barriers? The Japanese would have us believe so, and because of our mistrust of American industry, many Americans do. There is a modicum of truth in these arguments, but U.S.-Japan relations are much more complex, and Japan deserves as much of the blame for the problems as does the United States.

So far the problems and frustrations have been carefully contained. Close, friendly relations with Japan have been an unchallenged pillar of American foreign policy. Because of developments on both sides of the Pacific, however, those relations could be tested and even discarded over the next decade. This remains a minor possibility at the moment, but if the problems addressed below do not improve, that possibility will grow.

Such a scenario would be like the unfolding of a Greek tragedy. Both the United States and Japan benefit from their close economic relations. And yet, strong domestic imperatives may drive them apart, to the ultimate detriment of both.

Macroeconomics either bores most people to tears or confuses them, so they ignore it. But the big picture of what is happening to Japan and the United States can only be expressed in these terms, and the basic developments are quite simple.

For almost 30 years after the Second World War, Japan grew at an extraordinarily high rate—on average, 10 percent annually even after allowing for inflation. High growth requires heavy investment in plants and equipment, housing, roads, and other facilities. Investment must be financed by domestic savings or money borrowed from abroad. Rather than borrowing from abroad, as have many developing countries more recently, Japan had enough savings at home to fund its investment needs.

But Japan slowed down in the 1970s because it had caught up with the industrial world; adept at catching up rapidly, it was now constrained by the world technological frontier. From 1974, average economic growth in Japan has been under four percent annually. Slower growth means less need for investment.

So far so good. But Japan continued to save a lot. Those savings were a boon when the economy was growing rapidly, but now they had to go elsewhere in the economic system or Japan would slip into recession. During the late 1970s, the Japanese government absorbed most of those savings by running large government deficits and issuing government bonds. In the 1980s, though, the government reversed this policy and systematically cut its deficits by raising taxes and cutting spending.

Overseas Spending

This sounds like a good idea, one that the United States should follow but has trouble accomplishing. However, there is one catch: Japan was reducing its government deficit while the large surplus

---

BERRY'S WORLD By Jim Berry

© 1987 by NEA inc

Jim Berry. Reprinted by permission of NEA, Inc.

---

of savings over investment in the private sector continued. Therefore, those savings had to go somewhere. Where could they go? The only other outlet was overseas, showing up in the statistics as a current-account surplus (meaning that Japan exported more goods and services than it imported) and a capital outflow (meaning that Japanese savings were invested in other countries). This is what happened in the first half of the 1980s. Japan's current-account surplus rose from an actual deficit of over $10 billion in 1980 to an astronomical $86 billion in 1986.

Running a large surplus with the rest of the world is not a foregone conclusion. Luckily for Japan, the United States was moving in exactly the opposite direction: Large government deficits emerging were greater than the available pool of domestic savings, driving the United States into a current-account deficit and capital inflow. Let's put this in more elementary terms: The Japanese preferred to save their money rather than spend it, so they sent both the goods and the money to the United States, where people preferred to buy rather than to save.

Now this situation is beginning to unwind. The rapid rise of the yen against the dollar has slowed Japan's exports and increased imports. The weaker dollar will raise U.S. exports and slow U.S. imports. These effects have been slow to appear, but economists remain confident that they will. This poses a dilemma for Japan: If the excess savings can no longer be pushed abroad as a rising international surplus, where will they go? Japan is now confronting this problem, and is taking action to discourage saving, encourage investment, and even reverse its government fiscal policies by raising government spending and cutting taxes.

Why does all this matter? Even though the situation is now changing (and should continue to do so for several years), the United States has become the world's largest debtor and Japan the largest net creditor. For the first time since before the war (when Japan had extensive colonial holdings in Asia), Japan has been thrust into the position of owning and managing large assets abroad, many of them in the United States. This raises several potential problems.

Shifting Positions?

First, all nations are sensitive about foreign ownership. Both Japan and Europe restricted American investment in their economies in the 1950s, when we had the money to buy their assets. So far, Americans appear to welcome Japanese investment because it has helped hold U.S. interest rates down and has created jobs. But even the United States must have some threshold beyond which the (often irrational) fear of foreign domination comes to the fore. Japanese investment has certainly been quite visible as the Japanese have been buying banks, securities firms, familiar skyscrapers in Manhattan, and driving up the price of nineteenth-century art. It is only a small step from visibility to criticism.

Second, the dramatic shift in the positions of Japan and the United States complicates leadership and relations in the world. The United States remains a world leader in many significant ways. It is a large nuclear superpower capable of projecting a military presence around the world, and uses its position to take the lead in attempting to solve major world problems. Japan is a large economic power with no nuclear capability, which rarely thinks about anything except its own narrow economic interest. These are stereotypes that are not entirely true, but they come surprisingly close to describing accurately the positions of the two countries.

Role Reversal

Japan and the United States are going through a gigantic and painful role reversal. The United States, formerly the wealthiest nation on earth, has become the biggest debtor. Japan, for 40 years America's economic and geopolitical junior partner, has become the world's (and America's) biggest creditor. This switch is bound to have political and psychological ramifications. Debtors classically go hat-in-hand to their creditors, and feel resentment about it. Debtors who are used to being No. 1 feel the resentment even more deeply. The strain is showing on both sides of the Pacific.

The New Republic, June 15, 1987.

Moving to a debtor position impairs America's ability to play its leadership role, and moving to a creditor position raises the possibility that Japan will play a larger role, one for which it is ill-prepared. Being a leader implies formulating policies to deal with world problems and then trying to get others to go along with them. Telling Japan and other creditor nations what to do has a hollow ring to it when they hold the power of the purse.

Suppose Japan does not like some American policy toward the Middle East. Bombing Libya in retaliation for supporting terrorism would be a good example. Japan has little interest in anti-terrorism because anti-Western terrorism is virtually nonexistent in Asia and rarely affects any Japanese nationals. Japan may not really care who runs Libya or what his policies are as long as Japan can continue to do business there. If Japan were to object to aggressive American action against Libya, Japanese investors, perhaps with moral suasion from their government, could reduce the flow of investment to the United States enough to cause a jump in interest rates or a fall in the stock market. Such actions or the threat of such actions could have a serious impact on U.S. foreign policy.

The United States is not always wise or correct in its foreign policy decisions, but the problem of achieving consensus with other nations is difficult enough without giving veto power to our squabbling partners. Indeed, people on Wall Street are already voicing concern, warning Washington not to antagonize Japan and thus possibly slow the flow of money. They would rather have the money and accept constraints on policy.

Conversely, the rise of Japan as a strong creditor positions it to play a larger role in world policy. Japan has shown little inclination to do so, but that attitude could change. If it chooses to become more involved, we are likely to be profoundly disturbed by the results. Whether through active resistance to American foreign policy initiatives as described above, or through policies of its own, Japan could follow a course detrimental to U.S. national interest and possibly to world stability. The narrow economic self-interest that tends to guide Japanese policy may be only its lack of experience in broader world affairs, but do not count on this changing quickly. American government officials have been encouraging Japan to play a larger international role for many years in arenas such as the IMF [International Monetary Fund], GATT [General Agreement on Tariffs and Trade], and World Bank, but these officials assume that a larger Japanese role in setting policy would simply substitute for a portion of the U.S. role, with no real change in the decisions made. We should not make that assumption.

Even thoughtful Japanese now sometimes speak with open contempt about the United States. Some believe that American labor is lazy, sloppy, and poorly educated; that American firms are technologically inferior and inattentive to quality control; and that the U.S. government is run by misguided, incompetent amateurs. While this might sound no worse than the rhetoric of some of the American presidential candidates, Japanese attitudes have a harsh edge to them. Former Prime Minister Nakasone's comments about the inferiority of blacks and hispanics in the United States were not an aberration; most Japanese would agree with him and many were puzzled when Americans took offense. Japanese hubris is on the rise and represents a poor start for a nation embarking on a larger international role.

The Micro Picture

For more than 20 years the United States and Japan have been battling over a variety of specific trade disputes. Some have involved Japanese penetration of the U.S. market, with charges ranging from dumping to simply out-competing American firms and thereby grabbing "too much" of the market. Others point to the problems faced by American firms trying to enter Japan. The negotiations have often been noisy, nasty, and long-lasting.

Some American firms have attacked their Japanese competition simply because the courtroom offered a better chance to win than did the market place. And American consumers are right to buy Japanese products if they offer better prices, quality, and styling. But two fundamental facts must be recognized when dealing with these issues.

First, the United States remains a rather open economy and one that welcomes competitive foreign products, whereas Japan remains rather protectionist and rarely welcomes foreign competition on its home turf. Second, Japan has been moving toward a less protectionist position, but that movement has been slow, grudging, and often superficial. No Japanese claims to the contrary can contradict these facts. Even American businessmen who are successful in selling to Japan find it an extremely difficult place to do business.

A Collision Course

On a visit to Tokyo, I asked a cab driver what he thought about the growing tension between Tokyo and Washington. He said: *"Onbu ni dakko ni kataguruma* (Give them an inch and they'll take a mile)."

His point was that the traditional roles of the two countries are now being reversed and an increasingly dominant Japan will now no longer be willing to tolerate the demands of a declining America. That a Japanese cabdriver thought this was perhaps a sign that cracks in American hegemony are wider than one might think. But if Japan insists on neglecting that dynamic, regenerative power inherent in the American spirit, an even wider and more dangerous fissure could evolve, ultimately eroding the fragile *Nichibei* (Japan-America) alliance and putting the two nations on an unavoidable collision course either late in this century or early in the next.

Steven Schlosstein, *Business Tokyo*, March 1989.

Behind this contrast lie fundamental differences in attitude toward free trade. Throughout the postwar period, the United States has had a firm ideological commitment to the principle of free trade. Based on standard economic theories, we believe that free trade is good because it leads to efficient allocation of resources. We export those products in which we are the most competitive, and import those in which we are not. We have been willing to accept the basic concept that disinvestment must take place in those industries that are less productive because we are ultimately better off shifting that investment to more productive industries. The United States has often violated these principles and has put protectionist barriers in place to protect a number of products, including textiles and steel. But the principle remains and the departures are accompanied by great debate and some embarrassment.

Because Japan entered the postwar period believing that it was weak and unable to compete, it erected a massive array of barriers to keep out many foreign-manufactured products. By the mid-1960s, Japan was facing heavy international criticism over those barriers, and began a slow process of dismantling them. This process has been defensive, and has been undertaken because of foreign pressure and threats of retaliation against Japan's exports rather than out of any ideological or intellectual commitment to free trade. Japan wanted to export, and recognized that some opening of its home market was the price that it had to pay to continue to do so.

Japan and Trade

These attitudes remain, even though Japan is now a rich country with an enormous trade surplus. Virtually all of Japan's trading partners complain bitterly that its continued protectionism is a disgrace. Countries in Japan's position should be the moral leaders of the international trading system. Japan not only fails to provide moral leadership, it is one of the main problems. Japan still completely prohibits rice imports, despite a domestic price that is many times world levels. Furthermore, it changed the standards applying to skis last year on the grounds that Japanese snow is different than snow in other countries, drove American producers out of the aluminum baseball bat market by establishing a web of standards and rules deliberately designed so that American products would not be able to meet them, and locked American firms out of a multi-billion-dollar airport construction project in Osaka, despite the worldwide expertise of American firms in this field.

Japan's failure to change is one of the principal reasons that the U.S. commitment to free trade has been severely shaken in the United States. The foolish protectionist statements made by many members of Congress are deplorable, but the dilemma is that those in Congress, business, and academia who used to counter those initiatives strongly have been undercut. Japan's continued protectionist behavior has been so blatant and unrelenting that free traders in the United States find it increasingly difficult to oppose retaliation against Japan.

Should Japan continue this pattern much longer, a serious breakdown in the postwar movement toward freer trade could result. At the very least, the United States is likely to use targeted protectionism against Japan as a bargaining tool in its attempt to get Japan to open. This was done in 1987 when Japan failed to comply with a bilateral agreement on semiconductor trade. The original agreement can be faulted, but Japan did sign it and should have complied. In the face of overwhelming evidence that Japan was not complying, the United States imposed punitive tariffs on a small number of imports from Japan, with a promise to remove them when Japan complied. This form of careful, calculated pressure will become more frequent if Japan does not respond to negotiations.

A Brighter Side?

This has been a gloomy assessment of Japan's relations: The United States has damaged its world leadership position; Japan could use its creditor position in the United States in ways inconsistent with U.S. national interest; and protectionism threatens support for the postwar international trade system. Some or all of these developments could worsen in the future and push both countries to a more antagonistic and less productive relationship, but there are some rays of hope.

On the macroeconomic front, the enormous imbalances of the first half of the 1980s are coming down and should continue to do so. On the trade front, the strong value of the yen now makes imports look very inexpensive to the Japanese. This has led more and more Japanese to ask why those products should be so much more expensive in Tokyo than in other countries. Businessmen have similarly been questioning their commitment to expensive domestic suppliers and are increasingly making the switch to imports. These developments may bring about a domestic constituency that favors free trade for the first time since the war. If the Japanese themselves become serious about imports, then progress on removing barriers will be rapid and Japan could demonstrate the necessary moral leadership to reinforce the international trading system.

These developments are in their early phases. One hopes they will continue and offset the slide toward increased frustration and antagonism. The most important step the United States can take now is to continue cutting the federal budget deficit. This is critical. If we do, the United States can arrest the rise of its international debt and keep the yen strong to improve the atmosphere for resolving trade problems. Parts of the gloomy scenario may remain, but at least it can be contained. But if we do not cut the federal budget deficit, then our dependency on foreign capital will increase, the complications for American foreign policy will become worse, and Japanese contempt for the United States will reach disturbing levels.

"The relations of the United States and Japan are pivotal to sustaining the current balance of power in the [East Asian] region."

US-Japan Cooperation Improves Asian Security

Jerome K. Holloway

Jerome K. Holloway is a lecturer at the Naval War College in Newport, Rhode Island, and has served in the State Department and Foreign Service. In the following viewpoint, he argues that military cooperation between the US and Japan has maintained a stable balance of power in East Asia, and has served US interests. Holloway warns that focusing too much attention on trade disputes might jeopardize security ties.

As you read, consider the following questions:

1. What potential developments in Asia are most threatening to US interests, according to Holloway?
2. According to the author, what four factors could change the US-Japan relationship?
3. Why is Japan better than China as a strategic US ally in Asia, according to Holloway?

Jerome K. Holloway, "Japan and the East Asian Balance of Power," *Parameters*, September 1988.

$\mathbf{Y}$ears after the collapse of the American enterprise in Vietnam, there exists in East Asia a balance of power reasonably tolerable for the United States. Few would have predicted this when the last helicopter lifted from the roof of the American Embassy in Saigon. We would do well to recall that this balance contrasts with the situations that existed in 1946, 1953, and 1964 during which the United States, in following its 20th-century policy of opposing the hegemony of any single power in East Asia, embarked on quasi-hegemonic policies of its own. As of now, dangers to the East Asian balance of power seem remote, despite growing Soviet military power and increased political interest in the area. However, the relations of the United States and Japan are pivotal to sustaining the current balance of power in the region, and many Americans, including some of influence, do not recognize this. . . .

Taiwan remains separated from China. Korea is divided. The Vietnamese have shown a sharp appetite in Kampuchea and Laos. New Zealand and the United States have engaged in a mutually hobbling exercise over disclosure of nuclear weapons in US naval vessels calling at the former's ports. Unrest in the Philippines is serious. The Soviet Union has increased its military presence in East Asia and is trying to increase its political weight there. But in light of the predictions of disaster that followed the demise of the Saigon government in 1975, the present regional balance of power does not damage US interests.

Japan's Role

What could damage those interests is a change in Japan's role. In an illuminating book jointly prepared by American and Japanese contributors in 1975, this statement appeared: "The only remotely plausible change in the current alignment of nations that would threaten the security of the United States is for Japan to become hostile." The same statement would fit the 1980s and will probably fit the 1990s. Now, no one expects Japan to become hostile, but, substitute the words "indifferent," "neutral," "non-aligned," or "aloof," and the relationship is changed ominously.

What factors might change the Japanese-American relationship? First would be an attempt to revise the formal treaty status to expand the scope of Japanese military obligations in East Asia and to relate these to contingencies in the Middle East or Europe. No Japanese government or political party can risk "opening up" the present arrangements with the United States. The result would be not greater Japanese participation and responsibility: it would be a call from both intellectuals and the public for a decrease in Japan's security obligations. One may decry this, and most American politicians would, but the history of negotiations over the US-Japanese security relationship suggests that American attempts to get precise, legal language on Japanese commitments

222

usually fail. To get an expansion of those commitments both in concept and language that will make the bureaucrats and the military comfortable is self-defeating. This is not an exercise in Oriental pop-psychology, as many attempt to portray it. It is not that the Japanese prefer a vague, all-things-to-all-men formulation; it is a fact of political life. To attempt to change the present treaty arrangements is to risk the good in hopeless pursuit of the better or best.

The Trade Problem

The second danger is clearly trade and finance. One would think that enough has been written on this, and that there is sufficient objective evidence that the average man can see for himself (Japanese cars, cameras, and appliances work better and are cheaper than their American-made competition) to obviate ritualistic recounting of brutal truth about the decline of the American smokestack belt. But here we are in a world where emotions must be counted. No American policymaker can explain to the unemployed steelworker with a family that he is a victim of the international division of labor or even of the corporate blindness of his own business and labor leadership. His woes are a fact of life, as politically potent as Japanese distaste with commitments that could risk war. Hence, to try to suggest, as the US defense establishment must, that a trade war with Japan would endanger higher political and military interests is a difficult effort. But the effort must be made. . . .

The Defense Relationship

The U.S.-Japan Mutual Security Treaty is the foundation upon which our bilateral relationship rests. The interests of both the United States and Japan—and, indeed, the interests of the West, of which Japan is a part—are well served by it. Our security arrangements with Japan, including the presence of our troops and facilities there, are essential for the peace and security not only of Japan but of the entire Pacific region, including, of course, the United States.

Gaston J. Sigur, *Department of State Bulletin*, May 1988.

The average Japanese is an austere consumer; the Liberal Democratic Party cannot reduce substantially the agriculture subsidies that ensure the party's majority in the Diet; the Japanese bureaucracy changes no more quickly than other bureaucracies, and its ties to special interests in the business and political worlds bind it much the way many American regulatory agencies are bound; the labyrinth-like Japanese distribution system will change very slowly; and American manufacturers will still have difficulty getting their minds and efforts away from sole concentration on the huge, rich, and integrated market that is the US domestic economy. Japan has its bill of grievances against US policies, including a 1973 US embargo on the export of soybeans to Japan that was seen in Tokyo as analogous to the July 1941 US embargo.

Given the structure of US decisionmaking on trade and investment with Japan, the Pentagon's *locus standi* [standpoint] is weak, but the case of security considerations must be pressed.

Defense Spending

The third lever that might move Japan is related to the first—defense expenditures. . . . In the Pentagon we find flag officers planning ways to bring on Japanese involvement with strike group operations in the western Pacific and joint participation in carrier strike forces. Other planners devise force capabilities that Japan should purchase to meet an allegedly iron-bound commitment to 1000 miles of merchant ship protection. Meanwhile, on the wilder edges of planning, there is touted the idea that Japanese neutrality in a NATO [North Atlantic Treaty Organization]/Warsaw Pact war could be ended by a unilateral US strike against the USSR from Misawa.

No one argues that Japan should not be able to defend itself to the extent of making a would-be aggressor at least calculate his probable losses. But continuing attempts to co-opt a greatly augmented Japanese force into American operational plans risk alienation of the Japanese public and Japan's neighbors. Arguments that the Seventh Fleet is doing Japan's job in the Indian Ocean break down on the assumption that Japan sees a job that needs doing; it doesn't. One might also turn the problem around and ask what the United States would do differently if there were no Japanese armed forces at all.

China vs. Japan

Fourth, there is a remote danger that the United States might eventually seek a special relationship with the People's Republic of China as a substitute for the Japanese one. . . . The low priority given the defense establishment in China's Four Modernizations underlines the limitations to US-Chinese strategic cooperation. We learned, albeit at great cost, that we are ill-served by a friendly China and an unfriendly Japan, but that we can find bearable a hostile China and a friendly Japan. If both were hostile (a 21st-century scenario) there would be little point in US participation in the Asian balance of power, except, of course, as a partner of the Soviets, a dubious prospect.

Now none of this means that we should not pursue actively with Japan the enhancement of American political, economic and strategic objectives. But we should consider the extent to which we want to pursue the four courses warned of above. Japan's role now is comfortable to Japan; it is reasonably comfortable to the other noncommunist nations of East Asia. Perhaps we should accommodate ourselves to the present arrangements, however irksome they may seem to some elements of our government and society. A cold-eyed look at the Soviet menace to the balance of power in East Asia would help. The USSR has military power; but the Soviets have no political or economic power in the area, they have unresolved territorial problems with both China and Japan, and it would be a rare Asian who would find any attraction in Soviet society. True, if the balance of power in East Asia were to begin to turn against US interests, there would be opportunities for the Soviets. But the argument here is that this balance is now at risk only if the United States mishandles its relations with Japan.

> *"It is in the interest of the United States . . .
> to reduce and not increase military tensions in
> the Pacific."*

US-Japan Cooperation Harms Asian Security

Richard J. Barnett and Alan Geyer

Both Japanese and Americans have questioned whether the close military cooperation between their two countries truly benefits Japanese and Asian security. In Part I of the following viewpoint, Richard J. Barnett argues that the US emphasis on military ties with Japan has increased tensions in Asia and has harmed the US economy. Barnett is a senior fellow at the Institute for Policy Studies, a research organization in Washington, DC. In Part II, Alan Geyer argues that US-Japan military ties have not enhanced Japan's security and should be curtailed. Geyer is a contributing editor for *The Christian Century*, a liberal Christian magazine.

As you read, consider the following questions:

1. According to Barnett, how do American and Japanese views of national security differ?
2. How do the Japanese see themselves, according to Barnett?

Richard J. Barnett, "Japan and U.S. See Themselves as Victims of Same Relationship," *Los Angeles Times*, April 11, 1989. Reprinted with permission. Alan Geyer, "The US-Japan Military Alliance." Copyright 1989 Christian Century Foundation. Reprinted by permission from the April 26, 1989 issue of *The Christian Century*.

I

If the Cold War is over, the victor is Japan. The exertions of the United States in the 45-year struggle to contain Soviet communism created the indispensable conditions for Japan's emergence as an economic superpower. The American use of Japan as a base for its Korean War operations boosted Japanese recovery; the protracted Vietnam War brought prosperity to Japan even as it overheated the American economy and tore its social fabric. All during these years, Japan and the United States have pursued radically different national-security strategies.

The United States has consistently given priority to the military dimensions of national security, even at the sacrifice of economic advantage. True, the Korean War rearmament and subsequent military expenditures have at times provided crucial stimulus to the U.S. economy. But the concentration on fighting the Cold War to the neglect of the U.S. economy and its changing position in the world have seriously damaged national security. Japanese competition now inflicts greater damage and creates greater uncertainty about the future of the United States than anything the Soviet Union is doing or is likely to do.

Comprehensive Security

In contrast, the Japanese concept of "comprehensive security" has emphasized the race for markets, technological preeminence and a wide variety of sophisticated economic relationships with a wide range of partners. The United Staes has been the keystone of that strategy, both the military protector and the prime market. The strategy has been wildly successful. Japan has overtaken the United States as a supplier of investment capital and foreign aid and as the world's most successful producer and merchandiser of automobiles, machine tools, semi-conductors, robotics and other technologies that will shape the early decades of the new century.

The combined U.S. trade and budget deficits have created the conditions under which Washington is increasingly dependent on Japanese capital to pay its bills; and, because of the weakened dollar, the Japanese are picking up choice American assets—real estate, farm land, corporations—at bargain prices.

U.S.-Japanese relations are likely to deteriorate because both Japanese and Americans see themselves as victims. The Japanese attribute the astonishing turnabout in U.S.-Japanese relations to their success in following the rules laid down by the United States at the end of World War II. They became a peaceful trading nation. Why should they be blamed if they beat the United States at its own game?

Americans see themselves as victims of predatory Japanese trade practices and of Japan's monumental ingratitude for having had a "free ride" under the "nuclear umbrella" all these years. In both countries, nationalist sentiments fueled by radically different perceptions of the same reality are on the rise.

Soviet Disarmament

Unaccountably, despite growing tensions, U.S. policy continues to encourage Japanese rearmament. Soviet President Mikhail S. Gorbachev has made proposals to reverse the naval arms race in the Pacific and, according to the U.S. Navy's chief intelligence officer, the Soviets are pulling a significant number of surface ships out of service. (Decommissioning vessels makes the Soviet navy more efficient, the U.S. officer said, but this is not an argument he would extend to the U.S. Navy.)

Soviet sources say they have cut 40 surface vessels in the four years since 1985 and have hinted to a senior Pentagon consultant that they will remove as many as 50 attack submarines in the hope of inducing cutbacks in the U.S. carrier fleet. At the same time their naval exercises in the Pacific have become much more defensive and less provocative than in recent years.

Military Cooperation Harms Japan

East Asia and the Pacific are clearly a vital part of the United States' world nuclear strategy, and Japan apparently thinks the expansion and protection of its economic interests depend upon that strategy. While seeking domination over Asia, Japan itself, like the United States, has become quite undemocratic or reactionary. For example, Japan . . . has a world-famous constitution which totally denounces war and rearmament. That constitution has been violated, however, and Japan now has a very strong army and is part of U.S. military strategy. It is quite ironic to see the United States forcing Japan to undertake a huge military buildup, which goes along with the resurgence of reactionary tendencies in politics and society.

Oda Makoto, *Social Justice*, Spring 1989.

The United States response has been to schedule PACEX [Pacific Exercises], the most provocative naval exercise in many years, which will link the Japanese navy even more closely into U.S. naval strategy. The exercise will feature a U.S. naval foray into the Sea of Okhotsk, which borders Soviet territory and is a sanctuary for Soviet missile-launching submarines.

Inverted Priorities

It is in the interest of the United States, although not necessarily the self-defined interests of the U.S. Navy, to reduce and not increase military tensions in the Pacific. Once again national-security priorities are inverted. Reducing the costs of the military is a prerequisite for a successful economic strategy. Gorbachev offers the possibility of naval disarmament that could produce major savings for both countries.

It is not in the interest of the United States for Japan to become more of a military power than it already is. This is particularly true if we are unable to address the increasingly serious economic conflicts that threaten to turn ever close military allies into bitter commercial rivals.

II

On the enormous U.S. Air Force base at Yokota in suburban Tokyo, headquarters not only for the Fifth Air Force but for all U.S. forces in Japan, there is a seemingly incongruous United Nations liaison office. That office is a remnant of the Korean War, which was waged under the UN flag. It is also a poignant symbol of what might have been: a genuinely multilateral peace treaty for Japan after World War II. Such a treaty just might have prevented the Korean War, the remilitarization of Japan, and the present escalation of military confrontations in the Northwest Pacific. Those confrontations with Soviet naval deployments are a strange and disturbing contradiction to the thaw in East-West relations in Europe and in recent U.S.-U.S.S.R. summitry.

Many Japanese favored a neutral and demilitarized nation after 1945. Instead, Japan, while demilitarized for a time, was made the forward base for U.S. forces in East Asia and the staging area for the Korean War. In recent years, Japan has become one of the world's major military powers, spending $30 billion a year, more than any other Asian nation. . . .

Military Collaboration

The recent intensification of Japan-U.S. military collaboration in Asia and the Pacific [includes:] . . .

• The buildup of the Japanese military ("Self-Defense Forces"), with 250,000 personnel; a navy soon to have 60 destroyers (more than in the U.S. Pacific fleet), 14 submarines and 18 frigates; and an air force of more than 300 combat aircraft, including the newest U.S. fighters. This buildup certainly strains the Japanese constitution's renunciation of "land, sea and air forces."

• Nuclear collaboration with the U.S., which some are concerned violates not only the constitution's renunciation of war and armed forces but the 1951 Treaty of Peace and the 1967 "Three Non-Nuclear Principles" enunciated by Prime Minister Eisaku Sato—no possession, no production, no entry of nuclear weapons.

• Extensive and provocative Japan-U.S. naval exercises at a time when the Soviet Union is curtailing its Pacific fleet operations.

• Japan's participation since 1986 in research on the Strategic Defense Initiative, and the effort to conceal the nature of that research by enacting a state secrets law (such a law has not yet passed the Diet).

• Japan's funding of the U.S. budget deficit, which in practice means the purchase of many billions of dollars of U.S. bonds to pay for the U.S. military.

• The rapid economic growth of Japan, which allows for the escalation in military spending and which comes partly at the expense of less-developed countries, where Japanese development aid has been primarily geared to expand Japanese exports, invest Japanese capital, and purchase raw materials cheaply.

• Community-relations problems around U.S. bases, stemming especially from the deafening roar of night landing exercises at Atsugi and Miyake Jima, which has led local governments to file lawsuits. . . .

• The PACEX (Pacific Exercises) war games scheduled for September 1989. While there has been little notice of PACEX in the U.S., the Japanese press and various peace groups have reported the following: the war games will stretch from the South China Sea to the Bering Sea and will enter the Sea of Okhotsk, surrounded on three sides by Soviet territory; U.S. aircraft-carrier battle groups from both the Third and Seventh fleets, plus two army divisions, a Marine division and more than 500 combat aircraft will be joined by Japanese, Korean and Philippine forces in the month-long exercise; and the Japanese Maritime Self-Defense Force will participate in mock attacks (presumably on Soviet territory) that range far beyond the self-defense of the Japanese islands. . . .

A Shock Wave

In 1981 Japan made a deal with the United States to assume the defense of its sea lanes up to 1,000 miles from Japan proper. This sent a shock wave of alarm through the countries of South East Asia that suffered Japanese invasion in World War II, and where there are the greatest concentrations of Japanes foreign aid, trade, loans and investment. Japan's claim that its growing military strength is only for self-defense has been viewed with scepticism.

William Pomeroy, *People's Daily World*, August 3, 1988.

Such war games inevitably mean that Japan, Korea and the Philippines (all of whom have renounced nuclear weapons) are collaborating with the nuclear strategies of the U.S., since nuclear weapons are integrated with conventional weapons in all U.S. forces. Japan's nonnuclear status is further compromised by the U.S. nuclear command and control sites—as many as 28—in Japan. That concentration of nuclear software makes Japan the prime

Soviet target in East Asia. Moreover, the large naval bases at Yokosuka at the mouth of Tokyo Bay, which serves as headquarters for the Seventh Fleet, is the home port of the aircraft carrier *Midway* (presumably loaded with nuclear weapons) and the destroyer *Fife* and the cruiser *Bunker Hill*, both of which are now equipped for Tomahawk nuclear cruise missiles. Okinawa remains burdened with many U.S. nuclear facilities. As if more evidence were needed of the U.S. nuclear presence in Japan, the disclosures of elaborate contingency plans for coping with nuclear accidents and incidents surely provides it.

The invisibility of such issues in the American media and churches is startling. We know about the flood of Japanese goods and our huge trade deficit with Japan, the controversy over technology-sharing in the FSX fighter, the insider trading scandals in the Takeshita government, and congressional pressure for more "burden-sharing" by the Japanese military—as if Japan remained a disarmed pacifist state. The public and the churches do not seem to know the extent to which the U.S.-Japan alliance has become hostage to an anachronistic and perilous escalation of nuclear war-fighting strategies and deployments—a development demeaning to the Japanese and corrupting to our relationships. . . .

We would all do well to recall what might have been in Japan-U.S. relations, and reflect on what they might yet become if we are capable of alternative visions.

"If Japan cannot restrain the excesses of its own economy, then the United States ... should impose limits from outside."

The US Should Challenge Japan's Trade Policies

James Fallows

James Fallows is Washington editor of *The Atlantic Monthly*. Since 1986 he has lived in and reported from Japan. In the following viewpoint, he argues that Japan's continuing trade surplus with the US threatens both the US and the international economy. Fallows concludes that the US should pressure Japan to reform its economy and trade practices.

As you read, consider the following questions:

1. What is the basic conflict between the US and Japan, according to Fallows?
2. According to Fallows, what underlying theme of Japanese culture affects trade negotiations?
3. Why does the author believe that Japan's perception of US power is important?

Japanese-American relationships have a fragile, walking-on-eggs quality, which makes people think that it's dangerous to talk frankly in public. Many other international relationships are robust enough to survive open discussions of disagreements. . . . But the American fraternity of Japan-handlers, which includes most diplomats and a number of businessmen, scholars, and journalists, instinctively stifles outright complaints about Japan.

The impulse toward tact is understandable. Most Americans who have worked in Japan are aware of raw anti-Japanese prejudice in the United States and don't want to pander to it. They are also reluctant to do anything that would aggravate Japan's ever-present fears that the rest of the world is about to gang up on it and exclude it. The last time Japan felt left out was in the 1930s, when it started down the road to fascist nationalism after it suffered a number of international snubs. . . .

Now, however, Japan has become too important to be treated with such delicacy. Excessive politeness prevents Japan and the United States from facing the conflict that in the long run endangers their relations much more than the comments of any bigoted Japan-bashers could.

For the foreseeable future Japan will be America's single most valuable partner, because of what it can do in three areas. First is the U.S.-Japan military understanding, which prevents Japan from building as large an army as it would need on its own, leaves the United States as the reigning power in the Pacific, adds very little direct cost to the U.S. military budget, and prevents an arms race throughout Asia in which all other countries would try to defend themselves against the Japanese. Second is finance: Japan has become America's financier, providing investment capital and covering much of the U.S. government's debt. Third is business: Japanese-American business relations provide technology, markets, talent, supplies, and other essential elements to both nations' companies.

A Basic Conflict

These three realities tempt many people, especially American diplomats, to assume a fourth: that Japanese and American interests do not clash in any fundamental way. This assumption is wrong. There is a basic conflict between Japanese and American interests—notwithstanding that the two countries need each other as friends—and it would be better to face it directly than to pretend that it doesn't exist.

That conflict arises from Japan's inability or unwillingness to restrain the one-sided and destructive expansion of its economic power. The expansion is one-sided because Japanese business does to other countries what Japan will not permit to be done to itself. It is destructive because it will lead to exactly the international ostracism that Japan most fears, because it will wreck the postwar system of free trade that has made Japan and many other nations prosperous, and because it will ultimately make the U.S.-Japanese partnership impossible to sustain. . . .

Friends must sometimes help friends break destructive habits. Japan is in a good position to lecture the United States about its destructive business and financial habits, and more and more Japanese officials have been doing just that. But Japan's destructive habits are potentially more harmful to the rest of the world than America's are. If Japan cannot restrain the excesses of its own economy, then the United States, to save its partnership with Japan, should impose limits from outside.

Dick Wright reprinted by permission of United Feature Syndicate, Inc.

Is Japan's economic growth really unbalanced? One indication of imbalance is so obvious that it seems almost tasteless to bring it up. This is the gap between Japan's export success and its artificially suppressed consumption at home. The same country that has the biggest cash surpluses and the largest overseas investments in the world also has by far the highest consumer prices, the highest proportion of unpaved roads among developed countries, the lowest per capita endowment of parks, sporting areas, and other public facilities, and across the board the least materially bountiful life. . . .

The Dutch journalist Karel van Wolferen asks in the opening pages of his forceful and important new book *The Enigma of Japanese Power*, "For what ultimate purpose do [the Japanese] deprive themselves of comfort and risk the enmity of the world?" His answer is that individual Japanese, rather than depriving themselves, are deprived by the country's major power centers—the big corporations, the government regulators—which are always struggling to keep from losing ground to one another or to foreign competitors. . . .

A second, equally obvious indication of imbalance involves trade statistics. . . .

"If the United States were a well-run country, neoclassical economists would be hanging from the Capitol dome," Chalmers Johnson told me in 1989."They predicted that by the time the dollar got [down] to 190 yen, the trade deficit would have disappeared." The dollar crashed through the 190 level in 1986 and has spent most of 1988 in the 120s, and still Japan has the largest trade surpluses in the world. Johnson may sound intemperate, but his point is fair. Classic free-trade analysis has proved virtually useless in predicting how Japan's trade balances would respond to a rising yen. Although Japanese officials typically put less faith in free-market equilibrium than Americans do, they also were often surprised by the effects of *endaka* ("high yen"). . . .

Adversarial Trade

There is one further indication of economic imbalance: the continuing pattern of one-sidedness in many Japanese transactions. A few years ago the management expert Peter Drucker introduced the term "adversarial trade" to describe Japan's approach to commerce, which is characterized by resistance to high-value imports and by targeted attacks on established foreign industries. . . .

Even some of Japan's "market-opening" measures end up illustrating its adversarial tendencies. In 1988, Japan agreed to reduce its barriers against beef imports, in stages over the next few years. One immediate effect was to increase the sale not of U.S. beef in Japan but of U.S. beef *ranches*. (There is already significant Japanese investment in the Australian beef industry.) "The whole point in opening up the Japanese market was for American producers to be able to sell here," Billy Cody, of Oregon's Japan Representative Office, told Fred Hiatt, of *The Washington Post*. "So what is the mentality that refuses to buy our products? What is the necessity to come and buy our producers?" . . .

Taken together, these developments reveal the tension between free-trade theory and Japan's place in the world. Most economic forces are supposed to be self-correcting—if the price goes up enough, the demand goes down. In the case of Japan's trade balance, there was a powerful external shove toward correction, in the form of *endaka*. Yet on the evidence of what has happened since 1985, normal economic and business pressures are not going to balance Japan's trade accounts. Its surpluses, assets, and industrial strengths will continue to grow in a lopsided way. . . .

Why is Japan so unconcerned about the double standard of its trading policy? It has to do with the ultimate values of Japanese political life—or what can be called the lack of them. Japan is a highly honorable society, in which individuals are deeply bound by obligations of gratitude, loyalty, and deference. But Japanese society has always been short on abstract principles dictating proper treatment of those outside the network of obligations—such as foreigners. The result is Japan's distinctive view of "fair" competition and its seemingly clear conscience about one-sided behavior. . . .

Real Differences

For years we assumed we had created Japan in our own image after World War II and that it would respond to trade initiatives and rules as we do. Now we see that the problems there and with many other countries are much more complicated than that—and we must strive to execute a trade policy that attacks these real differences—and therefore barriers—and begin to change them.

Richard A. Gephardt, *Vital Speeches of the Day*, May 15, 1989.

As countless foreign observers have reported, the honor and discipline of Japanese life are based on highly personal loyalties— to the feudal lord, to the honor of the family, these days to the corporation. These are different from such abstract principles as charity, democracy, world brotherhood, and so on, and they lead to different kinds of behavior. The members of a tight-knit Japanese work group or neighborhood will spontaneously sacrifice more for one another than their counterparts in the United States will—but they are a lot less likely to sacrifice for someone outside the group. Volunteer work and charitable organizations, like the United Way and Community Chest, are virtually unknown in Japan, and there is little instinctive concern about starving children in Ethopia, earthquake victims in Armenia, or refugees from Indochina. On the other hand, people in Japan are more likely to take care of their own. . . .

To bring this back to trade: the standard complaint about Japanese trading practice is that it's hypocritical. Japanese manufacturers sell freely in the United States, but foreigners must fight their way through public and private cartels to compete in Japan. The very idea of hypocrisy, however, assumes that there is one rule of behavior, which should apply to everyone at all times. Japan's brand of morality is more "situational," applying rules that seem appropriate to each occasion. It is appropriate for American consumers to demand the best product for the money. It is also appropriate for Japan to promote its aircraft industry. My point is not to criticize the fundamentals of Japanese morality—on the whole they're less troublesome for the world than universal creeds that lead one society to try to convert everybody else. But they have an effect on Japan's international dealings that other countries, with different values, are foolish to ignore.

For example, when foreign negotiators ask Japan to embrace the principle of free trade, they run up against not only Japanese special interests that would be hurt by imports but also a broader Japanese discomfort with the very prospect of abiding by abstract principles. . . .

Might Makes Right

A willingness to overlook cold, pure principle and get down to practicalities can be seen as a virtue by Americans as well as Japanese. But Japanese society's lack of interest in principle has a profound effect that most Americans are slow to recognize. The lack of interest in principle makes sheer power the main test of what is "fair." Might makes right anywhere, but in Japan's dealing with the outside world it does so sweepingly.

In Western societies there is a constant tension between officially constituted authority and principles that reach beyond worldly authority ("Render unto Caesar . . ."). These principles become the main grounds for a challenge to authority. People can throw tea in Boston Harbor, or overthrow the Czar, or refuse to pay their taxes, or tack a list of theses on the door, on the grounds that the authorities are not living up to some higher standard. But to do so, they must first believe in abstract, transcendent principles. The weakness of such principles in Japanese life makes it much harder to lodge a legitimate challenge to authority. (The most famous and flamboyant rebellions in Japanese history have usually been gestures of personal or clan loyalty, or efforts to erase a stain on individual honor, as when the Minister of War committed suicide after Emperor Hirohito ordered surrender, in 1945.) As a result, the Japanese are more likely to believe that what *is* is right—and to adjust themselves to changing realities of power.

The most dramatic wartime example . . . is the lightning change in the Japanese public attitude after the army surrendered. Only weeks after women and children had been preparing to defend the home islands with bamboo swords, the public cooperated with the [U.S.] Occupation authorities with a minimum of insubordination and sabotage. . . .

The conclusion is not that average Japanese people are mindless followers but that, like Catholic priests and members of the Marine Corps, they live in a culture that honors authority. And what this means, in turn, for U.S.-Japanese relations is that the *appearance* of American power is more important than most Americans fully realize.

Government Favors Producers

It should be clearly understood that the economic war between Japan and America is a conflict between governments representing the interests of businesses and producers rather than those of consumers, that is, the general public. U.S. demands for greater access to the Japanese market may jeopardize Japanese producers, but many of the changes sought would be welcomed by consumers, and it is not surprising that many are quietly praying for an American victory.

Nakatani Iwao, *Japan Echo*, Fall 1987.

It's hard to imagine a strictly internal force that could push Japan off its current path, even though more and more Japanese realize that their lives would be easier and their country would be better liked if its economy were less lopsided. The political system is gridlocked by powerful moneyed groups, and the customs and the intellectual tradition of the country discourage those who otherwise might protest. (When I ask Japanese friends why they aren't angrier about anti-consumer policies or the increasingly visible political corruption, they often reply with a phrase that means "It's been arranged—there's nothing to be done.") What is left, then, as a way of changing Japan's internal behavior is pressure from outside. This principle is so widely recognized that the Japanese term *gaiatsu* is used much more frequently here than the comparable words, "outside pressure," are used in America. Since the end of the Second World War the main source of *gaiatsu* has been the United States, which first imposed a Constitution and a new social order on Japan, during the Occupation, and after that began "demanding" liberalizations in Japan's economic behavior. Many Japanese seem to understand why the constant nagging occurs and why it eventually improves their standard of living. ("Will people say they want imported rice or beef?" one Japanese friend said. "Of course not. Will they accept it when we 'give in' to American demands? Yes, and most will be grateful.") The problem with relying on *gaiatsu*, however, is that whoever is pushing from outside must be unchallengeably strong. If he seems to falter, he is like a rough-and-tough drill instructor who loses a fistfight with one of the recruits and can no longer intimidate by his mere stare. His main source of authority is gone. This is why the appearance of American economic decline and social disintegration, highly exaggerated as it may be in Japan, can do almost as much damage as the real thing. If America's strength seems to wane, so does the main hope for obtaining "normal" economic behavior from Japan. "The Japanese . . . are peculiarly sensitive to the smell of decay, however well screened," Kurt Singer, a German expatriate who lived in Japan before the First World War, said in his eloquent little book *Mirror, Sword, and Jewel*, "and they will strike at an enemy whose core appears to betray a lack of firmness." Of course Japan is not about to attack in any military or overtly hostile way. But the smell of decay that now seems to be wafting across the Pacific from America is a tremendous obstacle to Japanese liberalization. Most Americans living in Japan scan the news each day for industrial-output and trade figures, for signs of robust recovery and the appearance of strength from the United States. They know that the Japanese political system, like Japan's constellation of economic forces, cannot save Japan from its excesses. . . .

America's Interests

Unless Japan is contained, therefore, several things that matter to America will be jeopardized: America's own authority to carry out its foreign policy and advance its ideals, American citizens' future prospects within the world's most powerful business firms, and also the very system of free trade that America has helped sustain since the Second World War. The major threat to the free-trade system does not come from American protectionism. It comes from the example set by Japan. Japan and its acolytes, such as Taiwan and Korea, have demonstrated that in head-on industrial competition between free-trading societies and "capitalist developmental states," the free traders will eventually lose. The drive to break up the world into trading blocs—united Europe, North America, East Asia—is largely fueled by other countries' desire to protect themselves against Japan. . . .

Of course America needs to reform its own corporate practices, improve its schools, and reduce its debt. Of course our economic goal should be an open free-trading system around the world, not escalating trade barriers. Of course we have no business telling the Japanese how to run their own subtle, sophisticated society. But we do have the right to defend our interest and our values, and they are not identical to Japan's.

"The U.S. effort to brand Japan as "unfair" is needlessly antagonistic."

The US Should Not Challenge Japan's Trade Policies

Saburo Okita

Saburo Okita was the Japanese minister for foreign affairs from 1979 to 1980 and is currently chairman of the Institute for Domestic and International Policy Studies in Tokyo. In the following viewpoint, he argues that US criticisms of Japan's trade policies are unwarranted, and could significantly damage relations between the two countries. Okita asserts that the Japanese economy is moving faster towards free trade than Americans realize, and that America's trade deficit results from its own economic mistakes.

As you read, consider the following questions:

1. How has Japan's economy changed in recent years, according to Okita?
2. What important fact about Japan should foreigners remember, according to the author?
3. What does Okita predict will happen if the United States increases its trade demands on Japan?

Saburo Okita, "Crowbar Is Wrong Way To Prod Tokyo," *Los Angeles Times*, July 12, 1989.

Statistical weaknesses in America's collection of economic data are well demonstrated when it comes to Japan.

In February 1989, the Advisory Committee for Trade Policy and Negotiations submitted its analysis of the U.S.-Japan trade problem to President Bush's trade representative, Carla M. Hills. Among other things, the report stated that Japanese imports of manufactured goods were about 40% less than would be expected, a conclusion that is attributed to an analysis by Robert Z. Lawrence of the Brookings Institution.

While Japan's 1987 imports of manufactured goods were $59.6 billion, Lawrence's analysis indicated that they should have been $99.3 billion. That was 1987. With the increase in Japanese imports of manufactured goods over two years, the figure will top $100 billion. The Japanese economy has developed dramatically, and I fear that the current debate in the United States has failed to keep up with events. It is imperative that the United States and Japan use the latest data available.

Japanese Economy Changing

The Japanese economy is moving faster than Americans realize. In 1984, the 5.1% growth in real gross national product [GNP] was attributed to a 3.8% increase in domestic demand and a 1.3% gain in the demand for Japanese exports. Four years later, in 1988, the real GNP growth rate of 5.7% was the result of a 7.6% increase in the demand for domestic products, while the external demand contribution was minus 1.9%. The shift to a pattern of growth fueled by a demand for domestic goods is clear.

Perceptions are also out of phase. There has been conspicuous change in the ratio of the trade surplus to GNP; the 4.4% rate of 1986 was sharply reduced to 2.8% by 1988. This is vivid testimony to the fact that exchange-rate adjustment has not been wholly ineffective. Nevertheless, some people have pointed out that even if the trade surplus is reduced as a percentage of GNP, the Japanese trade surplus has stayed basically unchanged in dollar terms. To be sure, Japanese GNP doubled in dollar terms from 1984 until 1988. Yet there was only a 16% increase in yen terms. While the yen has been somewhat weaker on exchange markets, its astonishing appreciation in past years has meant that Japan's dollar-denominated GNP looks like a very inflated figure from the domestic Japanese perspective. Thus there is inevitably a yawning gap between the way the Japanese themselves see the economy and the way it looks to observers overseas.

Japanese exports will remain competitive, largely because of production expertise. In 1988, partly because of the yen's appreciation, Japanese private-sector capital investment in dollar terms was $498 billion, which topped even America's $488.4 billion. With this heavy investment, Japanese companies may become more quality-and price-competitive than American companies. Developments on exchange markets are also creating a situation conducive to Japanese exports.

Japan Has Met Demands

The United States has had justifiable complaints to bring against Japan and others who have benefitted from our relatively open and immense marketplace while not opening as wide their own markets to American interests. But we tend to overlook that in size and openness, the United States market is not a world model, but a uniquely deviant case; we also tend to exaggerate the utility of "bashing" our trade partners. It won't right the trade imbalance, and the tone of the bashing sometimes suggests that the U.S. is not only the self-appointed legitimate arbiter for all, but is also a poor loser when other nations have applied new technologies more widely than Americans, as in the steel and auto industries. Whatever Japan has done since the 1960s in response to our demands, we have found new cause for the trade imbalance.

Professor James Morley well summarizes the sequence:

> When this problem first appeared, the American charge was that Japan was unfairly protecting its market with tariffs and quotas. Since about 1965 Japan has restructured its tariffs until its average is lower than that of the United States. Quotas have been abandoned on many items though not on all . . . (such as a few) agricultural products. . . . We then found unfair competition in the American market, charging Japan with paying unfairly low wages, subsidizing its export industries, or "dumping" its goods abroad unfairly in order to gain unwarranted market shares. We went after threatening industries and still do. Then it was the exchange rate, pegged at a level that made Japanese exports unfairly cheap and American exports unfairly expensive. The rate has been brought down from 360 yen to the dollar to roughly 130 yen [123 yen at time of writing] to the dollar. Then we turned our attention back to the Japanese market to assault its inspection procedures and other internal restrictions. Now some Americans are complaining about the unfairness of Japan's having social values and institutions different from our own. . . .

What are we to do? What are the Japanese to do? Surely not play an endlessly bruising game of economic and political football to a scoreless tie. It will do no good to bash for bashing's sake.

Lawrence W. Beer, *Vital Speeches of the Day,* January 1, 1989.

While there is some concern that Japan does not shoulder responsibilities commensurate with its economic capability, or that it lacks the philosophy or principles needed to guide it in the years ahead, much of this criticism arises from the gap that has suddenly opened up between the way Japanese see Japan and the way foreign observers evaluate Japan.

Japan's Transitional Phase

Things are changing radically. It is important to recognize that Japan is in a transitional phase. Should not some consideration be given to how long a country has been a rich industrial country? Much of the criticism of Japan points to special features that are said to characterize Japan, but I wonder if the current problems are truly rooted in Japanese peculiarities or whether they are rooted in the fact that our two countries are at different stages of development and that Japan's situation is changing very rapidly.

Japan has been a latecomer to the club of industrial nations, and this has created conditions different from those at the time the United States and Western European countries achieved industrial status. This historical perspective is also important in understanding the problems that may arise between the industrial countries and the newly industrializing countries or other developing countries that have, or soon will achieve, rapid growth. In fact, I doubt there is much real difference between Japan today and the United States and Western Europe of a generation ago when it comes to working hours, productivity, living standards and all the rest. The features that seem so peculiar to Japan today are, in fact, transitional phenomena.

Political Costs

Americans should also weigh the political costs of its demands on Japan. These costs, incurred in responding to repeated American demands for more and more market openings, have begun to mount. We are very near the political limits to what Japan can do to accommodate these demands.

Liberalizing agricultural imports, for example, benefits urban dwellers but creates serious problems for farm families. As a result, the ruling Liberal Democratic Party's receptiveness to these demands has cost it votes in old rural strongholds. While it might conceivably be possible to offset these defections by picking up new votes in the urban areas that benefit from lower food prices, urban voters have been turned off by the new consumption tax and the Recruit corruption scandal.

Similarly, American demands to revise the Japanese law restricting the giant retail chains and restructure the distribution sector impose additional political costs on the Liberal Democrats. Large corporations benefit at the expense of smaller retailers.

While Washington is loudly and busily calling on everyone else to reduce trade surpluses, there is much that the United States could do to reduce its own trade deficit.

In testimony to the Senate Finance Committee in May 1989, Trade Representative Hills admitted that less than 20% of the United States' trade deficit is attributable to other countries' barriers; the remaining 80%-plus is due to the savings shortfall and other macroeconomic factors within the United States.

Little wonder so many Japanese suggest that the United States should get its own act together first—including better macroeconomic policies and greater corporate competitiveness—before it starts crying about how unfair others are.

Stop Blaming Japan

It is one thing to press Japan to play a more responsible role in international economic affairs. It is quite another to talk about Japan as if it were some kind of pariah in the world community whose ability to produce high-quality, low-cost goods and whose people's adherence to values of diligence, hard work, thrift and perseverance verge on the immoral. . . .

American leaders need to declare a cease-fire in the war of words with Japan and to stop thinking that the Japanese can somehow solve our problems.

Gerald L. Curtis, *The New York Times*, June 17, 1987.

Many in the United States who view Japan as a threat and contend that Japan engages in "adversarial trade" to deliberately destroy American industry sector-by-sector have also called for the two governments to reach agreements on Japanese industry's share of the U.S. market in each specific sector, or for Japan to enter into "voluntary export restraints" to limit the damage to American industry.

The behavior that looks so damaging to industry in the importing countries is a carry-over from the fiercely competitive climate that exists in the domestic Japanese market. However, it should be recognized that some Japanese companies are now moving to rein in their competition for market shares overseas. While this may be attractive in light of the political considerations involved, its implementation will require a deliberate shift to managed trade.

What Does America Want?

What does America really want? Japanese companies are damned for competing for market share and damned for anything that smacks of cartelization.

The United States has called Japan "unfair" and demanded that Japan increase its imports or else Washington will impose punitive measures. Such an approach simply inflames passions on both sides of the Pacific, imposing new costs on the crucial bilateral relationship.

Recognizing the two countries' different historical, social and institutional backgrounds, it is important that Japan and the United States attempt to find a constructive way out of their present impasse. In that sense, it should be noted that the U.S. effort to brand Japan as "unfair" is needlessly antagonistic—both for its connotations of immorality and for its blatantly arbitrary nature.

Ranking Foreign Policy Concerns

This activity will give you an opportunity to discuss the values you and your classmates consider important in foreign policy, and the values you believe are considered most important by the majority of Americans.

Makers of foreign policy often face conflicting goals, and must decide which ones are most important.

WHILE WE WERE BUSY SPENDING BILLIONS TO DEFEND MAIN STREET, THE JAPANESE BOUGHT IT !!

Cartoon by Mike Thompson, *The St. Louis Sun*. Reprinted by permission.

This cartoon illustrates one side of a recurring debate about US foreign policy concerns. Many people argue that the US should maintain strong and expensive armed forces to ensure US military strength and political influence in the world. But others argue that the emphasis on defense spending is misplaced. While the US worries about external threats from other countries, Japan, which spends less on its military, is busy buying US land and businesses. Some people argue that the economic threat Japan poses is more serious than the threat of foreign invasion. They argue that economic competition is a more important concern than maintaining military strength.

Part I

Step 1. The class should break into groups of four to six students. Each group should rank the foreign policy concerns listed below. Use 1 to designate the most important concern, 2 for the second most important concern, and so on.

_____ having a strong US military presence in Asia

_____ promoting American exports to reduce the US trade deficit

_____ ensuring that the Japanese continue to buy US government bonds

_____ protecting American jobs

_____ supporting friendship with Japan because of its power and strategic location

_____ supporting Japan's position as a nuclear-free country

_____ maintaining America's advantages in technology

_____ sharing military technology with Japan to improve the defense capabilities of the US and Japan

_____ making Japan pay more toward its own defense

Part II

Step 1. Each group should rank the listed concerns in what the group considers to be the order of importance to the majority of Americans. Again use 1 to designate the concern the group believes most important to the majority of Americans, and so on until all the concerns have been ranked.

Step 2. After ranking the concerns, the small groups should discuss the following questions:

1. What noticeable differences do you see between your own rankings in Part I and the perceived ranking of the majority of Americans in Part II?

2. How would you explain these differences?

Periodical Bibliography

The following articles have been selected to supplement the diverse views presented in this chapter.

Lawrence W. Beer — "The United States-Japan Partnership," *Vital Speeches of the Day*, January 1, 1989.

Robert C. Christopher — "Terms of Estrangement," *Newsweek*, February 27, 1989.

William Clark Jr. — "US-Japan Relations" *Department of State Bulletin*, December 1988.

John W. Dower — "Fear and Prejudice in US-Japan Relations," *Ethics & International Affairs*, vol. 3, 1989.

John Greenwald — "Friend or Foe?" *Time*, April 24, 1989.

Steve H. Hanke — "US-Japanese Trade: Yes, Blame America First," *The National Interest*, Winter 1987/1988.

Seiichi Kamise — "US and Japan Relationship," *Vital Speeches of the Day*, July 15, 1988.

Paul Magnusson — "Can the Pentagon Keep Shielding Japan?" *Business Week*, March 27, 1989.

Kazuo Nukazawa — "Japan & the USA: Wrangling Toward Reciprocity," *Harvard Business Review*, May/June 1988.

Hisahiko Okazaki — "The Restructuring of the US-Japan Alliance," *Japan Review of International Affairs*, Fall/Winter 1988. Available from the Japan Institute of International Affairs, 19th Mori Building, 1-2-20 Toranomon Minato-ku, Tokyo 105, Japan.

George R. Packard — "The Coming US-Japan Crisis," *Foreign Affairs*, Winter 1987/1988.

Robert Pear — "Confusion Is Operative Word in US Policy Toward Japan," *The New York Times*, March 20, 1989.

Wesley W. Posvar — "US-Japanese Relations in a Global Perspective," *Vital Speeches of the Day*, April 15, 1988.

Jerry W. Sanders — "America in the Pacific Century," *World Policy Journal*, Winter 1988/1989.

Organizations To Contact

The editors have compiled the following list of organizations which are concerned with the issues debated in this book. All of them have publications or information available for interested readers. The descriptions are derived from materials provided by the organizations. This list was compiled upon the date of publication. Names and phone numbers of organizations are subject to change.

American Chamber of Commerce in Japan (ACCJ)
Fukide Building No. 2
1-21, Toranomon 4-chome
Minato-ku, Tokyo 105
Japan

ACCJ consists of American citizens, companies, and organizations operating in Japan. It promotes commerce between the US and Japan, supports liberalizing the Japanese market, and aims to represent and express the opinions of the US business community regarding trade, commerce, and finance. It publishes a monthly journal, the book *Living in Japan*, and various reports on investment and trade.

American Enterprise Institute for Public Policy Research (AEI)
1150 17th St. NW
Washington, DC 20036
(202) 862-1239

The Institute sponsors research on a wide range of national and international issues. Its studies take a generally conservative stance on issues of politics, economics, and foreign affairs. The Institute publishes the journal *Public Opinion*, and has published several books and papers on Japan, including *Japan's Public Policy Companies* and *Sharing World Leadership? A New Era for America and Japan*.

American Federation of Labor/Congress of Industrial Organizations (AFL/CIO)
815 16th St. NW
Washington, DC 20006
(202) 637-5000

The AFL/CIO is made up of ninety labor unions with fourteen million total members, and is the largest federation of its kind. It believes the US should take measures in response to Japan's trade policies to ensure fair trade and protect US jobs. It has also worked in conjunction with Japanese labor unions. It publishes periodic reports and the weekly *AFL/CIO News*.

Asia Resource Center (ARC)
PO Box 15275
Washington, DC 20003
(202) 547-1114

ARC is an educational corporation formed in 1971 to bring the concerns of Asian people to the American public. It supports minority rights in Japan, and opposes enlarging the Japanese military. ARC provides publications and audiovisual resources, and distributes *AMPO*, a progressive Japanese-Asian quarterly review.

The Asia Society
725 Park Ave.
New York, NY 10021-5088
(212) 288-6400

The Asia Society works to increase American understanding of Asia and its growing importance to US and world relations. It publishes the journal *Focus on Asian Studies* and reports about Japan and other Asian countries. Books concerning Japan include *Japan's Economic Role in Northeast Asia* and *Japan, the United States, and a Changing Southeast Asia*.

Associated Japan-America Societies, Inc. (AJAS)
333 E. 47th St.
New York, NY 10017
(212) 832-1155

AJAS was formed in 1979 to provide a cooperative network among independent Japan-America Societies located in over twenty cities in the United States. Each AJAS member-society works to promote goodwill between Japan and its own community, and to promote better relations between the US and Japan by increasing American understanding of Japan. AJAS and its member-societies sponsor lectures on trade, Japanese relations with the US and USSR, Japanese women, and many other topics. It distributes films and publishes a guide to its activities and member-societies.

Association for Asian Studies (AAS)
1 Lane Hall
University of Michigan
Ann Arbor, MI 48109
(313) 665-2490

The Association is a group of educators, students, government officials, and others interested in the study of Asia. AAS publishes scholarly research and other material designed to promote Asian studies. Its quarterly publication is the *Journal of Asian Studies*.

The Brookings Institution
1775 Massachusetts Ave. NW
Washington, DC 20036
(202) 797-6220

The Institution, founded in 1927, is a liberal research and education organization that publishes material in the fields of economics, government, and foreign policy. The Institution publishes the quarterly *Brookings Review* and various books and reports, including *Japan: Facing Economic Maturity* by Edward J. Lincoln.

Cato Institute
224 Second St. SE
Washington, DC 20003
(202) 546-0200

The Institute sponsors and publishes research on public policy questions. It supports free trade and believes Japan should spend more on its defense. The Institute publishes the *Cato Journal* and books and reports, including *Collective Defense or Strategic Independence?*

Center for Teaching International Relations
University of Denver
University Park
Denver, CO 80208
(303) 871-3106

The Center works to promote international studies in elementary and high school classrooms. It publishes extracurricular teaching materials. Activity books on Japan include *Japan Meets the West* and *Teaching About World Cultures*.

Citizens Against Foreign Control of America (CAFCA)
PO Box 3528
Montgomery, AL 39109
(205) 279-0531

CAFCA urges US government restrictions of foreign investments, imports, and ownership of US corporations. It believes that unrestricted Japanese and other foreign investments threaten Americans' ability to control their own future. The organization lobbies for laws limiting foreign investment and sponsors research and lectures. It serves as an information clearinghouse on foreign investments, and publishes *CAFCA Newsletter* in addition to brochures including *Guess Who's Coming to Dinner.*

The Council on Foreign Relations
58 E. 68th St.
New York, NY 10021
(212) 734-0400

The Council is a membership organization composed of individuals with specialized knowledge of and interest in international affairs. It was formed to "study the international aspects of American political, economic and strategic problems." The Council publishes the journal *Foreign Affairs* and occasional books, including *The Future of U.S.-Japan Relations.*

Foreign Policy Association (FPA)
729 Seventh Ave.
New York, NY 10019
(212) 764-4050

The Foreign Policy Association is an educational organization founded in 1918. Its objective is to stimulate an informed and articulate public opinion on foreign policy issues facing the United States. A bibliography can be obtained of its books and publications. The Association's writings on Japan include *Japan: The Dilemmas of Success.*

The Foundation for Economic Education, Inc.
Irvington-on-Hudson, NY 10533
(914) 591-7230

The Foundation publishes information and research in support of capitalism, free trade, and limited government. It occasionally publishes articles on Japan in its monthly magazine *The Freeman.*

The Heritage Foundation
214 Massachusetts Ave. NE
Washington, DC 20002
(202) 546-4400

The Foundation is a conservative public policy research institute. It supports cooperation between the US and Japan to counter the Soviet threat in Asia, and opposes Japanese barriers to US exports. The Foundation has published information on Japan in its *Backgrounder* and *Heritage Lectures* series.

Japan-America Society of Washington (JASW)
Dacor-Bacon House Mews
606 18th St. NW
Washington, DC 20006
(202) 289-8920

The Society is a membership organization which promotes better understanding between the US and Japan, and sponsors a variety of exchange, cultural, and educational programs. It provides teaching materials to schools, and publishes proceedings of its conferences on teaching about Japan, including *US-Japan Science and Technology Exchange: Patterns of Interdependence.*

Japan Economic Institute of America (JEI)
1000 Connecticut Ave. NW, Suite 211
Washington, DC 20036
(202) 296-5633

JEI is a US research institute funded by the Japanese Ministry of Foreign Affairs. It works for improved business relations between the US and Japan by providing information and analysis on the Japanese economy. The Institute publishes the *JEI Report* and the *Japan-U.S. Business Report.*

Japan External Trade Organization (JETRO)
725 S. Figueroa St., Suite 1890
Los Angeles, CA 90017
(213) 624-8855

JETRO is a Japanese government agency that collects and distributes information to encourage Japan's overseas trade. It provides reports about Japan for businesses, sponsors seminars and trade fairs, and publishes pamphlets, surveys, economic data, and the periodicals *Focus Japan* and *Tradescope.*

Japan Publications Trading Co., Ltd.
PO Box 5030
Tokyo International, Tokyo 101
Japan

The company serves as overseas distributor of several English-language publications from Japan. Periodicals it distributes include the *Japan Quarterly* and the *Japan Echo,* a journal consisting of translations of articles and editorials by prominent commentators which originally appeared in leading Japanese publications.

Japanese American Curriculum Project (JACP)
414 E. Third Ave.
San Mateo, CA 94401
(415) 343-9408

JACP develops and distributes curriculum material on Asian Americans. It was originally founded to tell the histories of Japanese Americans interned in US camps during World War II. Books it sells about Japan through its annual catalog include *Japanese Culture and Behavior, Jobs in Japan—The Complete Guide To Living and Working in the Land of Rising Opportunity,* and *Japanese Women—Constraint and Fulfillment.*

National Association of Manufacturers (NAM)
1331 Pennsylvania Ave. NW, Suite 1500 N.
Washington, DC 20004
(202) 637-3000

NAM is a trade association which represents the interests of US manufacturers on national and international issues, and works to promote freer trade between the US and Japan. It reviews legislation, court decisions, and administrative rulings affecting industry. When Congress is in session it publishes *Briefing* weekly. Its other publications include the bimonthly journal *Enterprise,* and periodic policy statements, papers, and reports on many international economic issues relating to trade relations between Japan and the US.

Social Studies Development Center (SSDC)
Indiana University
2805 E. Tenth St.
Bloomington, IN 47408-2698
(812) 855-3838

SSDC is sponsored by the College of Arts and Sciences and the School of Education of Indiana University. It works to improve social studies education in elementary and secondary schools. It publishes and distributes a variety of materials on global education, including *Resources for Teaching About Japan* by Linda S. Wojtan.

US-Japan Culture Center (USJCC)
600 New Hampshire Ave. NW, Suite 750
Washington, DC 20037
(202) 342-5800

USJCC serves as a resource center on Japan and its relations with the US. It maintains a library of Japanese and American books and periodicals, sponsors exchange and research programs, and provides seminars and language classes. It sponsors an essay contest on relations between the US and Japan, and publishes winning essays. Its bimonthly publication *News* describes its activities.

The Washington Institute
1015 18th St. NW, Suite 300
Washington, DC 20036
(202) 293-7440

The Institute is an educational organization that conducts research on foreign policy issues. It specializes in Asian studies and has published research on Japan. It explores ethical values underlying public policy issues. The Institute publishes books, pamphlets, and monographs including *Japan's Defense* and *Human Rights in East Asia*.

World Policy Institute
777 United Nations Plaza
New York, NY 10017
(212) 490-0010

The Institute, founded in 1948, works to develop progressive solutions to war, poverty, social injustice, and ecological damage. It conducts research and makes policy recommendations on US and world economic and security issues. The Institute has published articles on Japan in its *World Policy Journal*.

Bibliography of Books

Amano, Ikuo — *Education and Examination in Modern Japan.* Tokyo: University of Tokyo Press, 1989.

Gail Lee Bernstein and Haruhiro Fukui, eds. — *Japan and the World.* Basingstoke, UK: Macmillan Press, 1988.

Theodore C. Bestor — *Neighborhood Tokyo.* Stanford, CA: Stanford University Press, 1989.

Daniel Burstein — *YEN!: Japan's New Financial Empire and Its Threat to America.* New York: Simon & Schuster, 1988.

William K. Cummings et al., eds. — *Educational Policies in Crisis: Japanese and American Perspectives.* New York: Praeger Publishers, 1986.

Gerald Curtis — *The Japanese Way of Politics.* New York: Columbia University Press, 1988.

Boye De Mente — *Made in Japan.* Lincolnwood, IL: Passport Books, 1987.

James Fallows — *More Like Us: Making America Great Again.* Boston: Houghton Mifflin Company, 1989.

David Friedman — *The Misunderstood Miracle.* Ithaca, NY: Cornell University Press, 1988.

Ellen L. Frost — *For Richer, For Poorer: The New U.S.-Japan Relationship.* New York: Council on Foreign Relations, 1987.

Tasdashi Fukutake — *The Japanese Social Structure.* Tokyo: University of Tokyo Press, 1989.

George Gamota and Wendy Frieman — *Gaining Ground: Japan's Strides in Science and Technology.* Cambridge, MA: Ballinger Publishing Company, 1989.

John L. Graham and Yoshihiro Sana — *Smart Bargaining: Doing Business with the Japanese.* Cambridge, MA: Ballinger Publishing Company, 1989.

David Halberstam — *The Reckoning.* New York: William Morrow & Co., 1986.

Kichiro Hayashi, ed. — *The U.S.-Japanese Economic Relationship: Can It Be Improved?* New York: New York University Press, 1989.

V. Daniel Hunt — *Mechatronics: Japan's Newest Threat.* New York: Chapman and Hall, 1988.

Muto Ichiyo — *Class Struggle and Technological Innovation in Japan Since 1945.* Amsterdam: International Institute for Research and Education, 1987.

Mamoru Iga — *The Thorn in the Chrysanthemum.* Berkeley: University of California Press, 1986.

Shotaro Ishinomori — *JAPAN INC.: An Introduction to Japanese Economics.* Berkeley: University of California Press, 1988.

Chalmers Johnson, Laura D'Andrea Tyson, and John Zysman — *Politics and Productivity: How Japan's Development Strategy Works.* Cambridge, MA: Ballinger Publishing Company, 1989.

Tetsuya Kataoka and Ramon Meyers	*Defending an Economic Superpower: Reassessing the U.S.-Japan Security Alliance.* Boulder, CO: Westview Press, 1989.
Douglas M. Kenrick	*The Success of Competitive Communism in Japan.* Basingstoke, UK: Macmillan Press, 1988.
Hiroshi Kitamura, Ryohei Murata, and Hisahiko Okazaki	*Between Friends: Japanese Diplomats Look at Japan-U.S. Relations.* New York: Weatherhill, 1985.
Jun-ichi Kyogoku	*The Political Dynamics of Japan.* Tokyo: University of Tokyo Press, 1987.
Edward J. Lincoln	*Japan: Facing Economic Maturity.* Washington, DC: The Brookings Institution, 1988.
Noboru Makino	*Decline and Prosperity: Corporate Innovation in Japan.* New York: Kodansha International, 1987.
Akio Morita, Edwin M. Reingold, and Mitsuko Shimomura	*Made In Japan: Akio Morita and Sony.* New York: E.P. Dutton, 1986.
Kenichi Ohmae	*Beyond National Borders: Reflections on Japan and the World.* Homewood, IL: Dow Jones-Irwin, 1987.
Daniel I. Okimoto and Thomas P. Rohlen, eds.	*Inside the Japanese System.* Stanford, CA: Stanford University Press, 1988.
Hugh Patrick, ed.	*Japan's High Technology Industries.* Seattle: University of Washington Press, 1986.
Jim Powell	*The Gnomes of Tokyo: Japanese Financial Power and Its Impact on Our Future.* New York: Dodd, Mead & Co., 1988.
Clyde Prestowitz	*Trading Places: How We Allowed Japan To Take the Lead.* New York: Basic Books, 1988.
Edwin O. Reischauer	*The Japanese Today.* Cambridge, MA: The Belknap Press of Harvard University, 1988.
Ryuzo Sato and John A. Rizzo, eds.	*Unkept Promises, Unclear Consequences: U.S. Economic Policy and the Japanese Response.* New York: Cambridge University Press, 1988.
Frederik L. Schodt	*Inside the Robot Kingdom.* New York: Kodansha International, 1988.
Yoshio Suzuki	*Japan's Economic Performance and International Role.* Tokyo: University of Tokyo Press, 1989.
Peter Tasker	*Inside Japan.* London: Sidgwick & Jackson, 1987.
E. Patricia Tsurumi	*The Other Japan.* Armonk, NY: M.E. Sharpe, Inc., 1988.
J. Marshall Unger	*The Fifth Generation Fallacy.* New York: Oxford University Press, 1987.
Karel G. van Wolferen	*The Enigma of Japanese Power.* New York: Alfred A. Knopf, 1989.
Ezra F. Vogel	*Japan as Number One: Revisited.* Singapore: Institute of Southeast Asian Studies, 1986.
Merry White	*The Japanese Educational Challenge: A Commitment to Children.* New York: Free Press, 1987.

255

Dick Wilson   *The Sun at Noon: An Anatomy of Modern Japan.* London: Hamish Hamilton, 1986.

Jon Woronoff   *The Japan Syndrome.* New Brunswick, NJ: Transaction Books, 1986.

Dennis T. Yasutomo   *The Manner of Giving: Strategic Aid and Japanese Foreign Policy.* Lexington, MA: Lexington Books, 1986.

Index

259

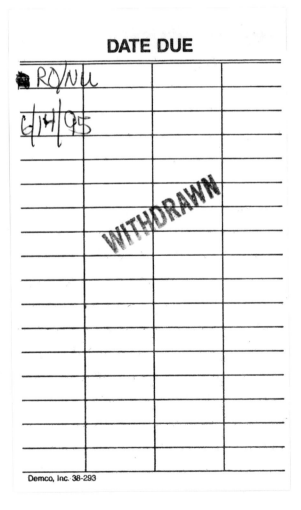

DATE DUE

R/NU			
6/14/95			
		WITHDRAWN	